ASCAP

CENTENNIAL SONGBOOK

SHEET MUSIC AND SONG NOTES FOR 55 CLASSIC SONGS

CELEBRATING **100 YEARS** IN SONG

ISBN 978-1-4803-5051-9

HAL•LEONARD®
CORPORATION

7777 W. BLUEMOUND RD. P.O. BOX 13819 MILWAUKEE, WI 53213

Visit Hal Leonard Online at
www.halleonard.com

ASCAP

The American Society of Composers, Authors and Publishers (ASCAP) is a not-for-profit membership association of nearly 500,000 songwriters, composers and music publishers of every kind of music. Our mission is to license the public performance of ASCAP music so that our members get paid fairly wherever their music is played – live, online or over the airwaves. For 100 years, we've made it possible for music to thrive by providing a livelihood to music creators, and offering businesses an efficient way to access our unmatched repertory of more than nine million musical works.

ASCAP members are the greatest names in American music – from Jay Z to Katy Perry, Duke Ellington to Hans Zimmer, Brad Paisley to Beyoncé and Bruce Springsteen to Leonard Bernstein. We also support the many thousands of songwriters and composers whose names you might not know, but whose music enriches our lives. As the only American performing rights organization owned and governed by its members, ASCAP keeps music and those that make it at the heart of what we do. We're committed to nurturing and advocating for music creators throughout their careers – after all, we are our members.

John A. LoFrumento

John A. LoFrumento
Chief Executive Officer
American Society of Composers, Authors and Publishers

FOREWORD

The American Society of Composers, Authors and Publishers (ASCAP) celebrates its centennial year in 2014. It is an organization I am proud to serve as President and Chairman because, for one hundred years, it has made a difference in the lives of its composer, lyricist and music publisher members ... and the music of our country.

The triumphs, trials and general history of ASCAP are explored in the new book, *A Friend in the Music Business: The ASCAP Story*, written by Bruce Pollock and published by Hal Leonard Books. The good people at Hal Leonard are also issuing this ASCAP Centennial Songbook as a sheet music companion to *A Friend in the Music Business*. It contains over 50 songs from all ten decades of the Society's existence, judged to be representative and historically important, but not necessarily the most performed or most honored. They do, however, provide a musical snapshot of the respective decades in which they became popular – from the glories of Tin Pan Alley to the Broadway stage to Hollywood's finest, from the Brill Building to Motown to disco, from Nashville to heartland rock to contemporary pop and R&B.

If we, as music creators, want to understand where we're going, this is a good time to look back at where our music has been for the past century. When ASCAP began, operettas, Tin Pan Alley and ragtime were the popular music of the day that could only be heard via live performances, gramophone records and piano rolls. Since 1914, new musical genres have emerged: the modern musical theater, cabaret, film and television music; blues, jazz, rhythm & blues, soul, funk and rap; folk, country and bluegrass; rock & roll, heavy metal, alternative and Americana; gospel and contemporary Christian. A lively and challenging American symphonic and concert music has also developed, along with a wide-ranging audience for America's Latin music. The ASCAP repertory reflects all of the above, containing literally millions of works in every genre and style.

And keeping pace with the proliferation of new genres have been dramatic changes in music delivery. Who would have thought that the parlor music of ASCAP's earliest days would give way to radio, television, cable and, now, the ubiquitous Internet? But I'm happy to say that the common denominator has always been and continues to be great music – provided by our composer, lyricist and publisher members.

On behalf of our growing musical family, I hope that you will find this ASCAP Centennial Songbook to be fun, informative and pleasantly nostalgic.

Paul Williams,
President & Chairman of the Board
American Society of Composers, Authors and Publishers

CONTENTS

1910s

Turner Layton

W.C. Handy

George M. Cohan

George W. Meyer & E. Ray Goetz

Victor Herbert & Rida Johnson Young

AFTER YOU'VE GONE – HENRY CREAMER & TURNER LAYTON

A classic written by the African-American songwriting team of Henry Creamer and Turner Layton, it was first recorded in 1918 by the white recording artist, Marion Harris, who was known for a time as "Queen of the Blues." The song's popularity has remained steady down through the decades with scores of recorded vocal and instrumental versions by a wide range of artists that includes Bessie Smith, Sophie Tucker, Al Jolson, Ella Fitzgerald, Nina Simone, Frank Sinatra, Paul Whiteman, Lionel Hampton and Loudon Wainwright III.

ST. LOUIS BLUES – W.C. HANDY

Possibly the definitive blues song, "St. Louis Blues" ranks as the second most recorded song (after "Silent Night") of the pre-Rock era. No less than sixteen versions of "St. Louis Blues" reached the Top 25, including renditions by Louis Armstrong, Rudy Vallée, Cab Calloway, Benny Goodman, Guy Lombardo, Billy Eckstine and composer W.C. Handy, himself. Bessie Smith's plaintive 1925 recording may be the most memorable of all.

OVER THERE – GEORGE M. COHAN

George M. Cohan was already known as one of Broadway's greatest entertainers and songwriters when America's entry into World War I in 1917 inspired him to write "Over There." A stirring anthem closely associated with early 20th Century vocalist Nora Bayes, the song was a boon to the war effort, promising that "the Yanks are coming" and "won't be back till it's over, over there!"

FOR ME AND MY GAL -- GEORGE W. MEYER, EDGAR LESLIE, E. RAY GOETZ

Three New York-based songwriters joined together to compose the 1917 standard, "For Me and My Gal," a Top Ten hit for four different artists that same year. The same tune became the title song of the 1942 Judy Garland / Gene Kelly film, and was also recorded by such stars as Guy Lombardo, Arthur Godfrey, Perry Como and rock & roll star Freddy Cannon.

AH! SWEET MYSTERY OF LIFE – VICTOR HERBERT & RIDA JOHNSON YOUNG

Naughty Marietta, one of the most famous American operettas, is where "Ah! Sweet Mystery of Life" originated in 1910. A 1935 film version of the operetta, starring Jeanette McDonald and Nelson Eddy, revived interest in "Ah! Sweet Mystery of Life." Eddy and Bing Crosby both enjoyed hit recordings of the song in the 1930s. Madeline Kahn performed it to great comic effect in Mel Brooks' *Young Frankenstein* in 1974.

Irving Berlin

Oscar Hammerstein II & Jerome Kern

George & Ira Gershwin

Hoagy Carmichael & Mitchell Parish

Ben Bernie & Maceo Pinkard

1920s

BLUE SKIES – IRVING BERLIN

"Blue Skies" is a timeless Irving Berlin song (inspired by the birth of his first child, Mary Ellin) that was first heard in 1926 as a last minute interpolation into the Rodgers & Hart musical, *Betsy*. Star Belle Baker was asked to perform 24 encores of the song on opening night. As a featured number in Al Jolson's 1927 smash "talkie," *The Jazz Singer*, "Blue Skies" received massive exposure worldwide. Fred Astaire and Bing Crosby co-starred in a 1946 film titled *Blue Skies* and Willie Nelson's 1978 recording reached the top of the country music charts.

OL' MAN RIVER – JEROME KERN & OSCAR HAMMERSTEIN II

Written for the great 1927 Broadway musical, *Show Boat*, "Ol' Man River" has remained one of America's most beloved and powerful songs. Its haunting melody and a lyric layered with yearning, resignation and deep meaning have attracted a stream of great interpreters. Paul Robeson is most closely associated with the song, but Bing Crosby, Al Jolson, Frank Sinatra, Ray Charles, Sam Cooke, the Beach Boys and Cher all recorded it, as well. The pioneering R&B vocal group, the Ravens, enjoyed a Top Ten hit with their version in 1948.

SOMEONE TO WATCH OVER ME – GEORGE & IRA GERSHWIN

A beautiful ballad taken from the musical, *Oh, Kay!*, "Someone to Watch Over Me" was originally conceived by George Gershwin as an up-tempo tune – his brother, Ira, advised him to slow the song down. *Oh, Kay!* star Gertrude Lawrence had the first in a long line of recordings by pop and jazz artists that includes Ella Fitzgerald, Chet Baker, Barbra Streisand, Linda Ronstadt, Sting, Oscar Peterson, Art Garfunkel and Amy Winehouse.

STARDUST – HOAGY CARMICHAEL & MITCHELL PARISH

Originally spelled as two words, "Stardust" began as an instrumental recording made by composer Hoagy Carmichael in 1927 that also featured his musician friends Tommy and Jimmy Dorsey. After Mitchell Parish added his poignant, poetic lyrics, the song sailed into immortality as one of the most recorded and performed songs of all time. Great versions have been recorded by Bing Crosby, Frank Sinatra, Louis Armstrong, Willie Nelson, Nat King Cole, Billy Ward and the Dominoes, Artie Shaw, Clark Terry and dozens more across the musical spectrum.

SWEET GEORGIA BROWN – BEN BERNIE, MACEO PINKARD & KENNETH CASEY

A 1925 #1 hit for Ben Bernie and the Hotel Roosevelt Orchestra, the song's goodtime jazz sound has made it a favorite ever since. Subsequent recordings have been numerous, but the most enduring version has been the 1949 recording by whistler Brother Bones, adopted as the theme song of the Harlem Globetrotters. The comic possibilities of "Sweet Georgia Brown" were explored further when stars Mel Brooks and Anne Bancroft performed it in Polish in their 1983 film, *To Be or Not to Be*.

Herman Hupfeld

Richard Rodgers & Lorenz Hart

Jimmy McHugh & Dorothy Fields

Cole Porter

E.Y. "Yip" Harburg & Harold Arlen

1930s

AS TIME GOES BY – HERMAN HUPFELD

Introduced in the 1931 Broadway musical, *Everybody's Welcome*, "As Time Goes By" attracted the interest of crooner Rudy Vallée, who quickly recorded a version that was a success but not a blockbuster. The performance of the song by singer Dooley Wilson (Sam) in the classic wartime film, *Casablanca* (1942), turned it into one of the most beloved of all song standards. It has since been recorded by a wide variety of artists, including Louis Armstrong, Willie Nelson, Carly Simon, Tony Bennett, Barbra Streisand, ZZ Top and Jimmy Durante.

MY FUNNY VALENTINE – RICHARD RODGERS & LORENZ HART

"My Funny Valentine" debuted in Rodgers & Hart's 1937 musical, *Babes in Arms*. Although it remains one of the best-known songs in the Rodgers & Hart catalog, with hundreds of recordings, it only reached the pop charts once—in a big band version by Hal McIntyre in 1945. The song's emotional lyrics and melody have attracted numerous great artists over the years, resulting in memorable recordings by Chet Baker, Ella Fitzgerald, Elvis Costello, Frank Sinatra, Miles Davis, among many others.

I'M IN THE MOOD FOR LOVE – DOROTHY FIELDS & JIMMY McHUGH

Frances Langford enjoyed a hit with "I'm in the Mood for Love" in 1935. The song reached an even wider audience when it was sung off-key by Carl "Alfalfa" Switzer in a Little Rascals short the following year. In the 1950s, James Moody swung the song in his jazz adaptation, "Moody's Mood for Love," inspiring a "vocalese" rendition by singers King Pleasure and Blossom Dearie.

NIGHT AND DAY – COLE PORTER

Fred Astaire introduced "Night and Day" in the 1932 Broadway musical, *Gay Divorce*, and his subsequent recording went to #1. Astaire sang it again in the 1934 film version, re-titled *The Gay Divorcee*. One of the standouts among Porter's large number of standards, "Night and Day" has been covered by pop, jazz and rock superstars, including Ella Fitzgerald, Tony Bennett, Charlie Parker and Ringo Starr. Frank Sinatra recorded five different versions of "Night and Day" over the years. The song's name was used as the title for the 1946 Hollywood biographical film about Porter.

OVER THE RAINBOW – HAROLD ARLEN & E.Y. "YIP" HARBURG

Judy Garland's signature song, "Over the Rainbow," was introduced by Garland in the 1939 movie classic, *The Wizard of Oz*, which contained an Arlen-Harburg song score. It certainly ranks as one the best-known American songs in the world. Both the Recording Industry Association and the National Endowment of the Arts ranked "Over the Rainbow" as #1 on their respective "Songs of the Century" lists, while the American Film Institute named it "the greatest movie song of all time." Ironically, "Over the Rainbow" was almost cut from *The Wizard of Oz* by the film's producer. Hit versions of "Over the Rainbow" have been recorded by Patti Labelle and the Bluebelles, Jerry Lee Lewis and the late Hawaiian superstar, Israel Kamakawiwo'ole.

1940s

Jack Lawrence & Walter Gross

"Duke" Ellington & Bob Russell

Harry Warren & Mack Gordon

Leigh Harline & Ned Washington

Irving Kahal & Sammy Fain

TENDERLY – JACK LAWRENCE & WALTER GROSS

"Tenderly," a sumptuously romantic ballad, was published in 1946. Among the first to record it was a young Sarah Vaughan. It was also closely associated with Rosemary Clooney, who enjoyed a Top 20 hit with "Tenderly" in 1952 and used it as the theme song to her television variety series. It has since become a jazz standard, with recordings by Bill Evans, Duke Ellington, Kenny Burrell, Chet Baker, Stan Getz, Billie Holiday and the duo of Louis Armstrong and Ella Fitzgerald.

DON'T GET AROUND MUCH ANYMORE – EDWARD KENNEDY "DUKE" ELLINGTON & BOB RUSSELL

Originally called "Never No Lament" when Duke Ellington recorded it in 1940 as a big band instrumental, it was given a new title after lyricist Bob Russell was inspired to add lyrics in 1942. In 1943, three different versions (by Ellington, the Ink Spots and Glen Gray) all reached the Top Ten of the pop charts. A long list of artists have made "Don't Get Around Much Anymore" their own, including Nat "King" Cole, June Christy, Paul McCartney, Willie Nelson, Ella Fitzgerald, Mose Allison, Sam Cooke, the Coasters and Michael Bublé.

AT LAST – HARRY WARREN & MACK GORDON

"At Last" made its first impact in the 1942 motion picture, *Orchestra Wives*, as performed by the Glenn Miller Orchestra with Ray Eberly sweetly crooning the lyrics. A #9 hit in 1942 for Miller, it became an even bigger hit with Ray Anthony's schmaltzy rendition in 1952. It was R&B great Etta James who gave the song a new lease on life with her powerfully soulful recording in 1960, still the definitive version. Divas Beyoncé Knowles and Céline Dion have also famously put their respective marks on the song, with Beyoncé invited to perform it at Barack Obama's 2008 inauguration.

WHEN YOU WISH UPON A STAR – LEIGH HARLINE & NED WASHINGTON

An Academy Award-winning song from the 1940 animated Disney classic, *Pinocchio*, "When You Wish Upon a Star" is still best known in the original version performed by singer Cliff Edwards in the role of Jiminy Cricket. More than 70 years after it was written, "When You Wish Upon a Star" is the Walt Disney Company's quasi-official anthem. Few songs specially written for children's films have been as popular with adult artists and audiences – Glenn Miller, Dion and the Belmonts, and Linda Ronstadt have all enjoyed hits with it. Louis Armstrong, Billy Joel, Brian Wilson, Manhattan Transfer, Keith Jarrett and dozens of others have recorded "When You Wish Upon a Star," as well.

I'LL BE SEEING YOU – SAMMY FAIN & IRVING KAHAL

Adopted as an anthem by sweethearts separated during World War II, "I'll Be Seeing You" was actually introduced in the 1938 Broadway musical, *Right This Way*. The song found a receptive audience after it was used in the 1944 romantic film, *I'll Be Seeing You*. Both Bing Crosby and the Tommy Dorsey Orchestra (featuring Frank Sinatra) enjoyed major hits with "I'll Be Seeing You." In the 1950s, the song found renewed popularity when Liberace used it as the closing theme to his weekly TV show. Virtually every major American vocalist has recorded "I'll Be Seeing You," from Jo Stafford to Willie Nelson to Ray Charles, Billie Holiday, Rickie Lee Jones and Tony Bennett.

Sammy Cahn & Jimmy Van Heusen

Arthur Hamilton

James E. Myers & Max C. Freedman

Adolph Green, Betty Comden, & Jule Styne

Cy Coleman & Carolyn Leigh

1950s

ALL THE WAY – SAMMY CAHN & JIMMY VAN HEUSEN

Introduced by Frank Sinatra in his 1957 film, *The Joker Is Wild*, "All the Way" was a major hit recording for the star and brought Sammy Cahn and Jimmy Van Heusen the Academy Award® for Best Original Song. A true standard, "All the Way" has been interpreted by a wide variety of artists in different genres, including stars of jazz (Billie Holiday, Wes Montgomery, Joe Lovano), country (Ray Price, Marty Robbins, Brenda Lee), R&B (James Brown, Lou Rawls, King Curtis) and pop (Neil Sedaka, Céline Dion, Barry Manilow).

CRY ME A RIVER – ARTHUR HAMILTON

Intended for Ella Fitzgerald to perform in the 1955 Jack Webb film, *Pete Kelly's Blues*, "Cry Me a River" was dropped. Chanteuse Julie London, backed only by guitar and upright bass, had an international hit with the song, the first of many memorable renditions, including versions by Dinah Washington, Barbra Streisand, Sam Cooke, Shirley Bassey, Joe Cocker, Crystal Gayle, Aerosmith, Norah Jones and Michael Bublé.

ROCK AROUND THE CLOCK
JIMMY DeKNIGHT (JAMES E. MYERS) & MAX C. FREEDMAN

"Rock Around the Clock," as recorded by Bill Haley & His Comets, was featured over the opening credits of the 1955 film, *The Blackboard Jungle,* and became a worldwide sensation. The recording became one of the biggest-selling of all time. Energetic, highly danceable and unforgettable, Haley's "Rock Around the Clock" remains quintessential rock & roll nearly 60 years after it was introduced.

JUST IN TIME – JULE STYNE, BETTY COMDEN, & ADOLPH GREEN

One of the enduring hits from the great musical, *Bells Are Ringing*, "Just in Time" was introduced on the stage by Judy Holliday and Sydney Chaplin in 1956. Tony Bennett recorded the song that same year. "Just in Time" became very popular after the film version of *Bells Are Ringing*, starring Holliday and Dean Martin, was released. Among the many artists who have recorded it are Mel Tormé, Nina Simone, Frank Sinatra, Oscar Peterson, Dick Hyman, Harry Connick, Jr. and Count Basie & His Orchestra.

WITCHCRAFT – CY COLEMAN & CAROLYN LEIGH

"Witchcraft" is most closely associated with Frank Sinatra, who released a multi-GRAMMY®-nominated hit recording of it in 1957. Since then, the song, with its swinging rhythm and clever and seductive lyric, has been covered and re-covered by dozens of artists. The list includes George Benson, Jim Reeves, Marvin Gaye, Peggy Lee, Robert Palmer, Bobby Short, George Maharis and Bill Evans.

1960s

Ronny White & Smokey Robinson

Burt Bacharach & Hal David

Valerie Simpson & Nick Ashford

Johnny Mandel & Paul Francis Webster

Henry Mancini & Johnny Mercer

Jimmy Webb

MY GIRL – SMOKEY ROBINSON & RONNY WHITE

A universally beloved Motown hit released in late 1964, "My Girl" was written by two members of the Miracles, Smokey Robinson and Ronny White. It was originally slated for the Miracles, but Robinson decided that it would be right for the Temptations with David Ruffin singing lead. "My Girl" became the first #1 song for the Temptations and remains the group's signature song to this day. The song has proved irresistible to artists from across the spectrum, with versions by many great R&B singers, rock bands, reggae acts and country stars – among them Otis Redding, Al Green, the Rolling Stones, Dennis Brown and Alabama.

RAINDROPS KEEP FALLIN' ON MY HEAD – BURT BACHARACH & HAL DAVID

"Raindrops Keep Fallin' on My Head" was written for the 1969 film *Butch Cassidy and the Sundance Kid* and was used in the famous scene with Paul Newman clowning around on a bicycle. B.J. Thomas was asked to record the song after it was turned down by Ray Stevens and Bob Dylan. Thomas's version of the Oscar-winning song went to #1 in the U.S. and was an international hit. Countless cover versions have been recorded, including memorable ones by Bobbie Gentry, Jose Feliciano, Ella Fitzgerald and even a Yiddish version by the Barry Sisters.

AIN'T NO MOUNTAIN HIGH ENOUGH – NICK ASHFORD & VALERIE SIMPSON

The 1967 recording of "Ain't No Mountain High Enough" by Marvin Gaye & Tammi Terrell is another timeless Motown smash, written by Ashford & Simpson shortly before joining the Detroit label's staff of songwriters. The song was the first of several Gaye-Terrell duets composed by Ashford & Simpson. A restructured arrangement of "Ain't No Mountain High Enough" became an even bigger hit for Diana Ross in 1970, early in her solo career, reaching #1 on both the pop and R&B charts. The Gaye-Terrell version was inducted into the GRAMMY Hall of Fame in 1999 and is frequently used on movie soundtracks.

THE SHADOW OF YOUR SMILE (LOVE THEME FROM *THE SANDPIPER*)
JOHNNY MANDEL & PAUL FRANCIS WEBSTER

"The Shadow of Your Smile," the 1965 "Love Theme from *The Sandpiper*" won Johnny Mandel and Paul Francis Webster the Academy Award® for Best Song and the Song of the Year GRAMMY. An unforgettable song, "The Shadow of Your Smile" is most closely associated with Tony Bennett. The song, a work of subtle beauty, has become a standard, with hundreds of cover versions recorded by artists ranging from Andy Williams, Barbra Streisand and Peggy Lee to country saxophonist Boots Randolph, mandolinist Jethro Burns and R&B vocal group, The Delfonics.

MOON RIVER – HENRY MANCINI & JOHNNY MERCER

"Moon River" was composed for the 1961 film, *Breakfast at Tiffany's*, bringing together two American masters – film composer Mancini and lyricist Mercer – for a legendary collaboration. The song won the Academy Award® for Best Song and also received the Song of the Year GRAMMY Award. It became the signature song for Andy Williams, who used it to open his popular TV variety show. R&B singer Jerry Butler enjoyed a major hit with "Moon River" in 1961.

WICHITA LINEMAN – JIMMY WEBB

"Wichita Lineman" was one of several Jimmy Webb songs made into standards by Webb's greatest interpreter, Glen Campbell. A major hit for Campbell on the pop, country and adult contemporary charts, it is unusual in that the music sounds so much like what the lyrics are about – the solitude of a lonesome telephone lineman. Billy Joel, a friend and admirer of Webb, once said, "'Wichita Lineman' is about an ordinary man thinking extraordinary thoughts." Among many recordings of the song, standouts include versions by Johnny Cash and REM.

1970s

Paul Williams & Roger Nichols

Don Schlitz

Billy Joel

Stevie Wonder

Alan & Marilyn Bergman & Marvin Hamlisch

Dino Fekaris & Freddie Perren

WE'VE ONLY JUST BEGUN – PAUL WILLIAMS AND ROGER NICHOLS

In 1970, actor and lyric writer Paul Williams joined composer Roger Nichols in writing a song for a bank commercial that featured a newly married couple. Williams' fellow A&M Records artist Richard Carpenter happened to see the commercial and asked if he and his sister Karen could record an expanded version of the jingle, which was called "We've Only Just Begun." It became the Carpenters' signature hit, rising to #1 on the easy listening chart and #2 on the Hot 100, spawned numerous covers and, above all, became a perennial wedding song.

THE GAMBLER – DON SCHLITZ

"The Gambler," an early songwriting effort by Don Schlitz, won him the GRAMMY Award for Best Country Song. Schlitz recorded the song in 1978 and enjoyed a minor chart hit, but when covered by Kenny Rogers later that year, it rose to #1 on the country chart and crossed over to the pop chart. A classic example of the story-song form, the lines, "You got to know when to hold 'em, know when to fold 'em, know when to walk away, know when to run," have entered the American lexicon. In addition to spawning many other recorded versions, "The Gambler" was dramatized as a TV mini-series with none other than Kenny Rogers in the title role.

JUST THE WAY YOU ARE – BILLY JOEL

Billy Joel's 1977 love song, "Just the Way You Are," struck a chord with the music audience and helped propel his career into superstardom, earning him GRAMMY Awards for Song of the Year and Record of the Year. It was notable for featuring a soaring saxophone solo by jazz star Phil Woods. Joel has said he didn't care for the song and was close to leaving it off his best-selling album, *The Stranger*. Many dozens of covers have been recorded, and it has been a particular favorite with jazz artists, including Joe Williams, Arturo Sandoval and Joe Pass.

YOU ARE THE SUNSHINE OF MY LIFE – STEVIE WONDER

At 22, Stevie Wonder was already a ten-year veteran of the music business when he wrote and recorded "You Are the Sunshine of My Life" for his *Talking Book* album in 1972. Inspired by his then-wife, Syreeta Wright, "You Are the Sunshine of My Life" was issued as a single in 1973 and was a GRAMMY-winning performance, topping the pop and easy listening charts. Artists as diverse as Perry Como, the Ventures, Stéphane Grappelli, T. Graham Brown and Arthur Fiedler and the Boston Pops are among the many who have recorded "Sunshine."

THE WAY WE WERE – MARVIN HAMLISCH, MARILYN & ALAN BERGMAN

With "The Way We Were," the title song for a 1973 romantic movie classic, Marvin Hamlisch and Marilyn & Alan Bergman crafted a titanic hit, winning the Best Song award from both the Oscars® and the Golden Globes®. The film's star, Barbra Streisand, enjoyed a #1 single with the song in 1974, as did Gladys Knight & the Pips (in a medley titled "Try to Remember/The Way We Were"). The American Film Institute has ranked "The Way We Were" as the eighth among the "100 Greatest Movie Songs of All Time."

I WILL SURVIVE – DINO FEKARIS & FREDDIE PERREN

"I Will Survive," a 1978 release for Gloria Gaynor, was written by Dino Fekaris and Freddie Perren. It is the anthemic and very danceable account of a woman finding the strength to go on following the end of a heartbreaking relationship. A #1 hit for Gaynor, it received the Recording Academy's first and only GRAMMY for Best Disco Recording. When first released, "I Will Survive" was the "B" side of the single, made into a hit by disc jockeys who turned it over. Still heard constantly on dance floors to this day, "I Will Survive" is one of the disco genre's ultimate classics.

1980s

Jon Bon Jovi, Richie Sambora & Desmond Child

Jerry Herman

John Mellencamp

Lionel Richie

Tom Kelly & Billy Steinberg

LIVIN' ON A PRAYER
DESMOND CHILD, JON BON JOVI, RICHIE SAMBORA

New Jersey's Bon Jovi is one of the most successful of all rock bands and "Livin' on a Prayer" is the band's signature tune. Released as a single from the *Slippery When Wet* album, it soared to the top of the pop charts in 1986. "Livin' on a Prayer" is the story of a struggling working-class couple, trying to make ends meet during an economic downturn and it resonated with listeners. Nearly three decades after its debut, it remains one of rock's most stirring anthems.

THE BEST OF TIMES – JERRY HERMAN

"The Best of Times" is a song highlight from *La Cage Aux Folles*, the 1983 Broadway musical of the French stage comedy of the same name, with a score by Jerry Herman. Herman received Tony® Awards for Best Musical and Best Score. Veteran Broadway composer-lyricist Herman had previously created musical theater magic with his exuberant musicals, *Mame* and *Hello, Dolly!* With the effervescently positive sound and lyric of "The Best of Times," a timeless sing-along for joyous occasions of all kinds was born.

SMALL TOWN – JOHN MELLENCAMP

As a native of Seymour, Indiana, heartland rocker John Mellencamp comes honestly by the sentiments expressed in "Small Town," which appeared on Mellencamp's critically-acclaimed 1985 album, *Scarecrow*. The good-humored song has indelibly linked Mellencamp with small town-America and is among the star's personal favorites. "Small Town" has been adopted by no less an American institution than the Green Bay Packers football team and is played after every home game.

ALL NIGHT LONG (ALL NIGHT) – LIONEL RICHIE

One of the singles released from Lionel Richie's mega-Platinum 1983 album, *Can't Slow Down*, "All Night Long (All Night)" added a dance-oriented, sweetly Caribbean inflection to the star's musical palette. The single hit the top position on the pop, R&B and adult contemporary charts and was a worldwide smash as well. The international flavor of the song led to Richie being invited to perform it during the closing ceremonies of the 1984 Olympic Games in Los Angeles.

LIKE A VIRGIN – TOM KELLY & BILLY STEINBERG

"Like a Virgin" became an iconic hit for Madonna but it was not written with her (or any specifically female artist) in mind. However, it became the title track of her 1984 album and the first #1 single of her career and the beginning of her superstardom. While the recording and accompanying video outraged conservative groups, the song was a key factor in establishing Madonna as a role model for legions of young female fans around the world. Musical parodist Weird Al Yankovic enjoyed a hit with his 1985 rewrite titled "Like a Surgeon."

1990s

Robert Clivilles & Freedom Williams

Prince

Mike Reid & Allen Shamblin

Shawn Colvin & John Leventhal

Diane Warren

GONNA MAKE YOU SWEAT (EVERYBODY DANCE NOW)
ROBERT CLIVILLES & FREEDOM WILLIAMS

"Gonna Make You Sweat (Everybody Dance Now)" was the debut hit for the C & C Music Factory, released in 1990. An exciting and intense dance floor number featuring rapping by Freedom Williams and powerful vocals by Martha Wash, it was the first major house music hit, reaching the top of the pop, dance and R&B charts. In the years since, it has been featured in numerous films and television programs, including *Sister Act*, *Jarhead*, *Fresh Prince of Bel Air*, *The Simpsons* and *The Office*.

NOTHING COMPARES 2 U – PRINCE

"Nothing Compares 2 U," a great ballad of heartbreak, was originally written by Prince for his backing band, the Family, in 1985. The song became a worldwide hit in 1990 when it was recorded by the young Irish artist, Sinéad O'Connor, who took it to #1 in the U.S, and several other countries. O'Connor's striking and much-seen video of the song helped to create the phenomenon. Prince later recorded the song himself.

I CAN'T MAKE YOU LOVE ME – MIKE REID & ALLEN SHAMBLIN

"I Can't Make You Love Me" was originally conceived by its writers, Mike Reid and Allen Shamblin, as an up-tempo country song. By the time it appeared on Bonnie Raitt's best-selling album, *Luck of the Draw*, it had become a slow, emotionally powerful ballad with a memorable piano solo by Bruce Hornsby. The song was a chart hit for Raitt and has become a standard, evidenced by the numerous cover versions by artists that range from Nancy Wilson to George Michael to Bon Iver.

SUNNY CAME HOME – SHAWN COLVIN & JOHN LEVENTHAL

On rare occasions, songs dealing with revenge or murder capture the popular imagination. "Sunny Came Home" was the centerpiece of Shawn Colvin's 1996 album, *A Few Small Repairs*. A story song, its plot deals with a woman who burns down her house. The lyrics of destruction and desperation are in counterpoint to the inviting acoustic arrangement and the sweetness of Colvin's vocals. A chart-topper for Colvin, it earned Colvin and her co-writer and producer, John Leventhal, GRAMMY Awards for Song of the Year and Record of the Year.

BECAUSE YOU LOVED ME – DIANE WARREN

The Oscar-nominated and GRAMMY-winning "Because You Loved Me" is just one of scores of hit songs created by Diane Warren, perhaps the most prolific and successful songwriter of the past three decades. Written for the soundtrack of the 1996 film, *Up Close and Personal*, it was recorded by Céline Dion and spent six weeks at the top of the charts. The lyrics are a thank you to someone for guidance, encouragement and protection; Warren has said that her feelings for her father inspired the song.

2000s

Josh Kear & Chris Tompkins

Alicia Keys

Stephen Schwartz

Kuk Harrel & Beyoncé Knowles
Christopher "Tricky" Stewart & Terius Nash

Jason Mraz

BEFORE HE CHEATS – JOSH KEAR & CHRIS TOMPKINS

"Before He Cheats" was recorded by country star Carrie Underwood for her debut album in 2006 and released as a single. The story of pre-emptive revenge for potential unfaithfulness was a national sensation and is among the best-selling country singles of all time. It won GRAMMY Awards for Country Song of the Year and Best Country Vocal Performance. R&B singer Joe subsequently recorded a version titled, "Before I Cheat."

IF I AIN'T GOT YOU – ALICIA KEYS

The second Alicia Keys album, *The Diary of Alicia Keys*, contained the song, "If I Ain't Got You," released as a single in early 2004. Keys has said that she wrote it after the sudden death in 2001 of fellow singer Aaliyah, a tragic event that helped Keys understand "what matters and what doesn't." The recording topped the R&B singles chart for six weeks and reached #4 on the Hot 100, remaining on that chart for 40 weeks. "If I Ain't Got You" was nominated for the 2005 GRAMMY Award for Song of the Year and won Best Female R&B Vocal Performance.

DEFYING GRAVITY – STEPHEN SCHWARTZ

Stephen Schwartz's smash Broadway musical, *Wicked*, includes the showstopper, "Defying Gravity," sung by the characters Elphaba (The Wicked Witch of the West) and Glinda, played by Idina Menzel and Kristin Chenoweth, respectively, in the original cast. A dance remix of the song featuring vocals by Menzel reached #5 on the Hot Dance Club Songs chart in 2007. The cast of Glee also recorded the song. In an "art meets life meets science" moment, "Defying Gravity" was used to wake up astronauts aboard a space shuttle mission in April 2010 in honor of the day's planned extra-vehicular activity.

SINGLE LADIES (PUT A RING ON IT) – BEYONCÉ KNOWLES, KUK HARREL, CHRISTOPHER STEWART, TERIUS NASH

Among the biggest hit songs of the early 21st Century is "Single Ladies (Put a Ring on It)" recorded by Beyoncé for her 2008 album *I Am...Sasha Fierce*. A clever and contagious look at the reluctance of men to commit, the single was a worldwide phenomenon, topping charts in a number of countries. A triple GRAMMY winner, "Single Ladies" and its viral video have been covered and/or parodied by numerous singers, dancers and comedians.

I'M YOURS – JASON MRAZ

Jason Mraz's 2008 single, "I'm Yours," from his album *We Sing. We Dance. We Steal Things.*, is that artist's breakthrough hit. The irresistible, reggae-inflected tune spent a record-breaking 76 weeks on the Billboard Hot 100 and was an international hit, as well. In an appearance on *Sesame Street*, Mraz performed a rewritten version of the song, titled "Outdoors." He also issued a remix of "I'm Yours" that included vocals by rapper Li'l Wayne and Reggae star Jah Cure.

Ashley Gorley, Kelley Lovelace & Brad Paisley

Ari Levine, Bruno Mars & Philip Lawrence

Ryan Tedder

2010s

AMERICAN SATURDAY NIGHT
BRAD PAISLEY, ASHLEY GORLEY & KELLEY LOVELACE

"American Saturday Night" is the title track of Brad Paisley's 2009 album. It was released as a single and rose to #2 on the country chart. It is distinctive in the way it boasts of American cultural diversity by listing, as songwriter Ashley Gorley has said, "the things that are borrowed from other countries and traditions that make America great."

LOCKED OUT OF HEAVEN
BRUNO MARS, PHILIP LAWRENCE & ARI LEVINE

"Locked Out of Heaven" a reggae and new wave-infused single from the 2012 Bruno Mars album, *Unorthodox Jukebox*, spent six weeks at the top of the Hot 100 and was a Top Ten hit in 20 other countries. Written by Mars and the other two members of the Smeezingtons writing-production team (Ari Levine and Philip Lawrence), the song celebrates a love both sensual and spiritual with a sonic nod to one of Mars's favorite bands, the Police.

SECRETS – RYAN TEDDER

"Secrets," a song on OneRepublic's 2009 album, *Waking Up*, was a Top 5 adult contemporary hit after being released as a single in 2010. It was particularly popular in Germany, Austria and Poland. The song's unique combination of a cello, booming drums and plaintive vocals make it memorable. It was prominently featured in the film *The Sorceror's Apprentice*, a promotional campaign for the final season of the TV series, *Lost*, and in the launch of Ralph Lauren's "Big Pony" fragrance line.

AH! SWEET MYSTERY OF LIFE

Lyrics by RIDA JOHNSON YOUNG
Music by VICTOR HERBERT

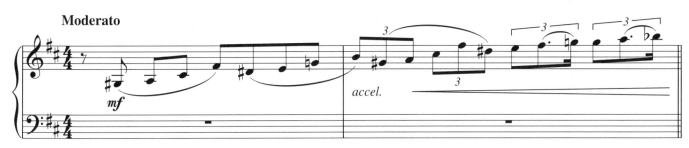

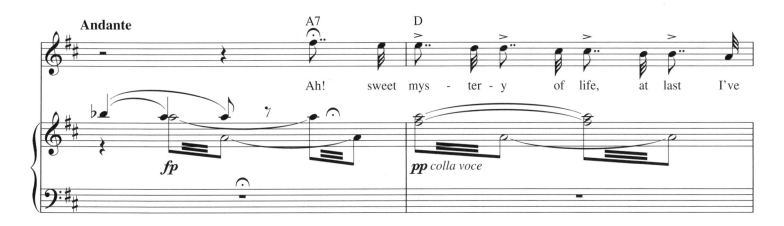

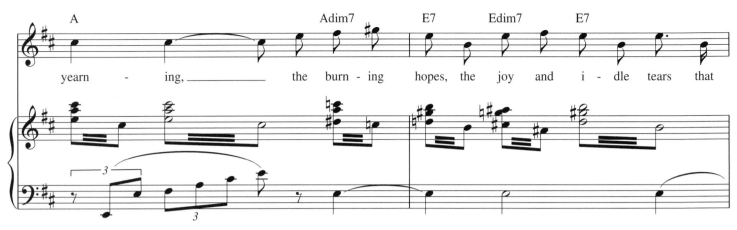

yearn - ing, _____ the burn - ing hopes, the joy and i - dle tears that

fall! _____ For 'tis love, and love a- lone, the world is

seek - ing; And 'tis love, and love a- lone, that can re-

pay! 'Tis the an - swer, 'tis the end and all of liv - ing, ___ for it is

AFTER YOU'VE GONE

Words by HENRY CREAMER
Music by TURNER LAYTON

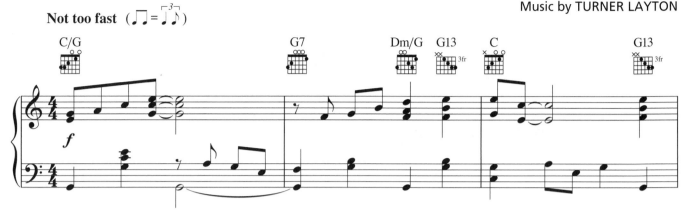

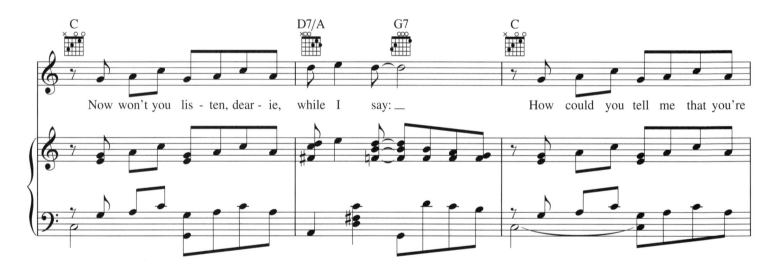

Now won't you lis - ten, dear - ie, while I say: — How could you tell me that you're

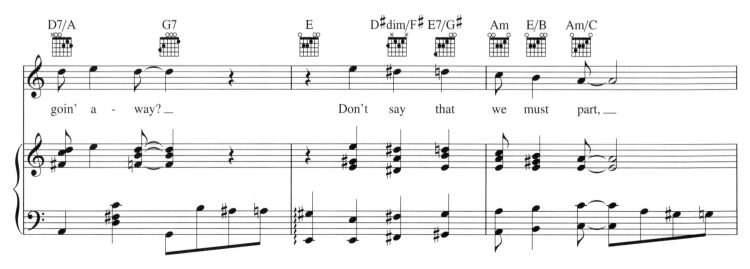

goin' a - way? — Don't say that we must part, —

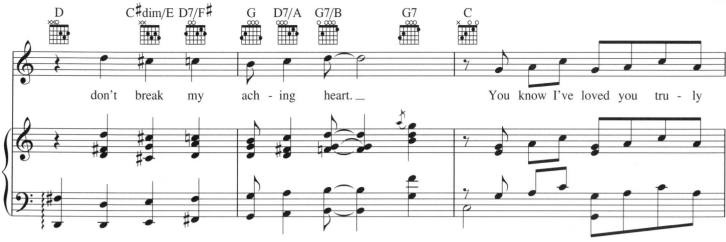

don't break my ach - ing heart. __ You know I've loved you tru - ly

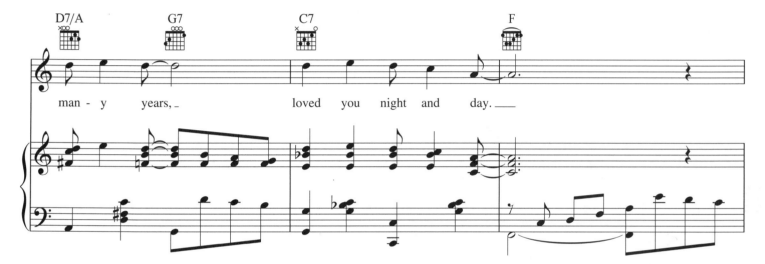

man - y years, __ loved you night and day. __

How can you leave me, can't you see my tears? __ Lis - ten while __ I

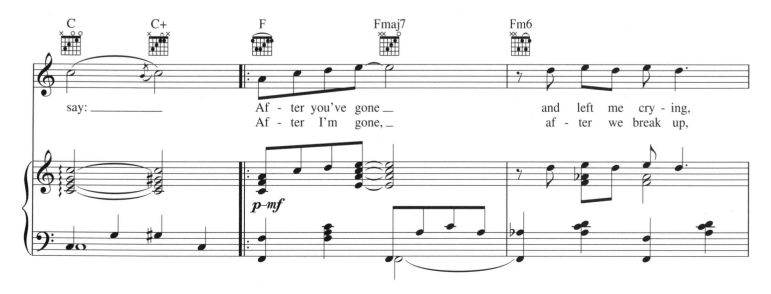

say: _____

Af - ter you've gone __ and left me cry - ing,
Af - ter I'm gone, __ af - ter we break up,

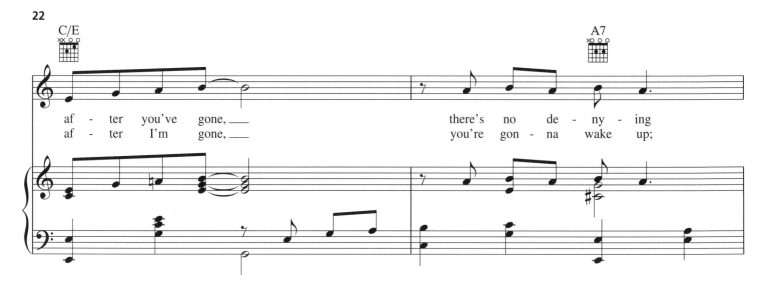

C/E

af - ter you've gone, ___ there's no de - ny - ing
af - ter I'm gone, ___ you're gon - na wake up;

A7

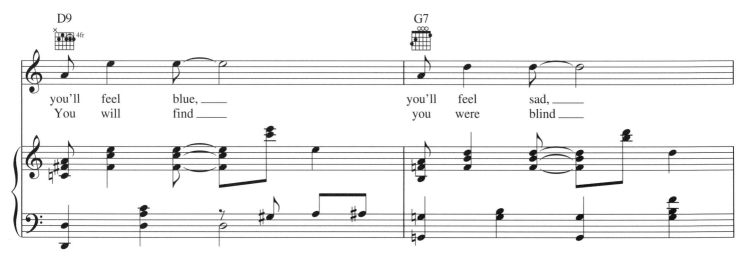

D9

you'll feel blue, ___ you'll feel sad, ___
You will find ___ you were blind ___

G7

C6

you'll miss the dear - est pal you've ev - er had. ___
to let some - bod - y come and change your mind. ___

C   **C7**

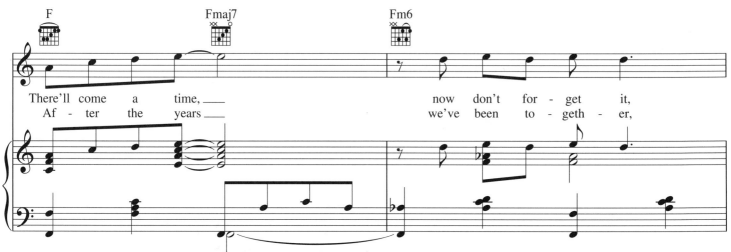

F   **Fmaj7**   **Fm6**

There'll come a time, ___ now don't for - get it,
Af - ter the years ___ we've been to - geth - er,

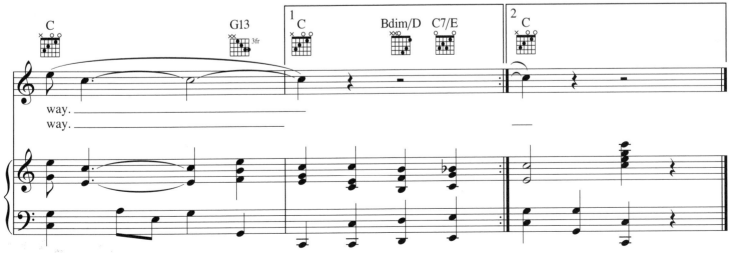

AIN'T NO MOUNTAIN HIGH ENOUGH

Words and Music by NICKOLAS ASHFORD
and VALERIE SIMPSON

With a steady beat

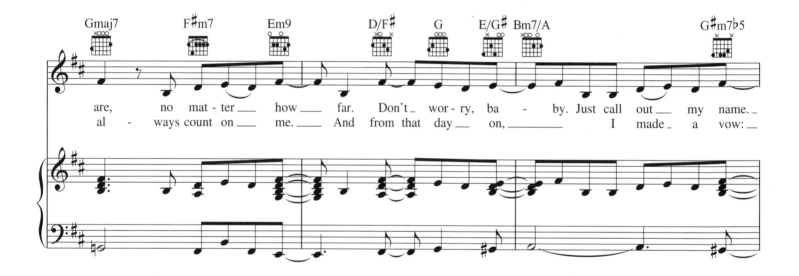

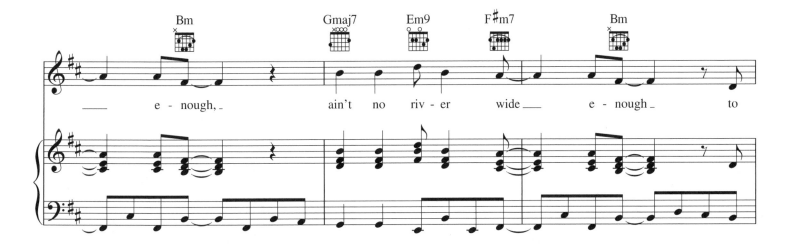

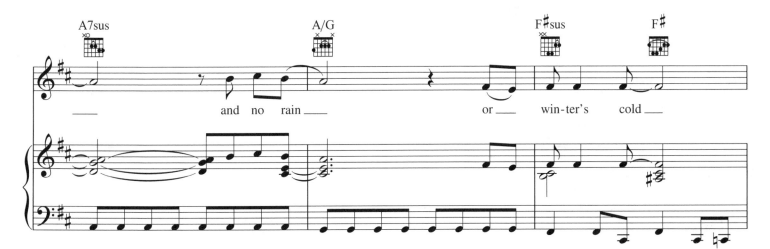

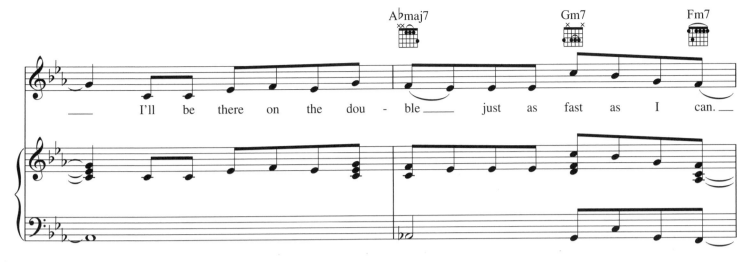

I'll be there on the dou - ble ___ just as fast as I can. ___

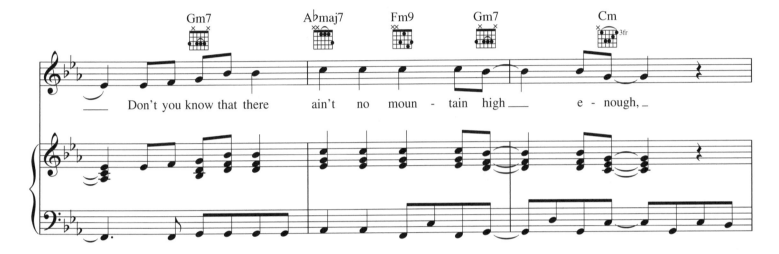

___ Don't you know that there ain't no moun - tain high ___ e - nough, _

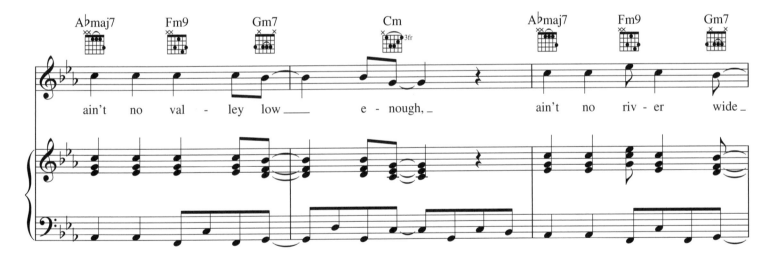

ain't no val - ley low ___ e - nough, _ ain't no riv - er wide _

___ e - nough ___ to keep me from get - ting to you, ___ babe.

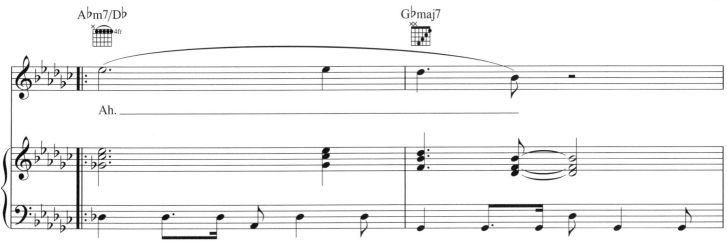

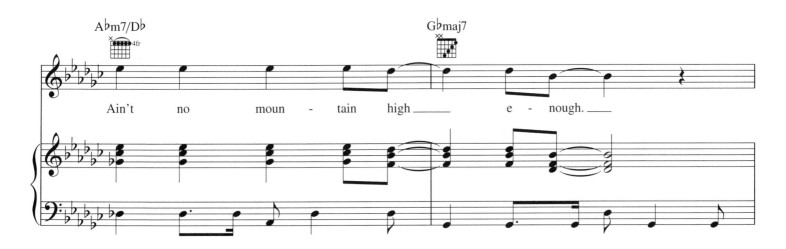

Repeat and Fade

ALL NIGHT LONG
(All Night)

Words and Music by
LIONEL RICHIE

Moderate Caribbean feel

Da da __

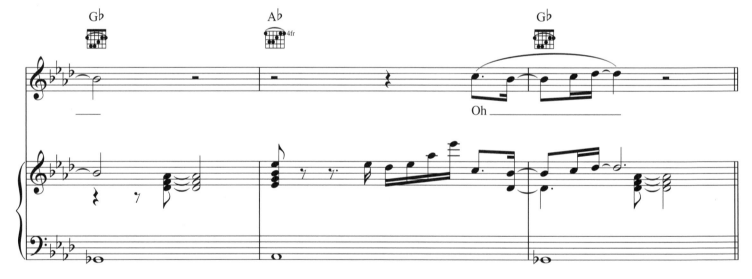

Oh _____

Well, my friends, __ the time has come.
Peo - ple danc - ing all in the street,

Raise the roof and
see the rhy - thm all

have some fun. / in their feet.

Throw a - way / Life is good,

the work to be done. __ / wild, and sweet. __

Let the mu - sic / Let the mu - sic

play on. (Play on, play on.) / play on. (Play on, play on.)

Ev - 'ry - bod - y sing, __ / Feel it in your heart

__ ev - 'ry - bod - y dance. / and feel it in your soul.

Lose your - self in wild ro - mance. We're going to / Let the mu - sic take con - trol. We're going to

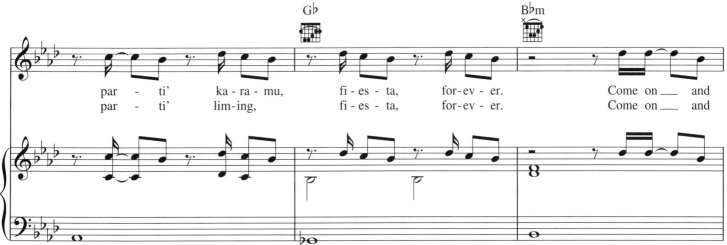

par - ti' ka - ra - mu, / par - ti' lim - ing,

fi - es - ta, / fi - es - ta,

for - ev - er. / for - ev - er.

Come on __ and / Come on __ and

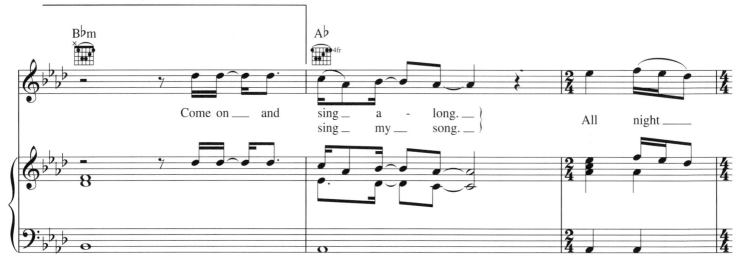

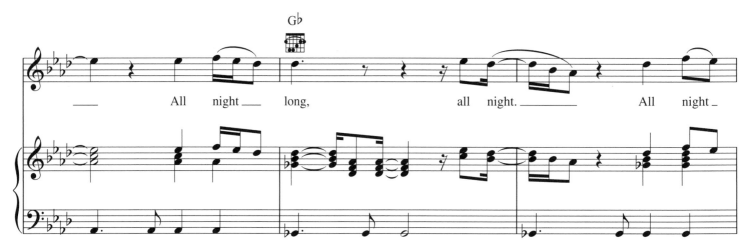

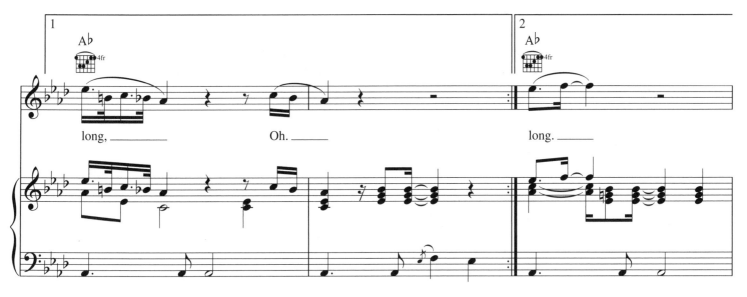

long, _____ Oh. _____ long. _____

Yeah! Once you _ get start - ed _ you can't sit _ down. _

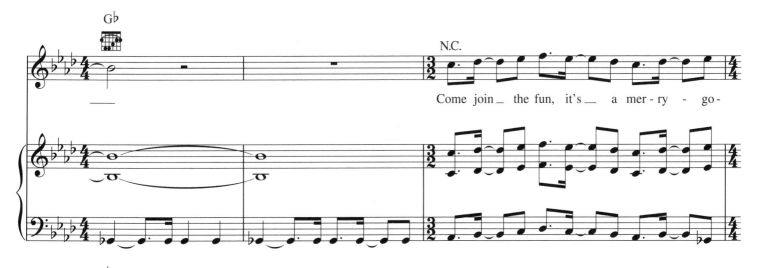

Come join _ the fun, it's _ a mer - ry - go-

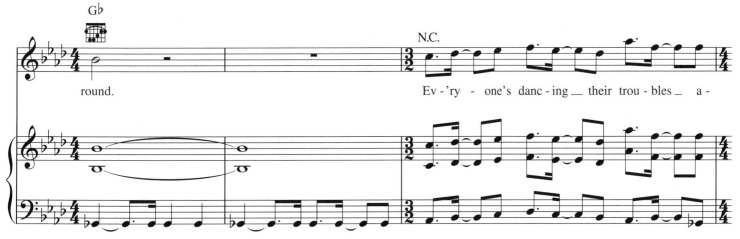

round. Ev -'ry - one's danc - ing _ their trou - bles _ a-

way.

Come join __ our par - ty, __ see __ how we play!

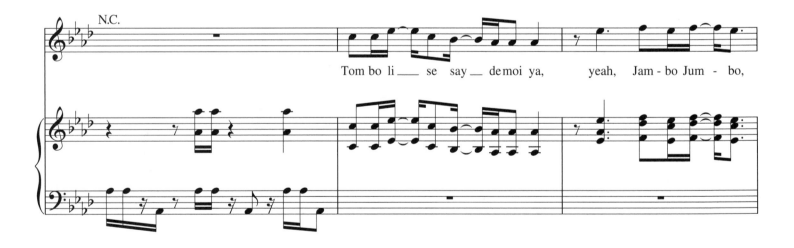

Tom bo li __ se say __ de moi ya, yeah, Jam - bo Jum - bo,

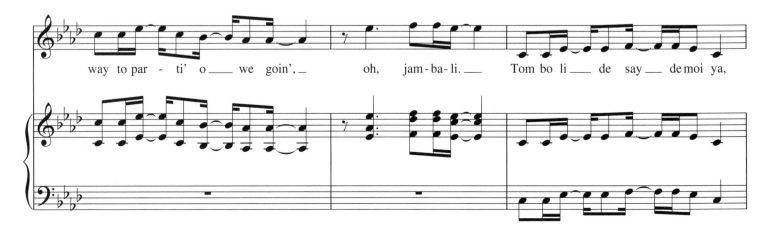

way to par - ti' o __ we goin', __ oh, jam - ba - li. __ Tom bo li __ de say __ de moi ya,

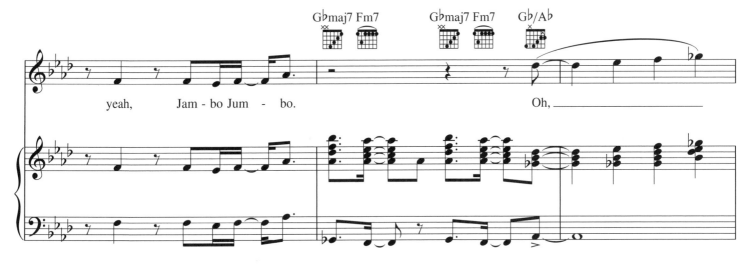

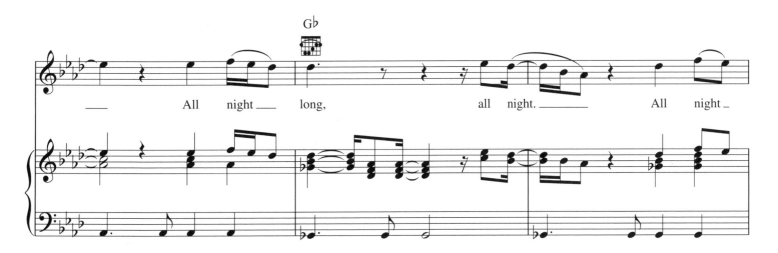

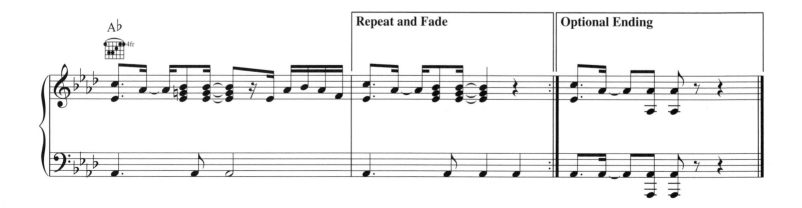

Because You Loved Me

from UP CLOSE AND PERSONAL

Words and Music by
DIANE WARREN

Slowly

For all ___ those times you stood ___ by me, for all ___ the
wings and made ___ me fly. You touched ___ my

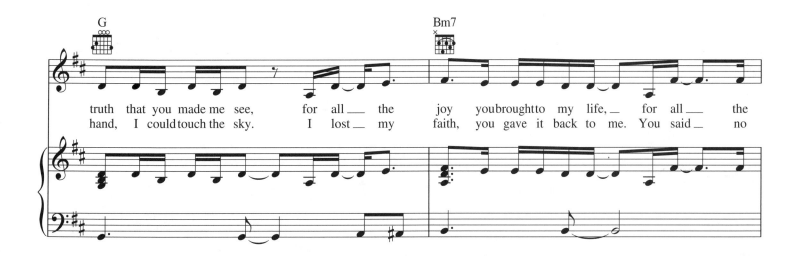

truth that you made me see, for all ___ the joy you brought to my life, ___ for all ___ the
hand, I could touch the sky. I lost ___ my faith, you gave it back to me. You said ___ no

wrong that you ___ made right, for ev - 'ry ___ dream you made ___ come true, for all ___ the
star was out ___ of reach. You stood by ___ me and I ___ stood tall. I had ___ your

*Recorded a half step lower.

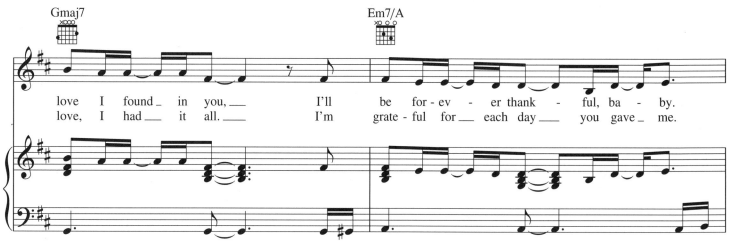

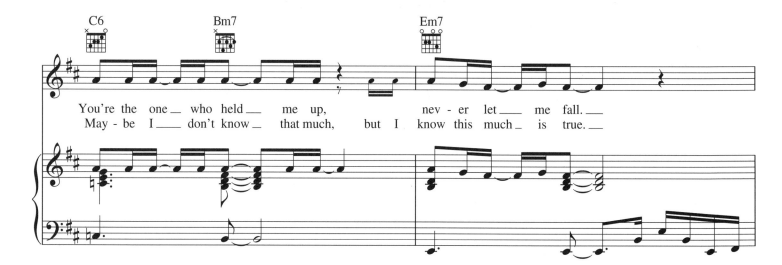

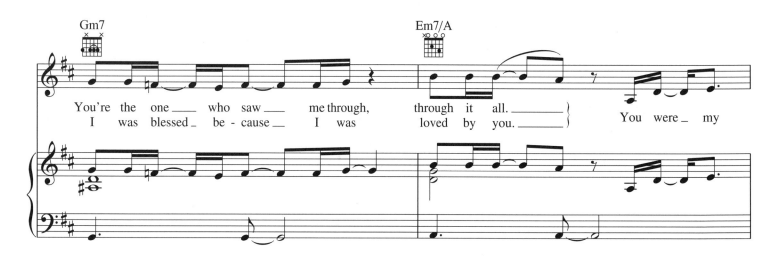

light in the dark, __ shin - ing your love __ in - to my __ life. _____ You've

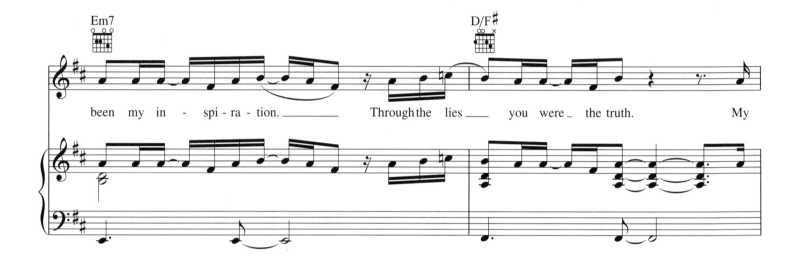

been my in - spi - ra - tion. _____ Through the lies __ you were __ the truth. My

world is a bet - ter place be - cause __ of you. ___ You were __ my

D.S. al Coda

CODA

loved __ me. You were __ my strength when I ___ was weak. You were __ my

voice when I could-n't speak. You were _ my eyes when I could-n't see. You saw _ the

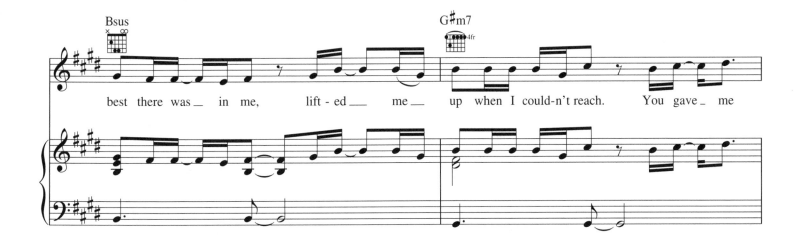

best there was _ in me, lift-ed __ me __ up when I could-n't reach. You gave _ me

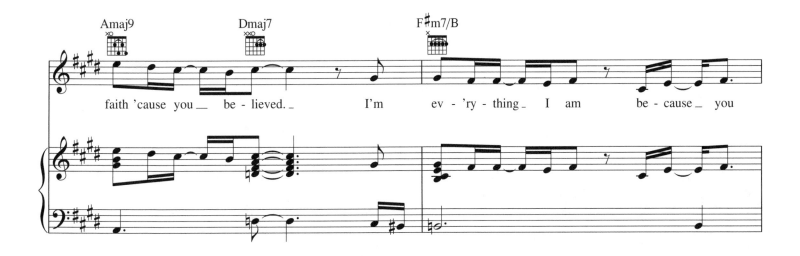

faith 'cause you _ be - lieved. _ I'm ev -'ry-thing _ I am be - cause _ you

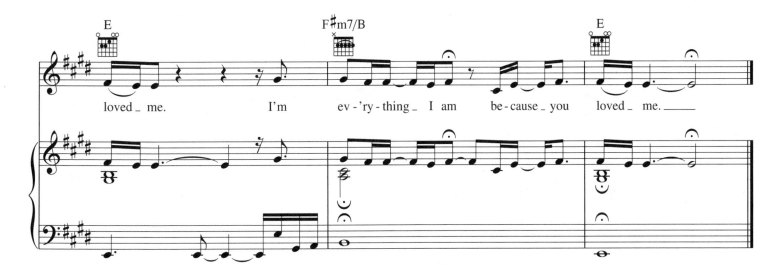

loved _ me. I'm ev -'ry-thing _ I am be - cause _ you loved _ me. _

ALL THE WAY
from THE JOKER IS WILD

Words by SAMMY CAHN
Music by JAMES VAN HEUSEN

AMERICAN SATURDAY NIGHT

Words and Music by BRAD PAISLEY,
KELLEY LOVELACE and ASHLEY GORLEY

Moderately fast

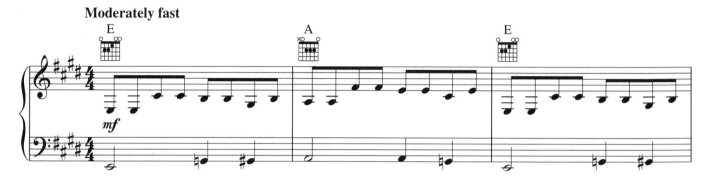

Whoa.

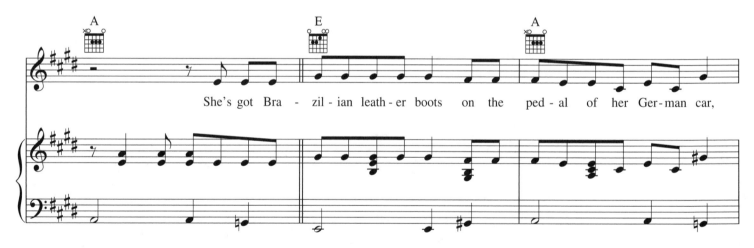

She's got Bra - zil - ian leath - er boots on the ped - al of her Ger - man car,

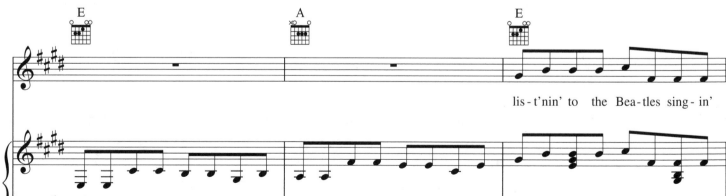

lis - t'nin' to the Bea - tles sing - in'

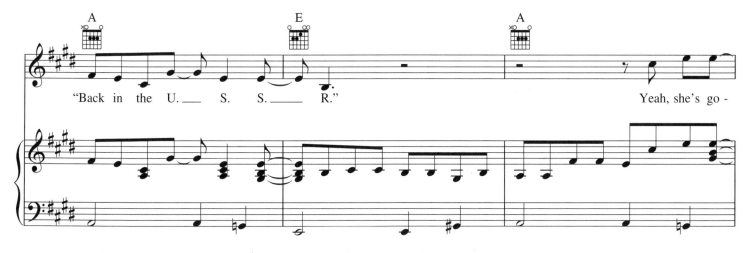

"Back in the U.___ S.___ S.___ R." Yeah, she's go-

- in' 'round the world ___ to-night, ___ but she ain't ___ leav-in' here. ___

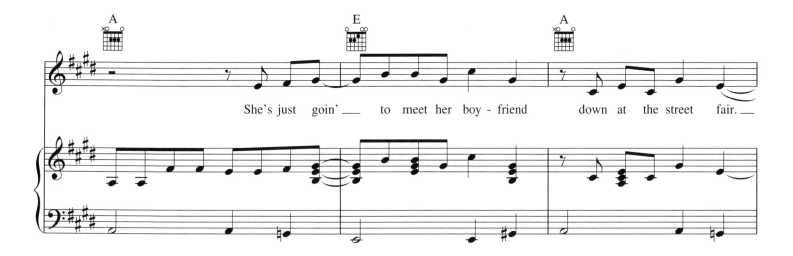

She's just goin' ___ to meet her boy-friend ___ down at the street fair. ___

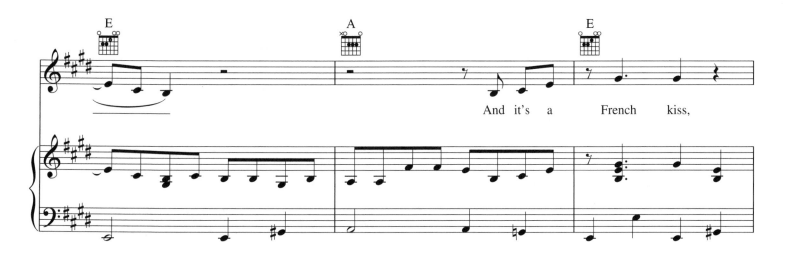

And it's a French kiss,

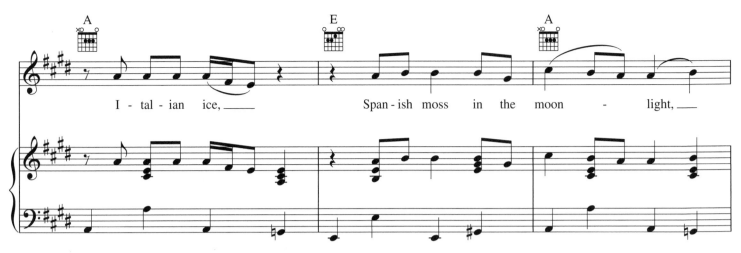

I - tal - ian ice, _____ Span - ish moss in the moon - light, _____

just an - oth - er A - mer - i - can Sat - ur - day night. _____

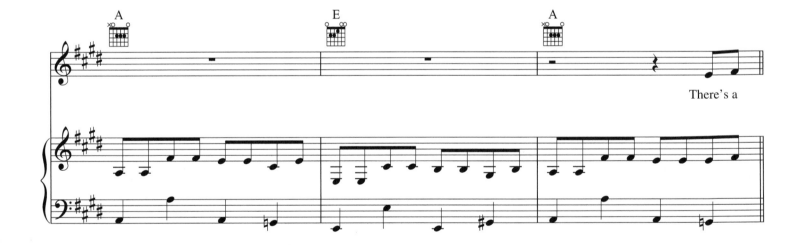

There's a

big to - ga par - ty to - night _____ down at Del - ta Chi.

mix it all up. It's a French kiss, I - tal - ian ice, ____

mar - ga - ri - tas in the moon - light, ___ just an - oth - er A - mer -

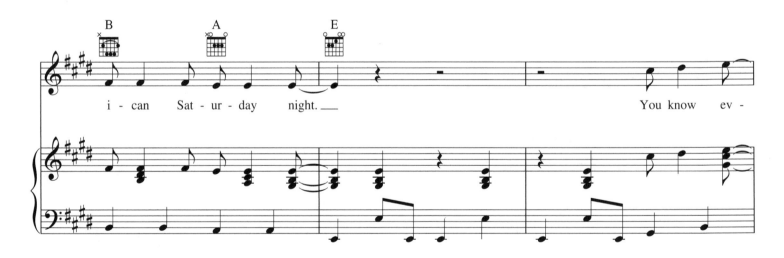

i - can Sat - ur - day night. ___ You know ev -

- 'ry - where _ has some - thin' _ they're _ known _ for,

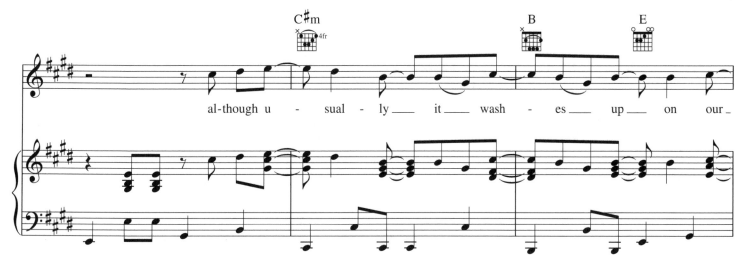

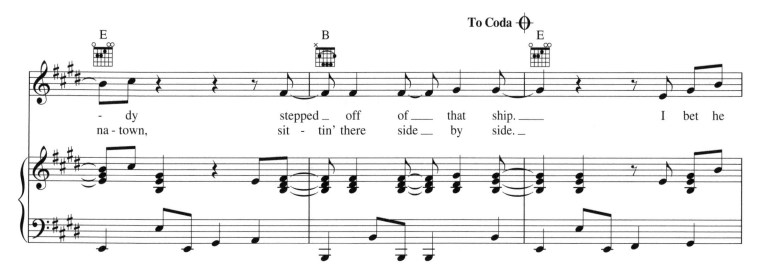

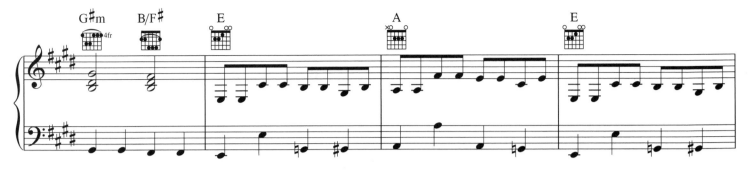

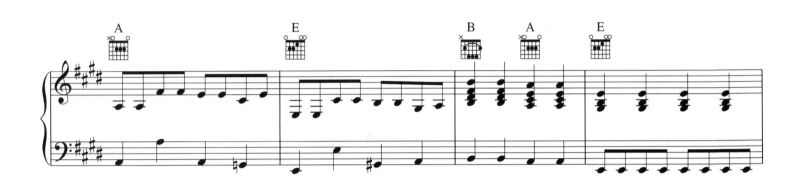

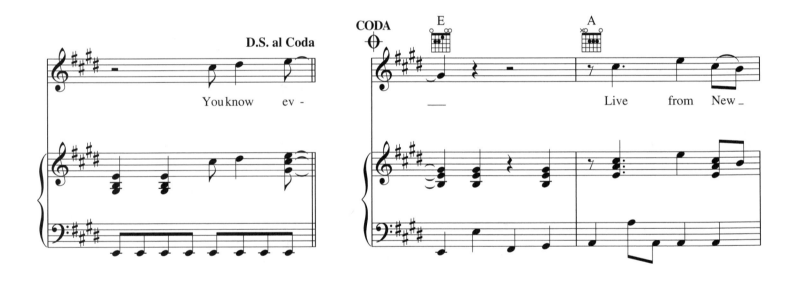

You know ev -

CODA

Live from New _

York,   It's a   French   kiss,   I - tal - ian   ice, _____

(it's Sat - ur - day   night!)

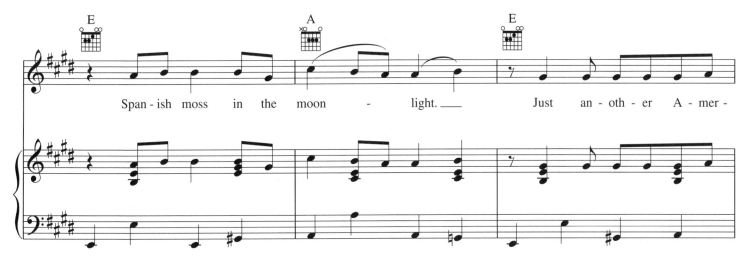

Span- ish moss in the moon - light. ___ Just an - oth - er A - mer -

i - can, just an - oth - er A - mer - i - can, _____ it's

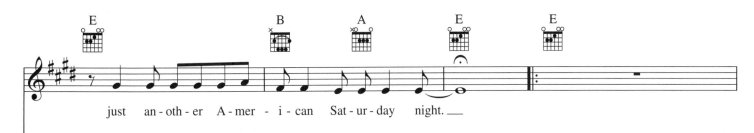

just an - oth - er A - mer - i - can Sat - ur - day night. ___

Optional Ending

Repeat and Fade

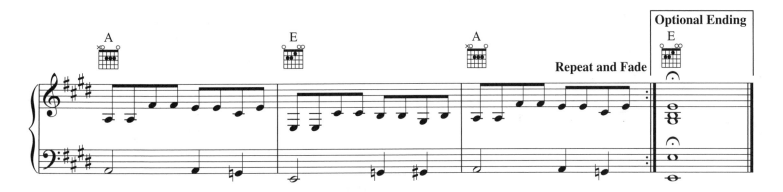

AS TIME GOES BY

from CASABLANCA

Words and Music by
HERMAN HUPFELD

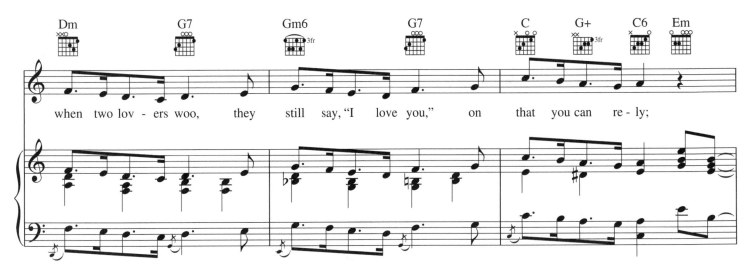

when two lov - ers woo, they still say, "I love you," on that you can re - ly;

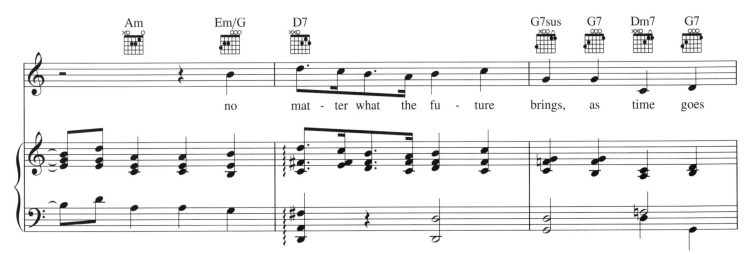

no mat - ter what the fu - ture brings, as time goes

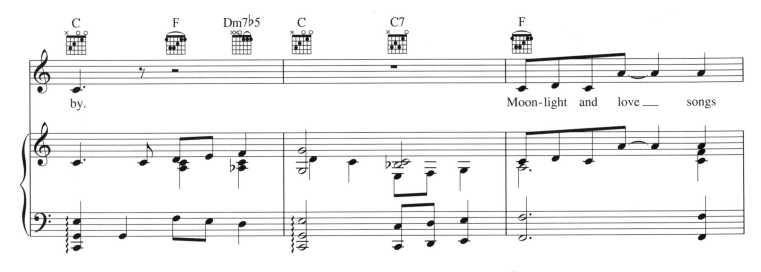

by. Moon-light and love ___ songs

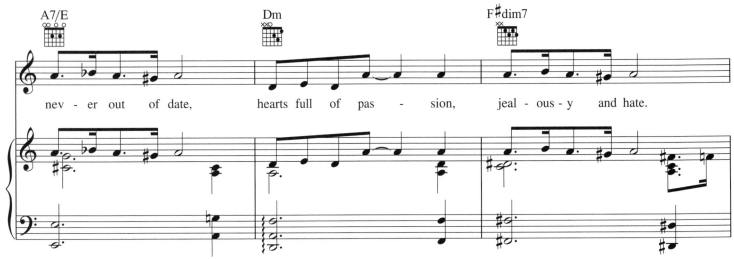

nev - er out of date, hearts full of pas - sion, jeal - ous - y and hate.

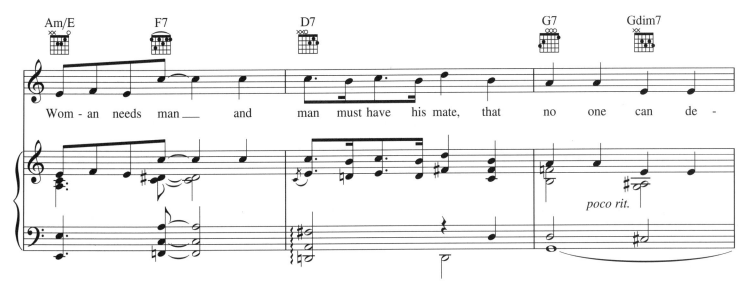

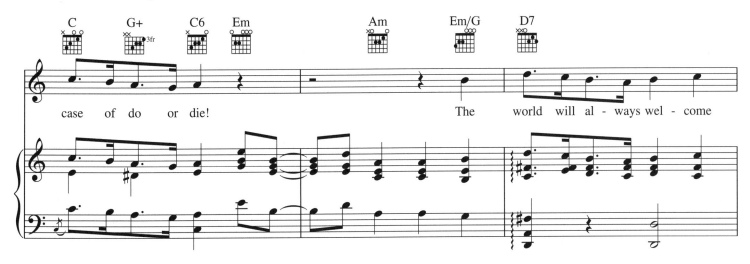

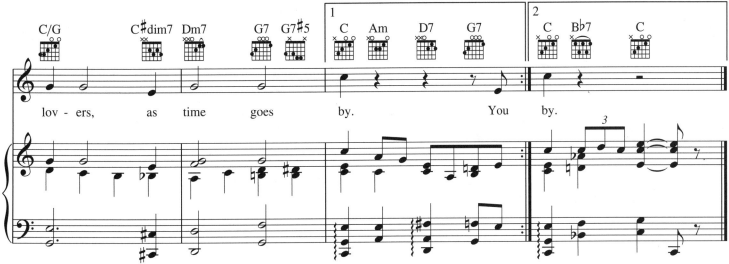

AT LAST

Lyric by MACK GORDON
Music by HARRY WARREN

Slowly and freely

mp

With pedal

Slowly, in four

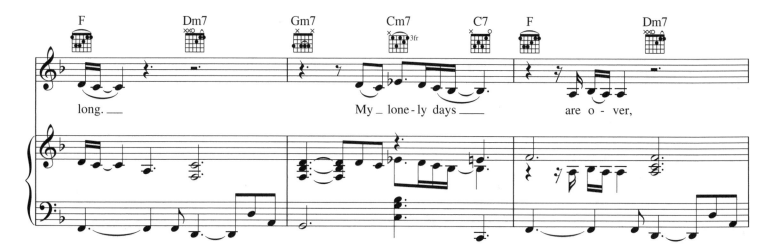

At last, my love _____ has come a-

long. _____ My lone-ly days _____ are o-ver,

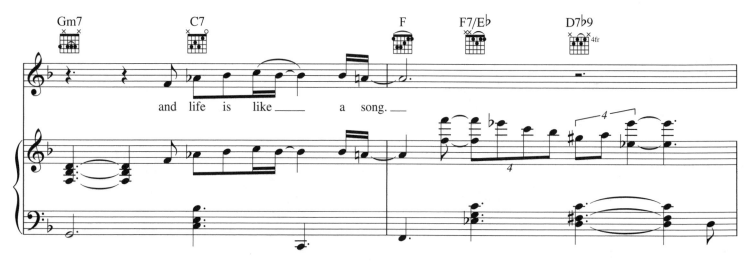

and life is like _____ a song. _____

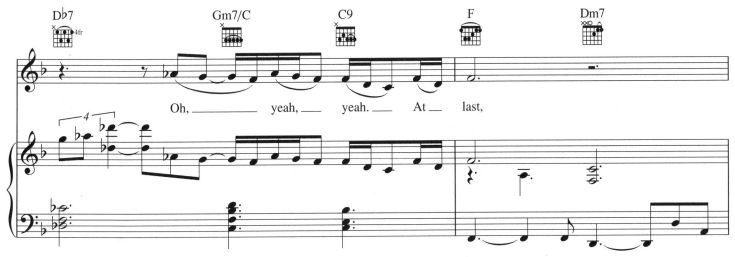

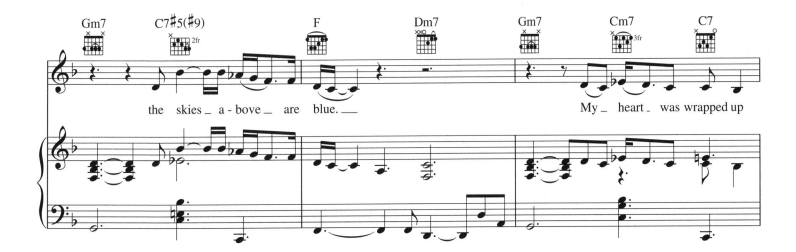

58

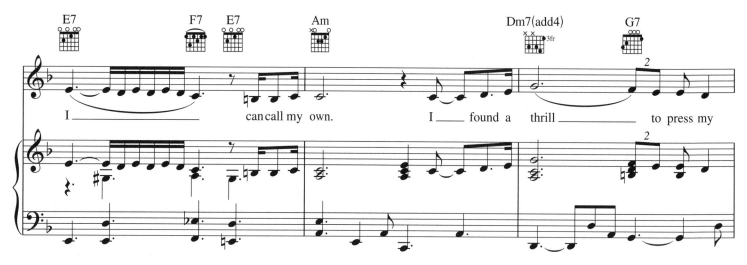

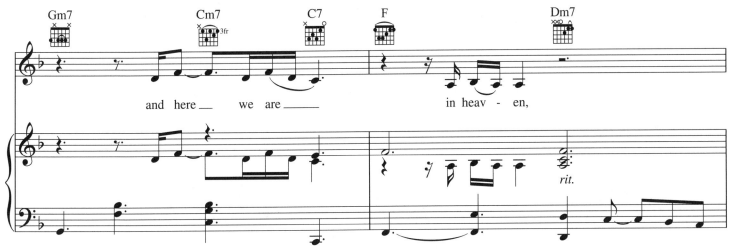

and here __ we are __ in heav - en,

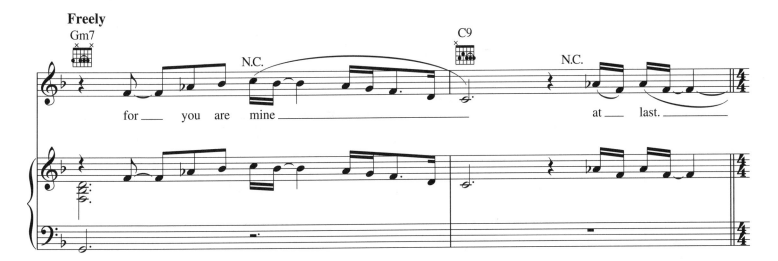

Freely

for __ you are mine _____ at __ last. _____

a tempo

Freely

BEFORE HE CHEATS

Words and Music by JOSH KEAR
and CHRIS TOMPKINS

Steady Country Swing-Rock

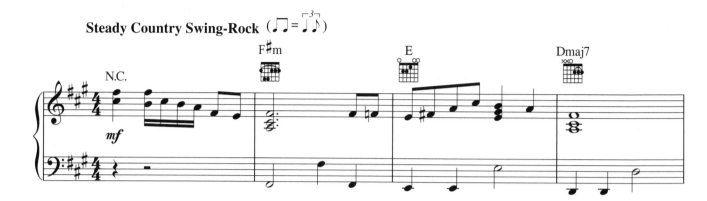

Right now he's prob-'ly slow danc-ing with a bleach-blonde tramp and she's
Right now, she's prob-'ly up sing-ing some white trash ver-sion of Sha-

prob-'ly get-ting frisk - y. Right now, he's prob-'ly buy-ing her some
ni - a ka-ra-o - ke. Right now, she's prob-'ly say-ing, "I'm drunk"

carved my name in - to his leath-er seat. _____ I took a

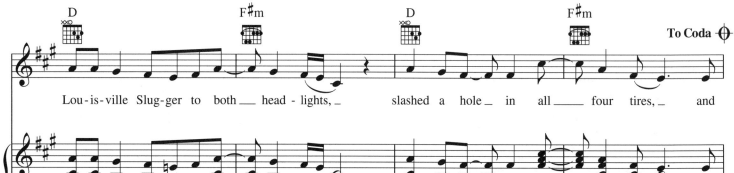

Lou-is-ville Slug-ger to both ___ head - lights, _ slashed a hole ___ in all _____ four tires, ___ and

may-be next time _ he'll think _____ be - fore _ he _____ cheats.

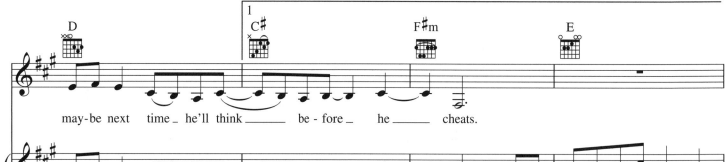

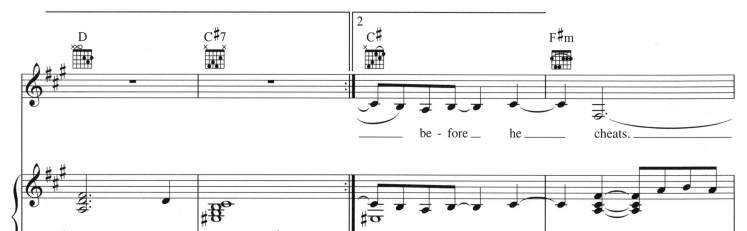

_____ be - fore _ he _____ cheats. _____

I might have saved a lit-tle trou-ble for the next girl, _____

'cause the next time that he cheats, _____ oh, you know _

_____ it won't be on _____ me. _____ No, _____

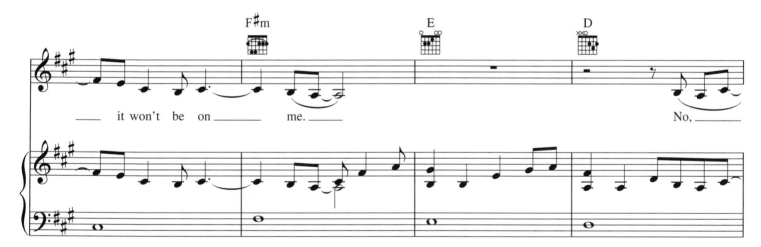

_____ not on _____ me. _____

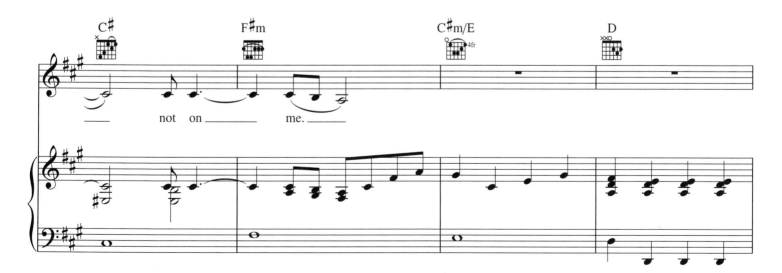

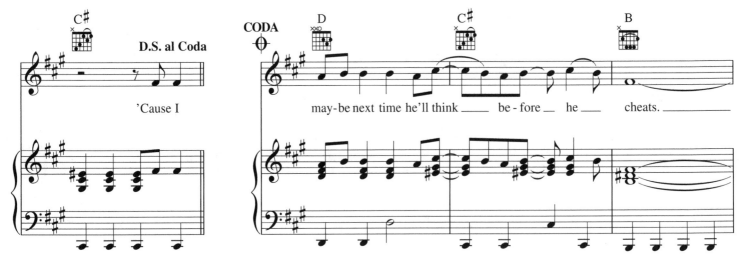

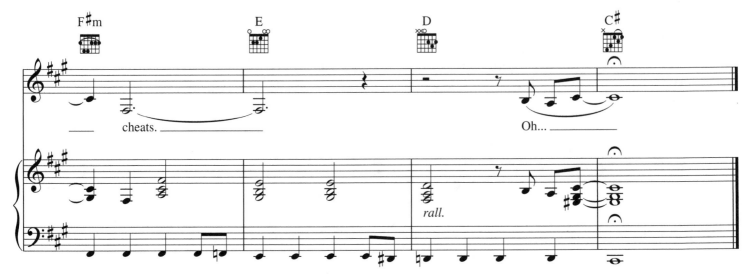

THE BEST OF TIMES
from LA CAGE AUX FOLLES

Music and Lyric by
JERRY HERMAN

Simply

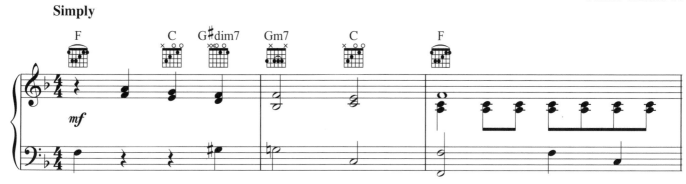

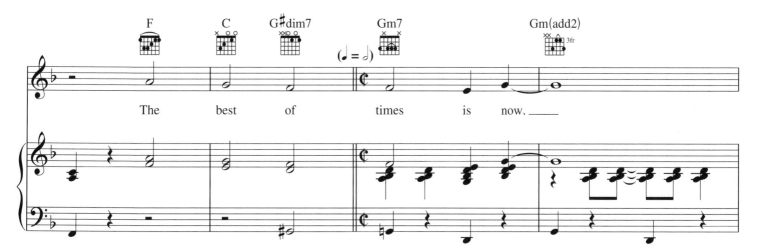

The best of times is now.

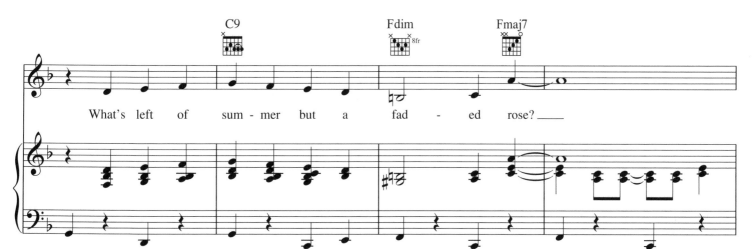

What's left of sum-mer but a fad-ed rose?

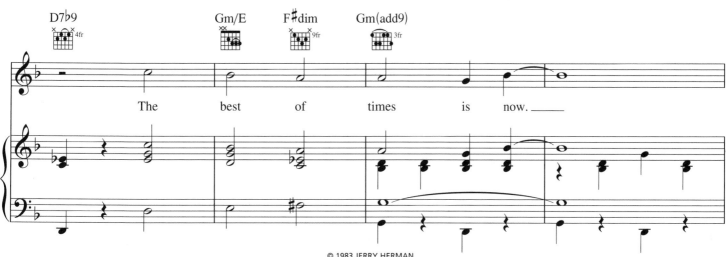

The best of times is now.

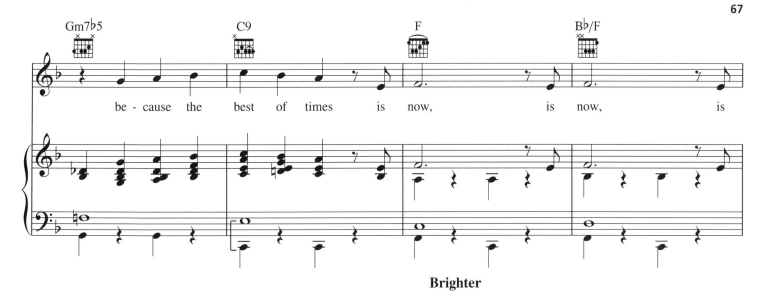

Brighter

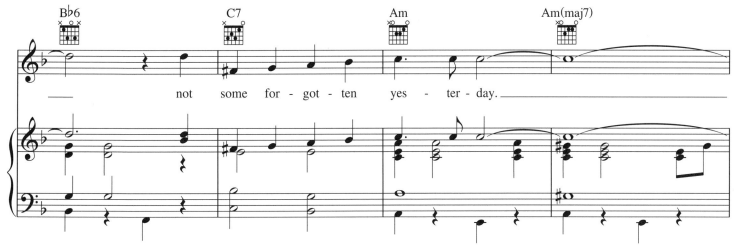

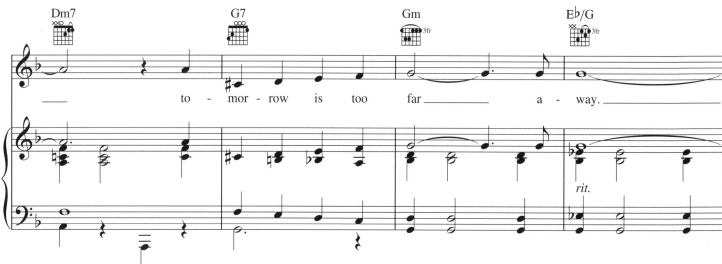

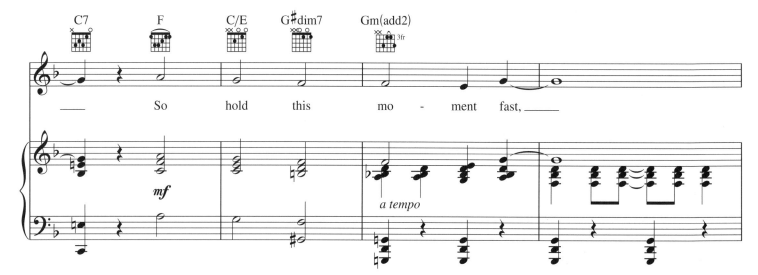

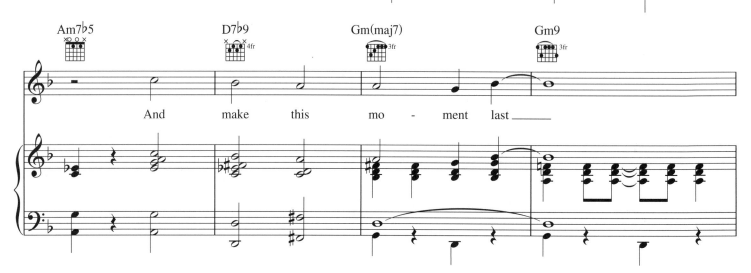

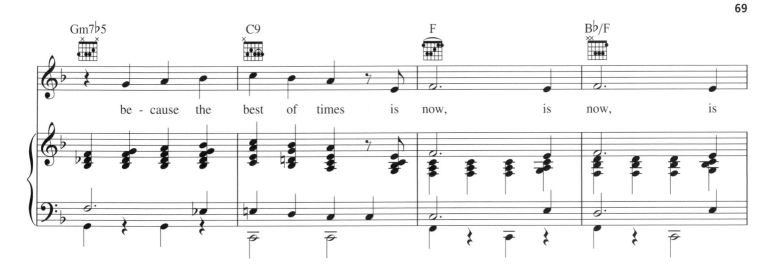

be - cause the best of times is now, is now, is

now. The best of

molto ritard.

Slower

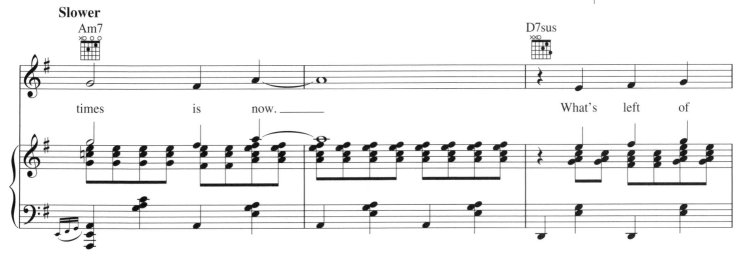

times is now. _____ What's left of

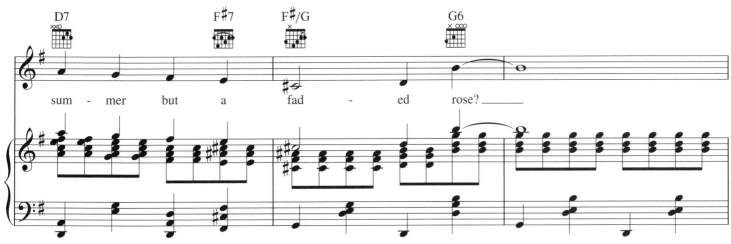

sum - mer but a fad - ed rose? _____

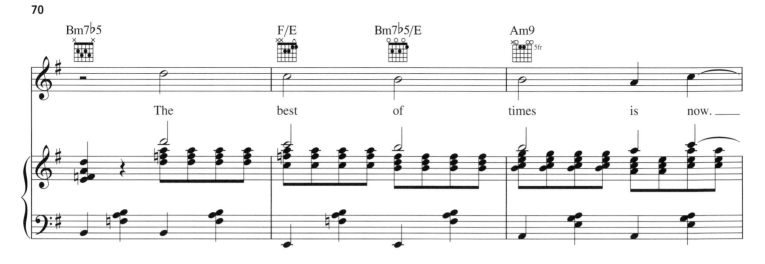

The best of times is now. _____

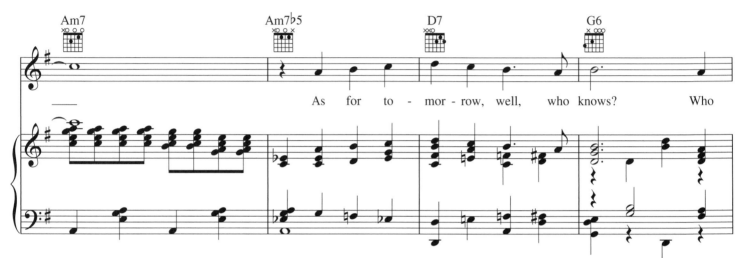

_____ As for to - mor - row, well, who knows? Who

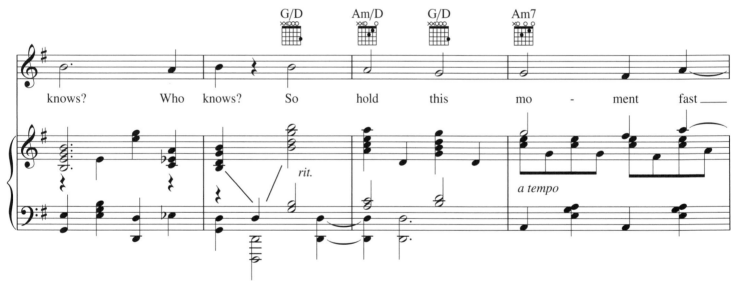

knows? Who knows? So hold this mo - ment fast _____

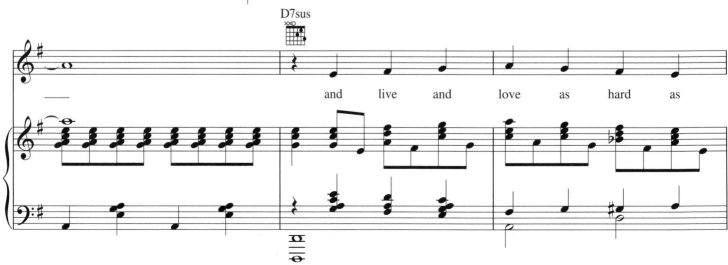

and live and love as hard as

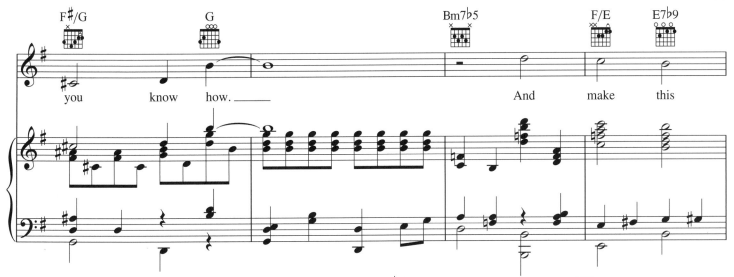

you know how. _____ And make this

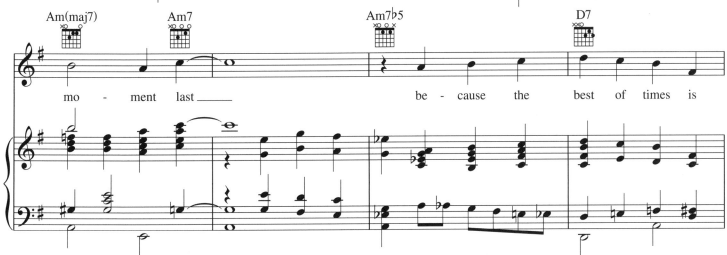

mo - ment last _____ be - cause the best of times is

now, is now, is now, is now, is

rit. poco a poco

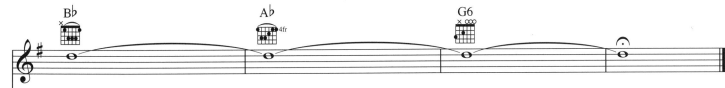

now. _____

BLUE SKIES

from BETSY

Words and Music by
IRVING BERLIN

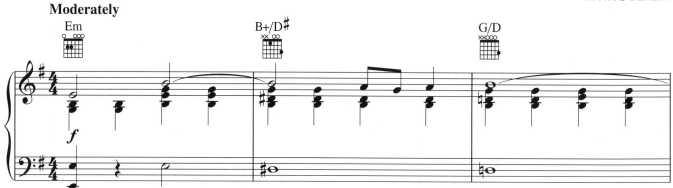

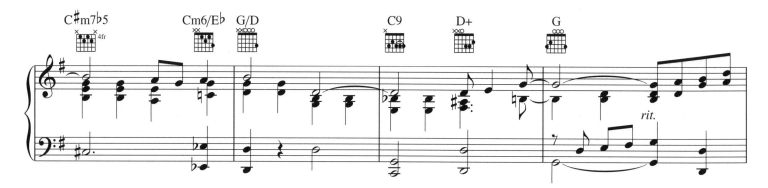

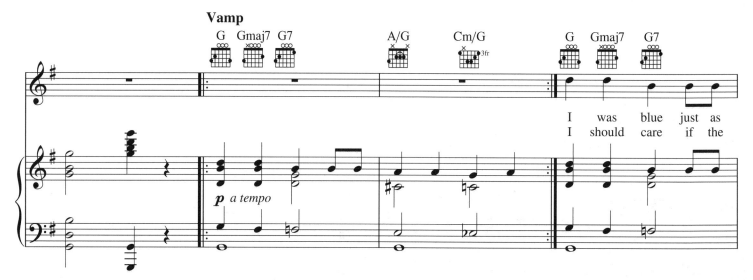

I was blue just as
I should care just if the

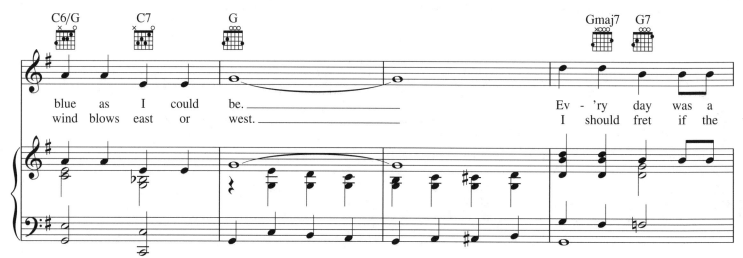

blue as I could be. _____
wind blows east or west. _____

Ev - 'ry day was a
I should fret if the

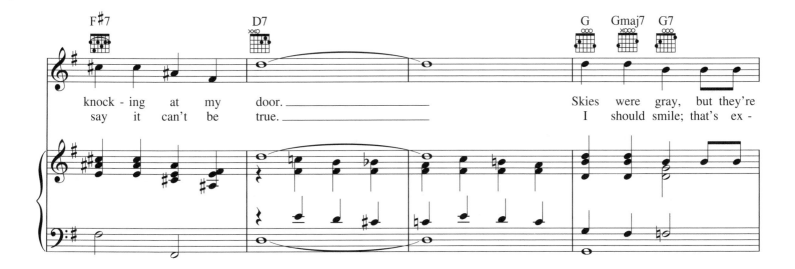

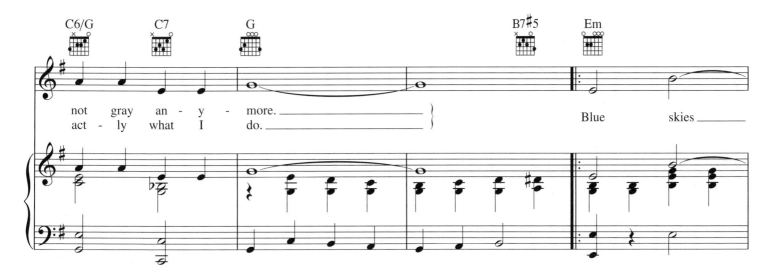

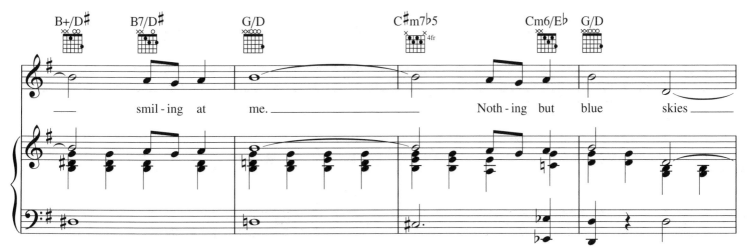

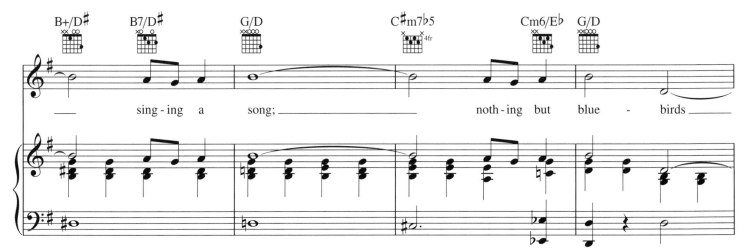

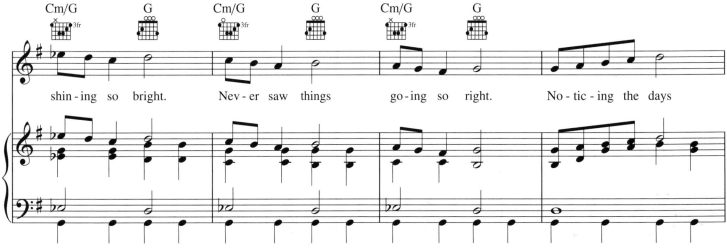

hur - ry - ing by; when you're in love, my, how they fly.

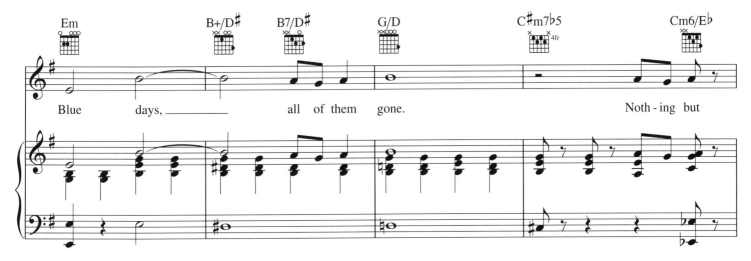

Blue days, _____ all of them gone. Noth - ing but

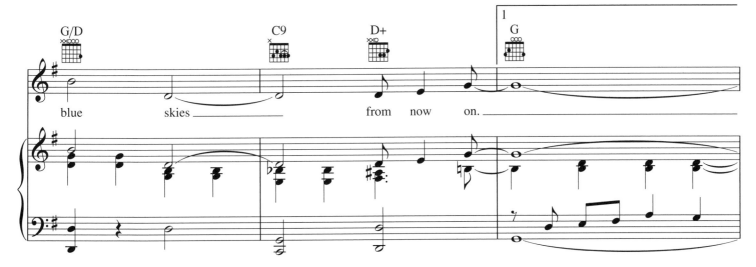

blue skies _____ from now on. _____

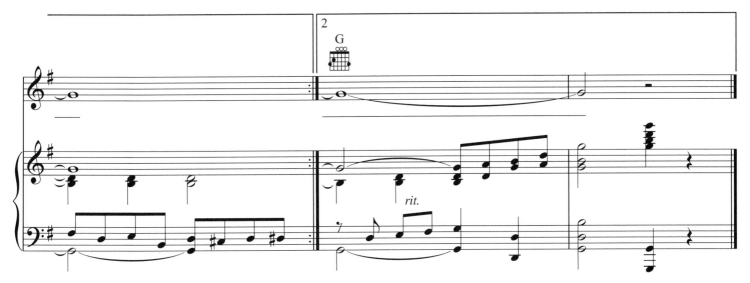

rit.

CRY ME A RIVER

Words and Music by
ARTHUR HAMILTON

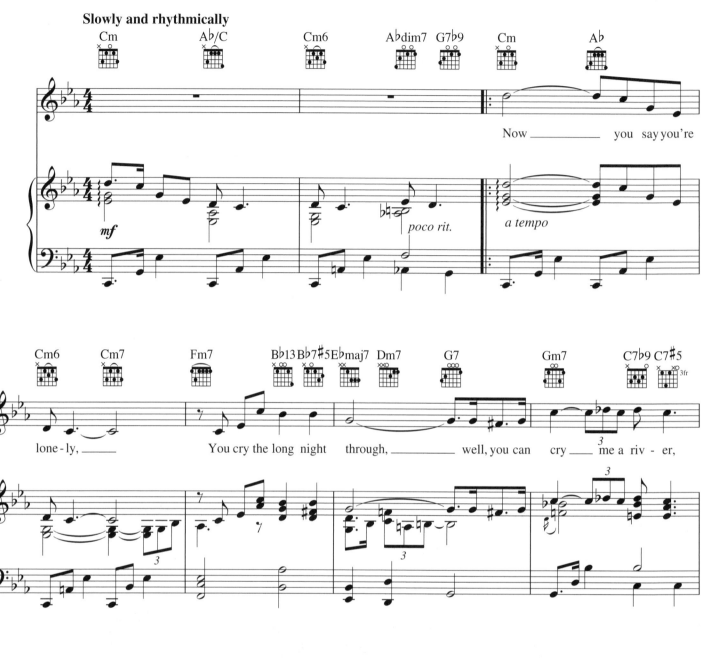

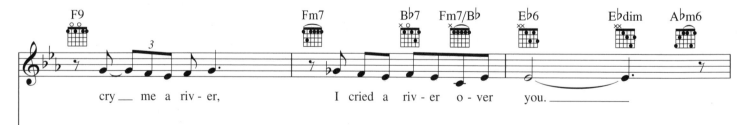

DEFYING GRAVITY
from the Broadway Musical WICKED

Music and Lyrics by
STEPHEN SCHWARTZ

Freely, with quiet intensity

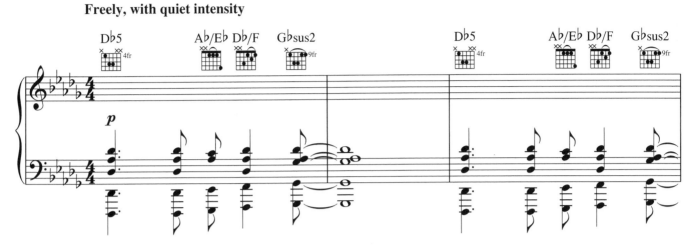

ELPHABA:

Some-thing has changed ___ with-in ___ me

some - thing is not ___ the same

I'm through with play -

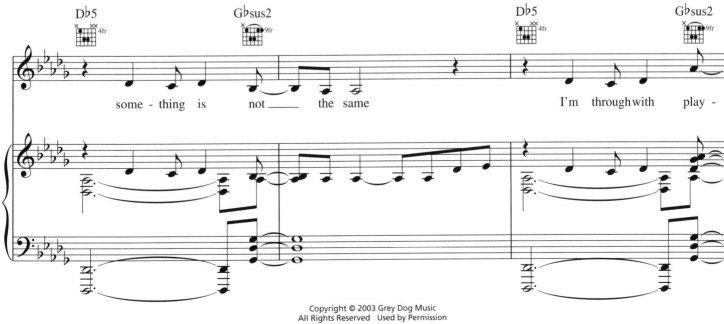

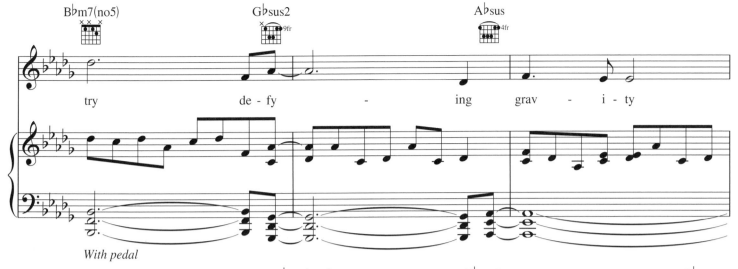

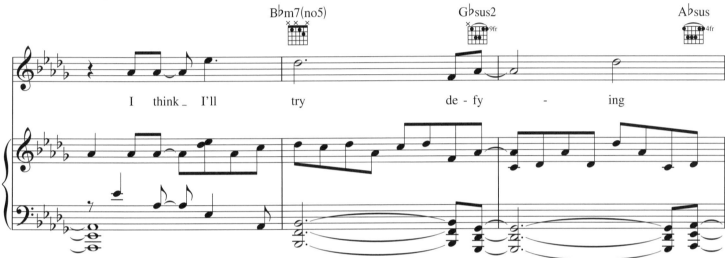

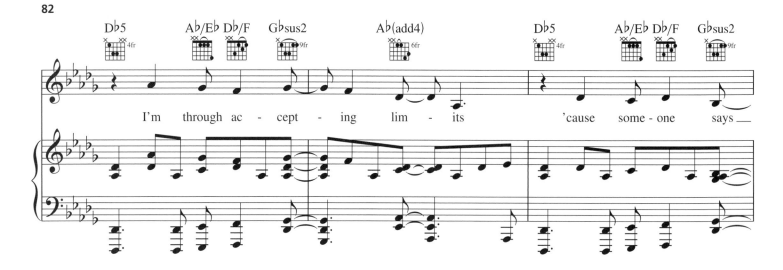

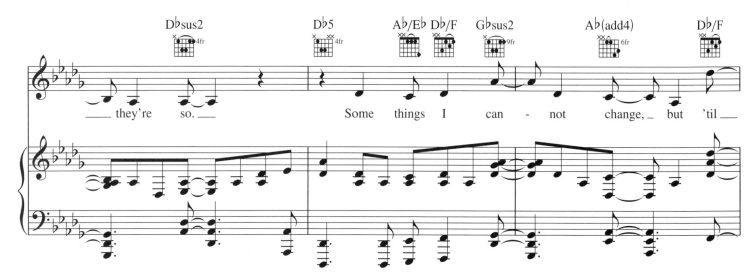

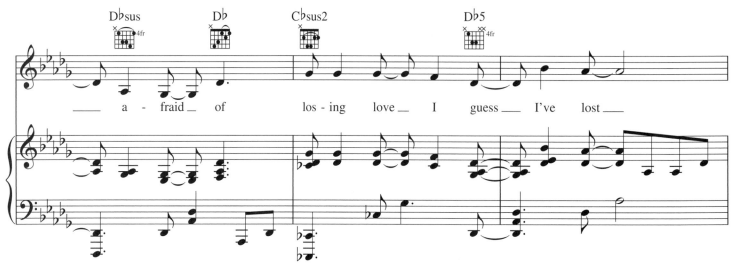

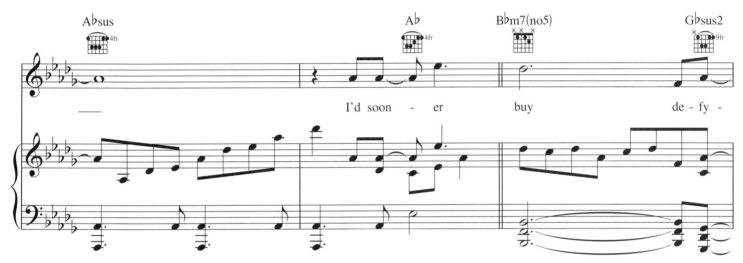

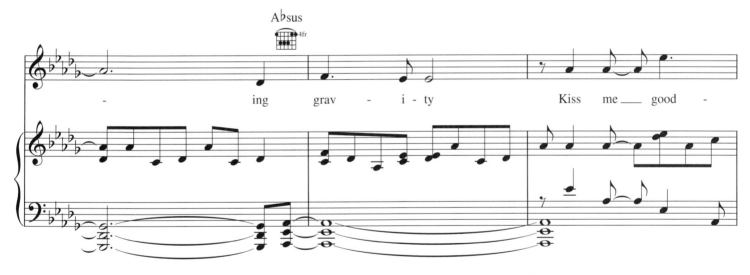

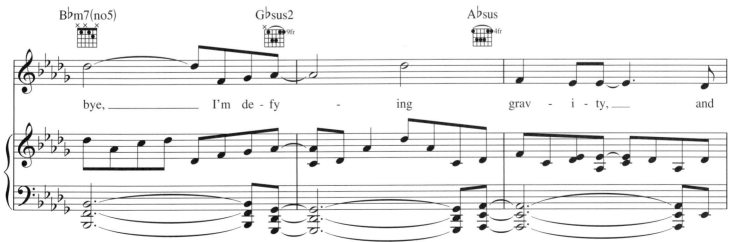

Moderato, dreamily

you can't pull __ me down. _____

Un - lim - it - ed... _____ My fu-ture is

un - lim - it - ed And I've just had a

vi - sion al - most like a proph - e - cy, I know—

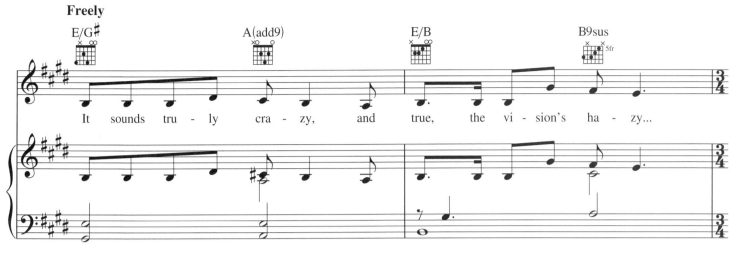

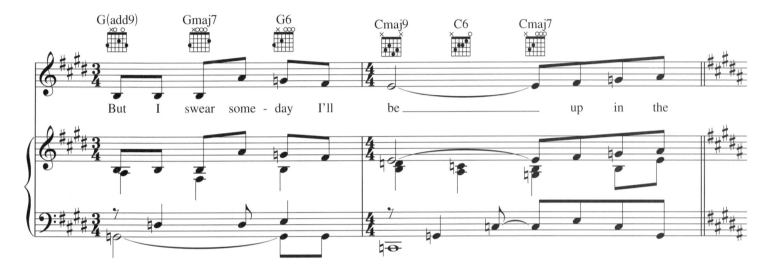

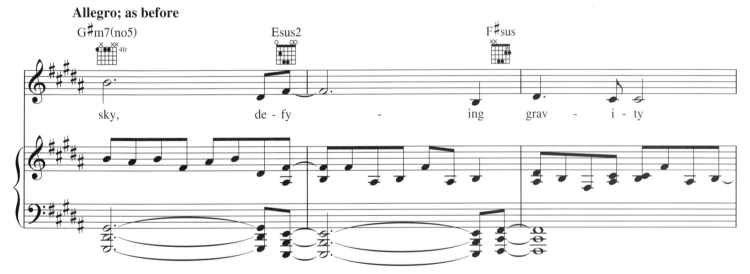

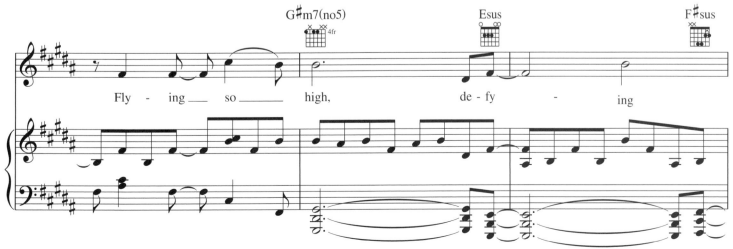

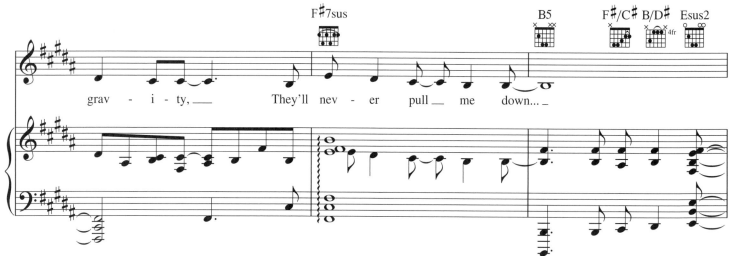

gravi-ty, ___ They'll nev-er pull ___ me down... ___

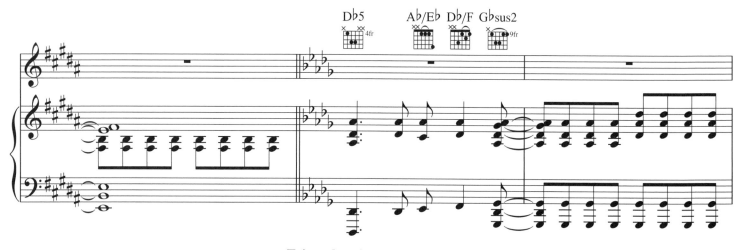

Triumphantly

So if ___ you care ___ to find ___ me,

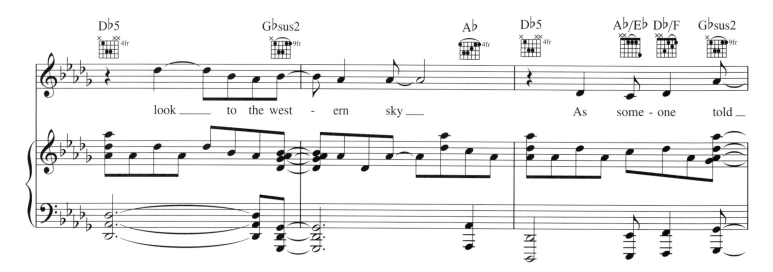

look ___ to the west-ern sky ___ As some-one told ___

all of Oz, no Wiz - ard that there is or was is ev - er gon - na

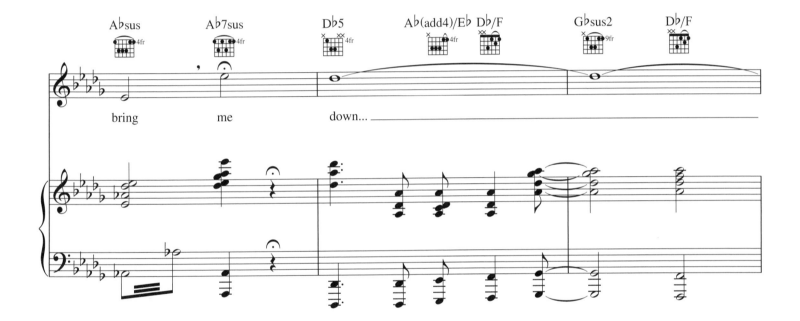

bring me down... _____

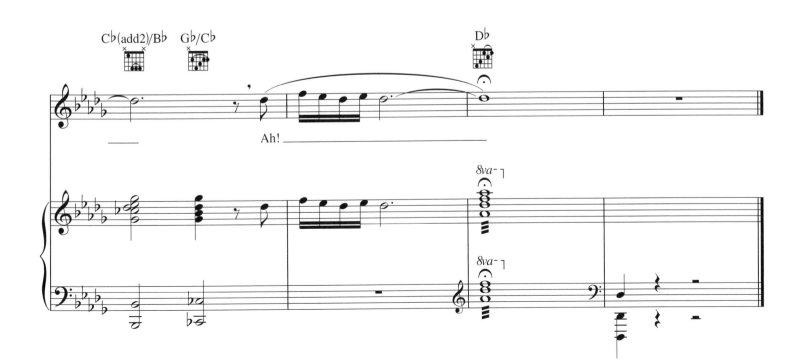

_____ Ah! _____

DON'T GET AROUND MUCH ANYMORE

Words and Music by DUKE ELLINGTON
and BOB RUSSELL

Medium Swing

Lyrics:

When I'm not play-ing sol-i-taire, __ I take a book down from the shelf, and what with pro-grams on the air, __ I keep pret-ty much __ to my-

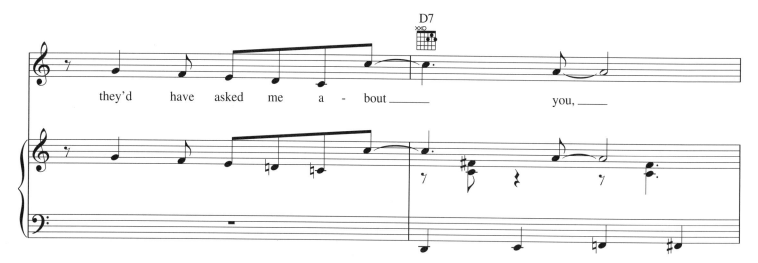

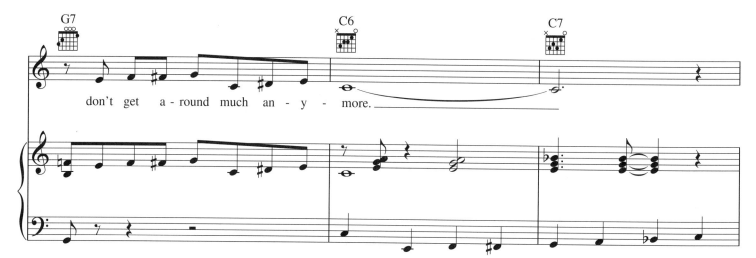

FOR ME AND MY GAL

Words by EDGAR LESLIE and E. RAY GOETZ
Music by GEORGE W. MEYER

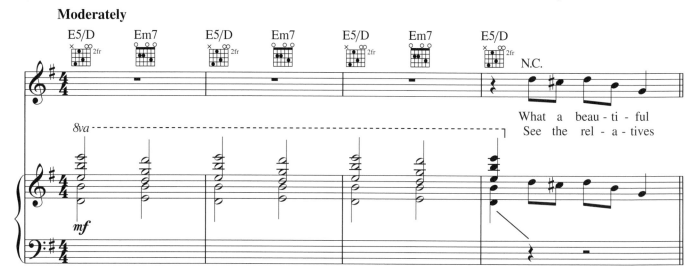

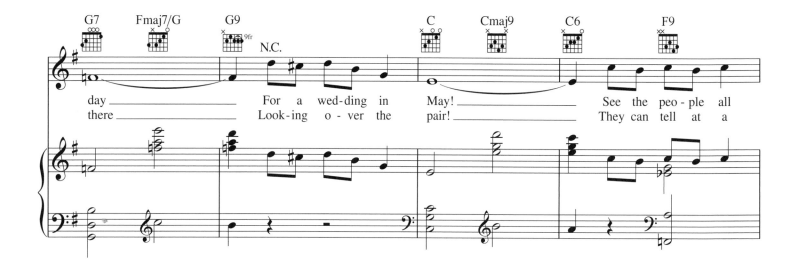

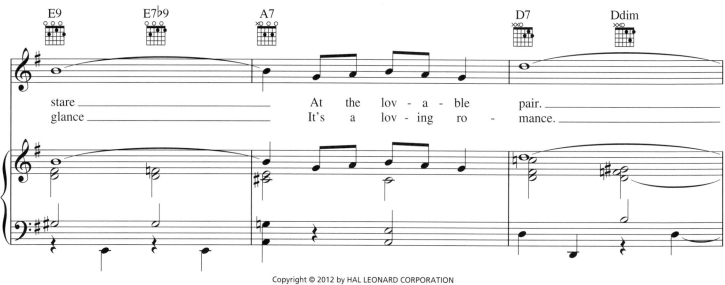

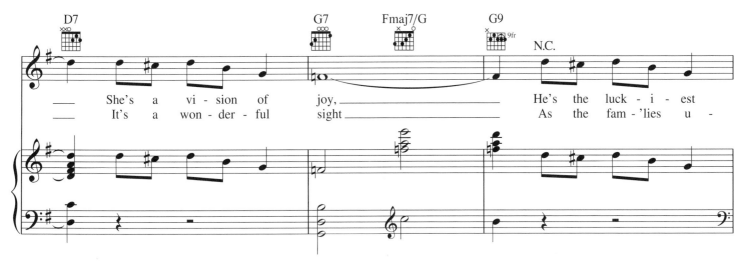

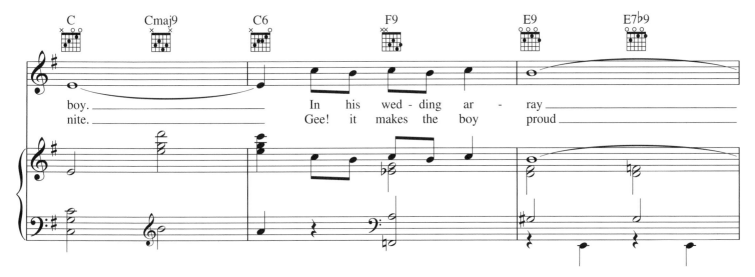

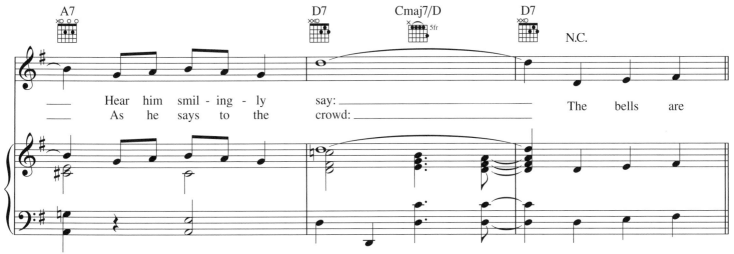

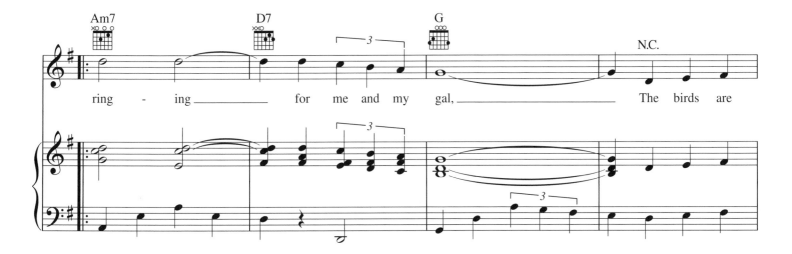

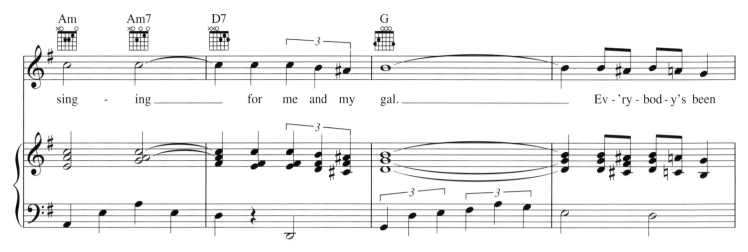

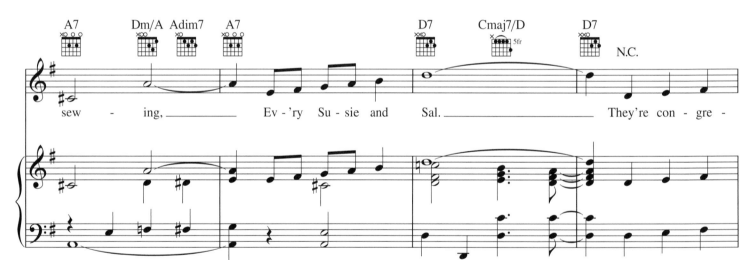

THE GAMBLER

Words and Music by
DON SCHLITZ

Moderate Country 2

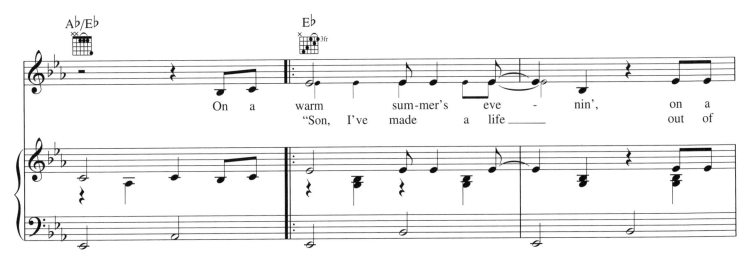

On a warm sum-mer's eve-nin', on a
"Son, I've made a life ___ out of

train bound for no-where, I met up with the gam-
read-in' peo-ple's fac-es and know-in' what their cards

-bler, we were both too tired to sleep. ___
___ were by the way they held ___ their eyes. ___

So
And if

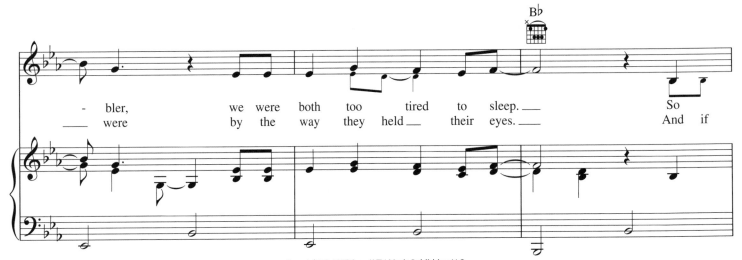

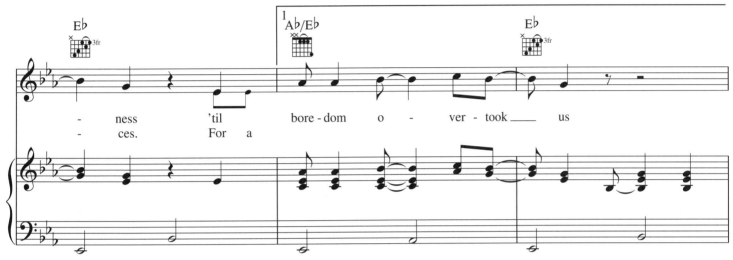

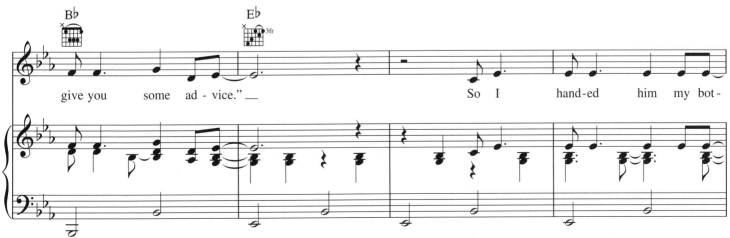

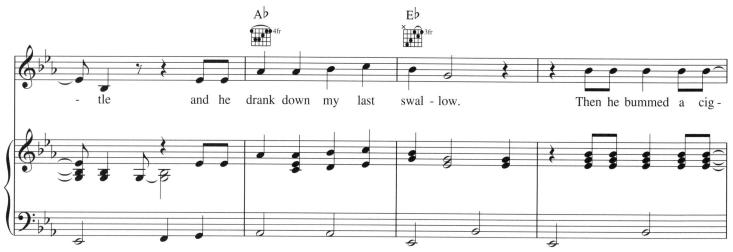

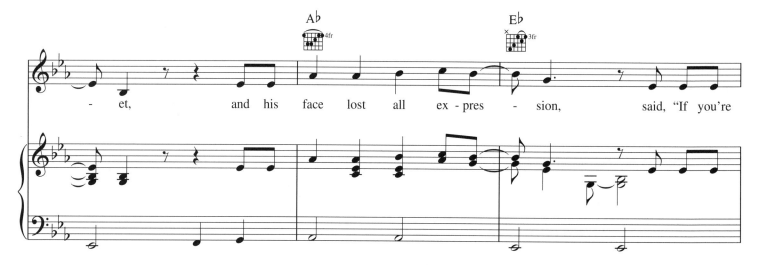

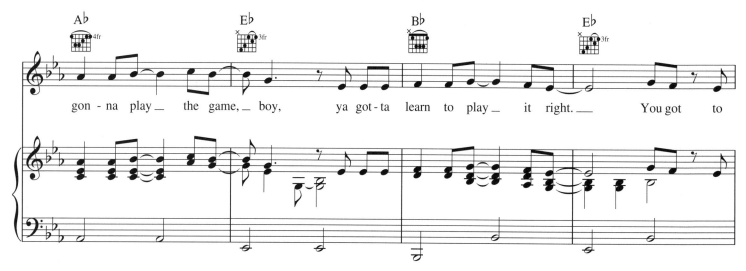

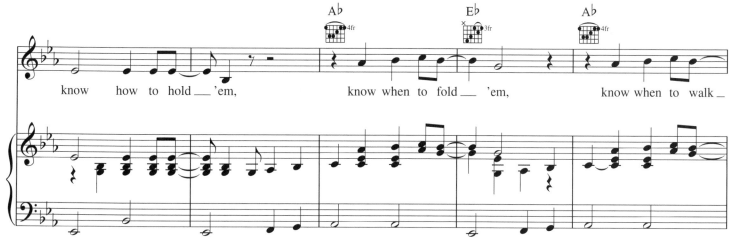

know how to hold __ 'em,   know when to fold __ 'em,   know when to walk __

__ a - way __   and know when to run. __ You nev - er count your   mon-ey   when you're

sit - tin'   at the ta - ble.   There'll be   time e - nough __   for count - in'

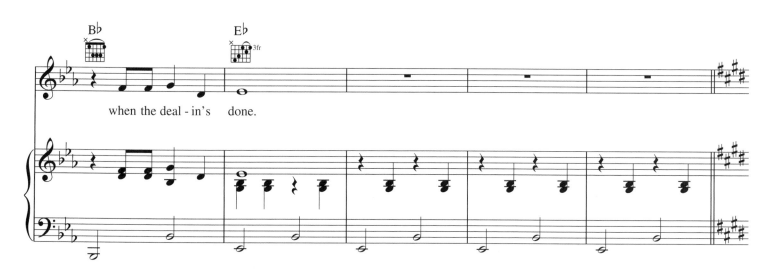

when the deal - in's   done.

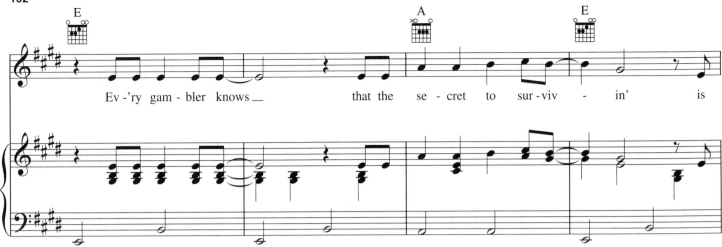

Ev-'ry gam-bler knows __ that the se-cret to sur-viv -in' is

know-in' what to throw a-way __ and know-in' what to keep. __ 'Cause

ev-'ry hand's a win- -ner and ev-'ry hand's a los- -er and the

best that you __ can hope for is to die in your sleep." And

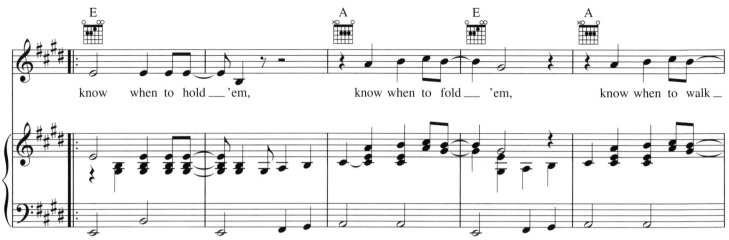

know when to hold __ 'em, know when to fold __ 'em, know when to walk __

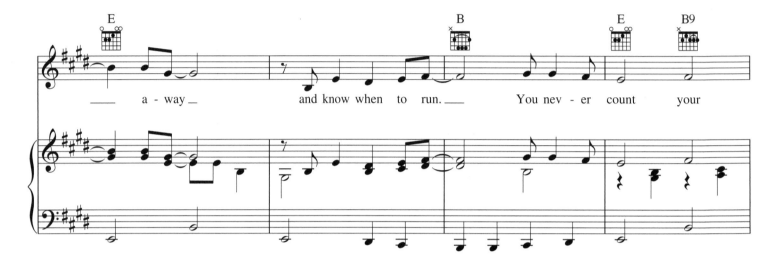

__ a - way __ and know when to run. __ You nev - er count your

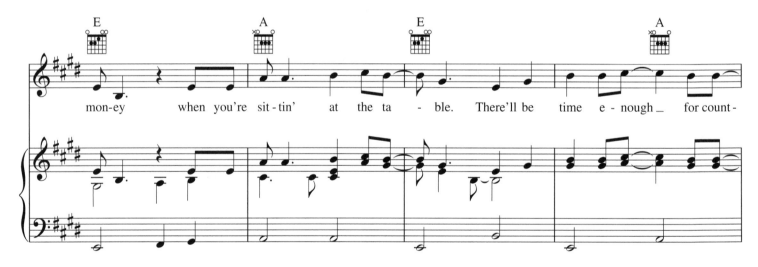

mon-ey when you're sit-tin' at the ta - ble. There'll be time e - nough __ for count-

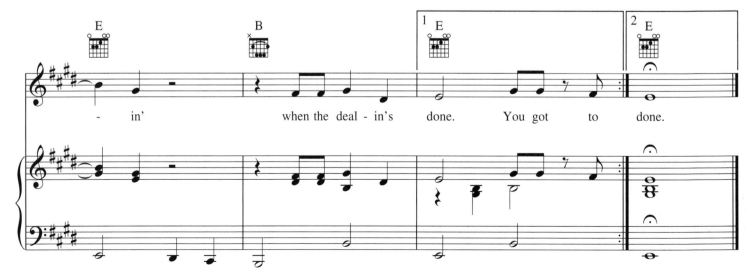

- in' when the deal-in's done. You got to done.

GONNA MAKE YOU SWEAT
(Everybody Dance Now)

Words and Music by ROBERT CLIVILLES
and FREDERICK B. WILLIAMS

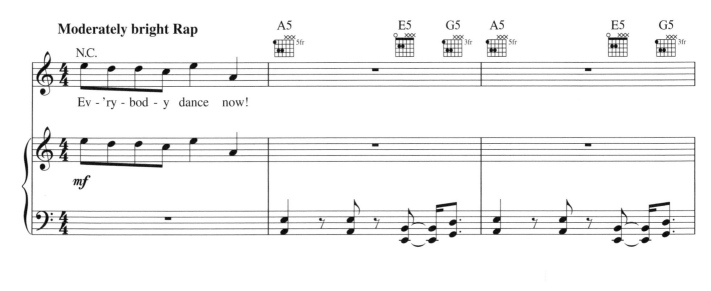

Ev-'ry-bod-y dance now!

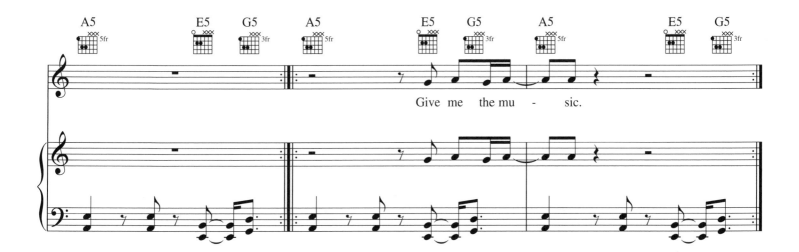

Give me the mu - sic.

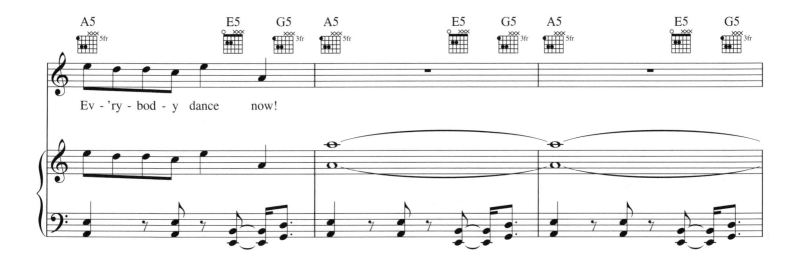

Ev-'ry-bod-y dance now!

Ev -'ry - bod - y dance now! Yeah. __

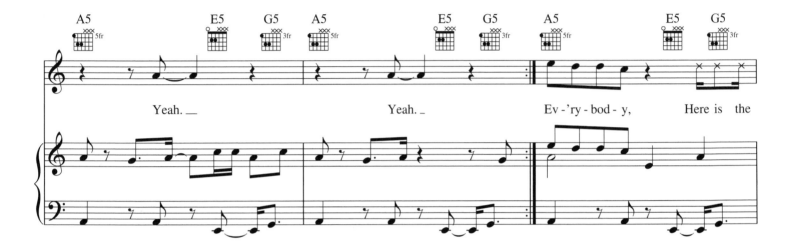

Yeah. __ Yeah. _ Ev -'ry - bod - y, Here is the

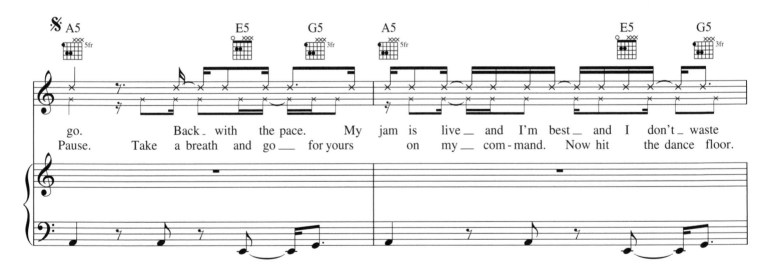

go. Back _ with the pace. My jam is live __ and I'm best __ and I don't _ waste
Pause. Take a breath and go ___ for yours on my __ com - mand. Now hit the dance floor.

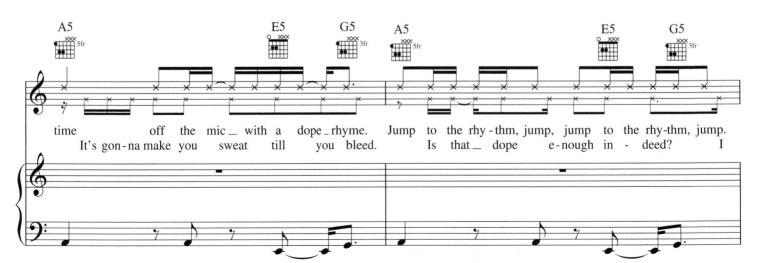

time off the mic _ with a dope _ rhyme. Jump to the rhy - thm, jump, jump to the rhy-thm, jump.
It's gon-na make you sweat till you bleed. Is that _ dope e-nough in - deed? I

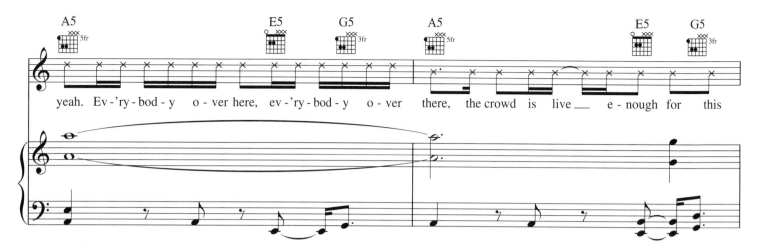

yeah. Ev-'ry-bod-y o-ver here, ev-'ry-bod-y o-ver there, the crowd is live __ e-nough for this

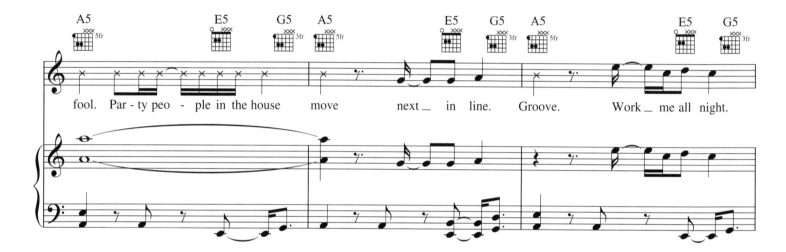

fool. Par-ty peo-ple in the house move next __ in line. Groove. Work __ me all night.

Come on, __ let's sweat, ba - by. __ Let the

mu-sic take __ con-trol. __ Let the rhy-thm move __ you. __ Sweat,

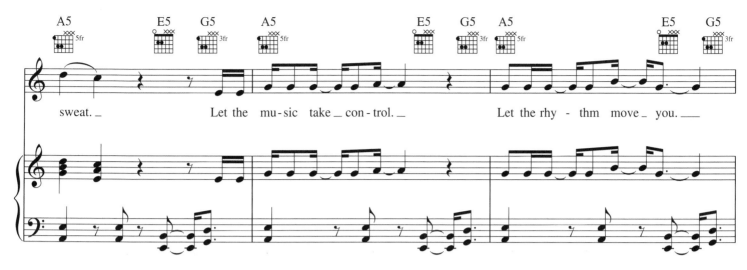

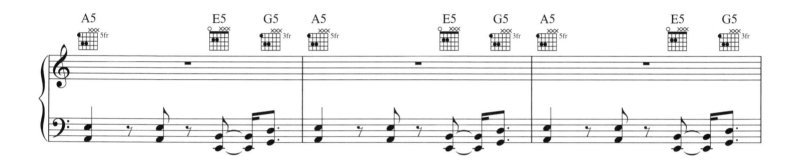

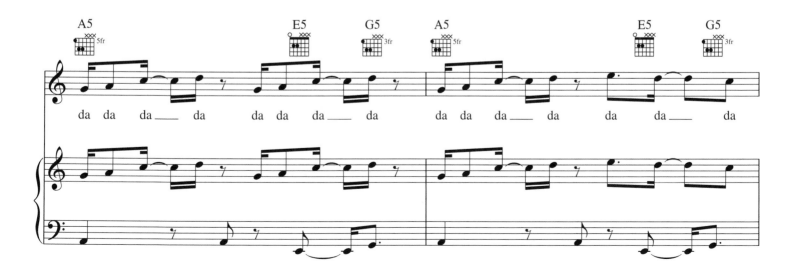

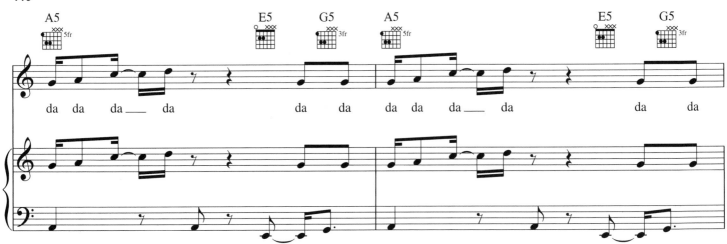

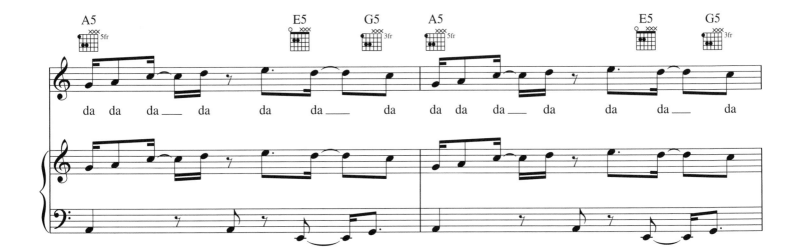

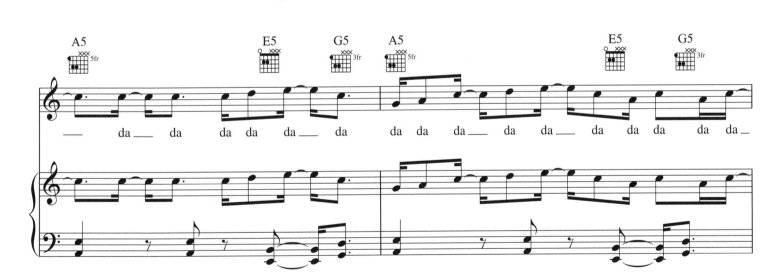

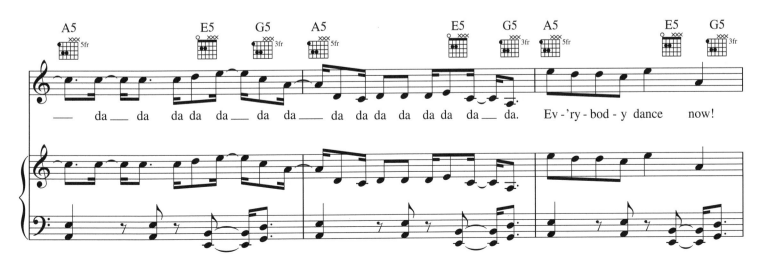

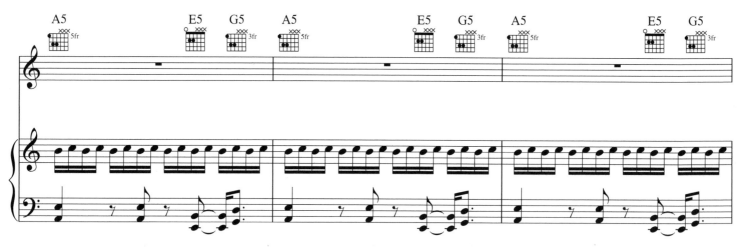

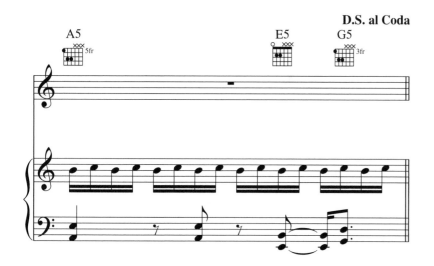

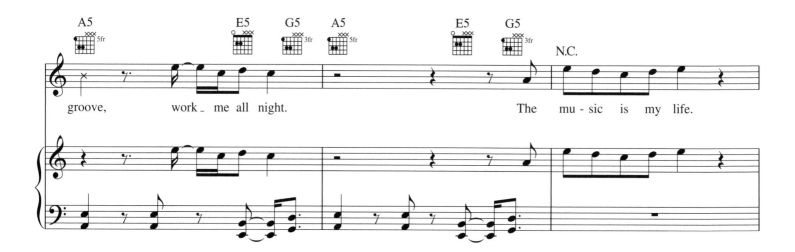

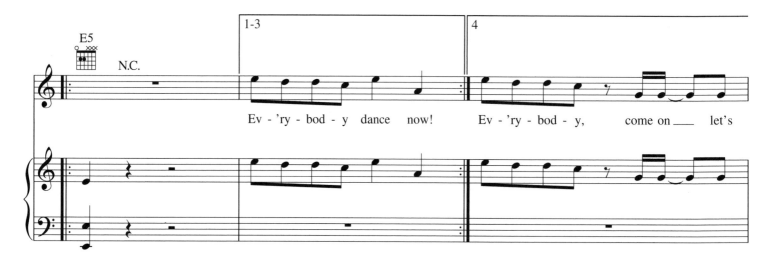

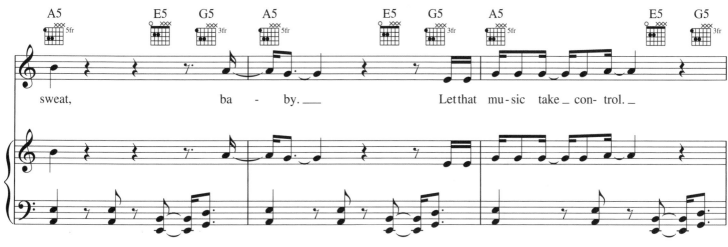

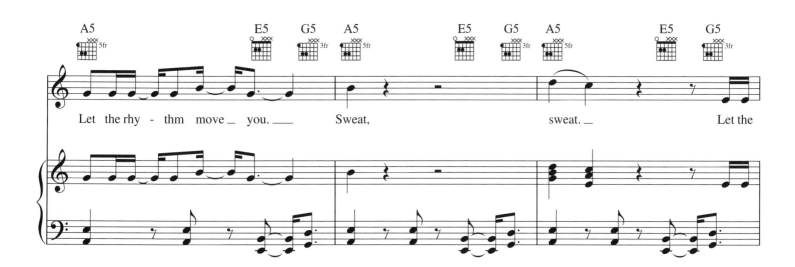

I CAN'T MAKE YOU LOVE ME

Words and Music by MIKE REID
and ALLEN SHAMBLIN

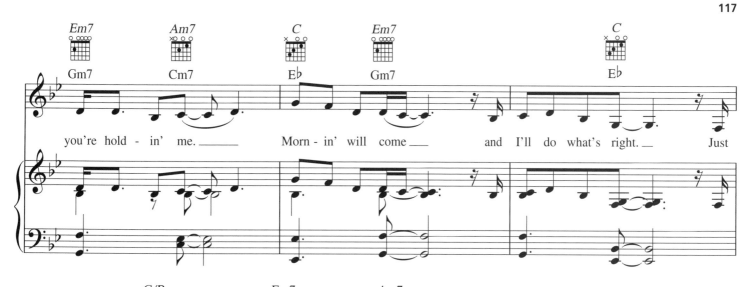

you're hold - in' me. _____ Morn - in' will come _____ and I'll do what's right. _____ Just

give me till then _____ to give up _____ this fight. _____ And I will give up this fight. _____

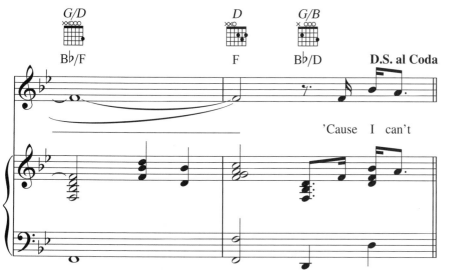
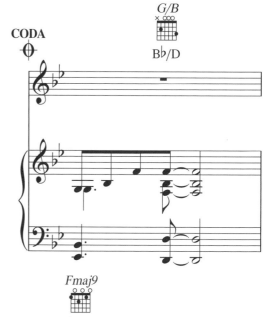

'Cause I can't

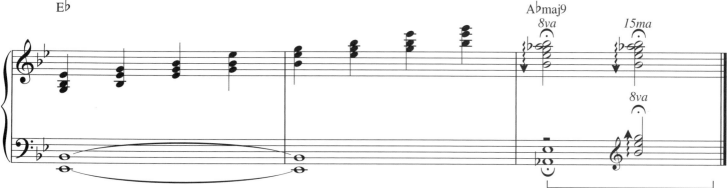

I WILL SURVIVE

Words and Music by DINO FEKARIS
and FREDERICK J. PERREN

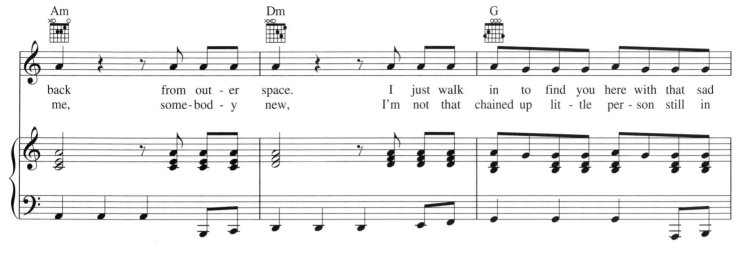

back — from out-er space. I just walk in to find you here with that sad
me, some-bod-y new, I'm not that chained up lit-tle per-son still in

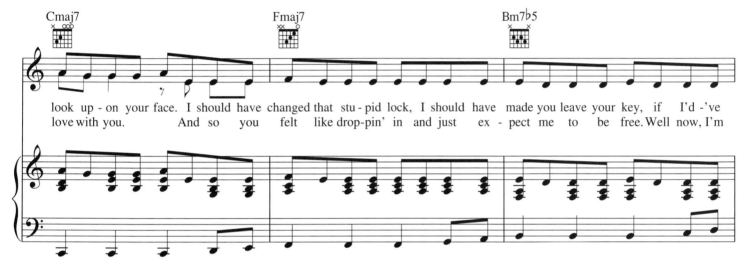

look up-on your face. I should have changed that stu-pid lock, I should have made you leave your key, if I'd-'ve
love with you. And so you felt like drop-pin' in and just ex-pect me to be free. Well now, I'm

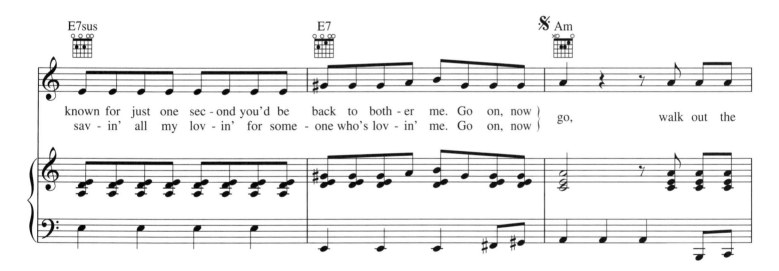

known for just one sec-ond you'd be back to both-er me. Go on, now } go, walk out the
sav-in' all my lov-in' for some-one who's lov-in' me. Go on, now }

door; just turn a-round, now, 'cause you're not wel-come an-y-more.

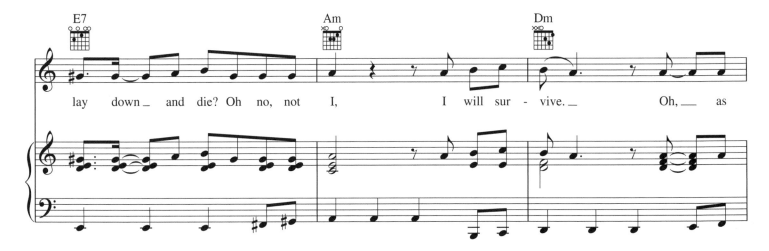

I'LL BE SEEING YOU

Written by IRVING KAHAL
and SAMMY FAIN

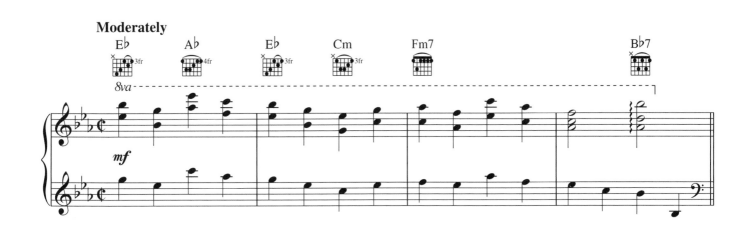

Ca - the-dral bells were toll - ing _____ and our hearts sang

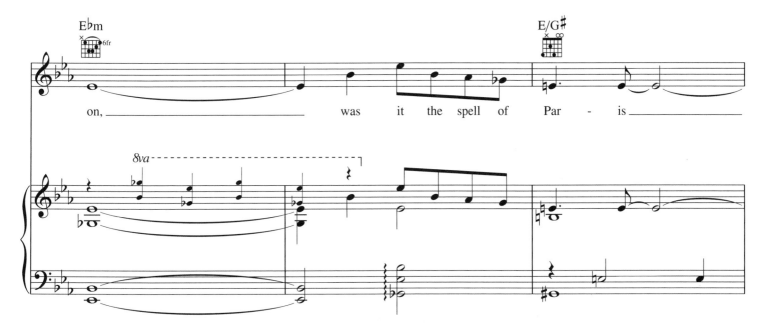

on, _____ was it the spell of Par - is _____

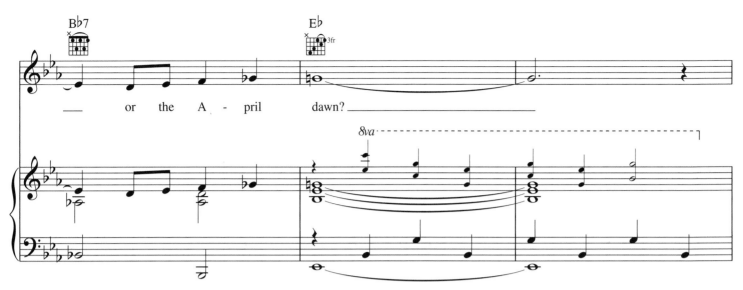

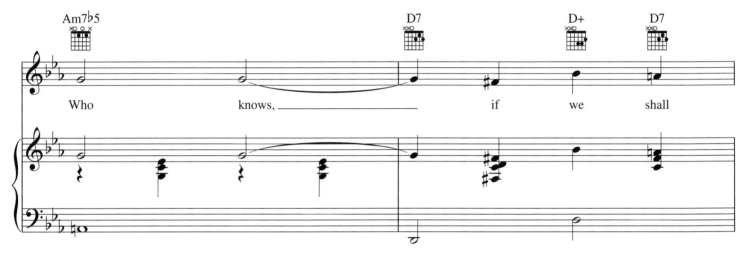

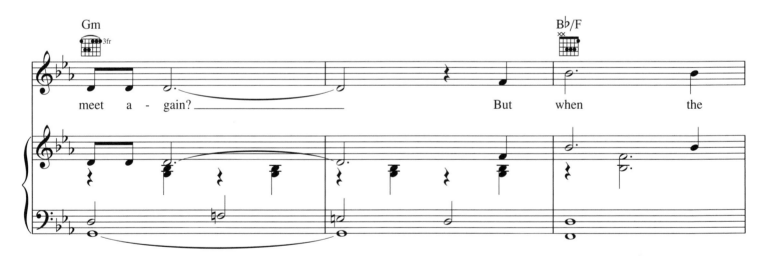

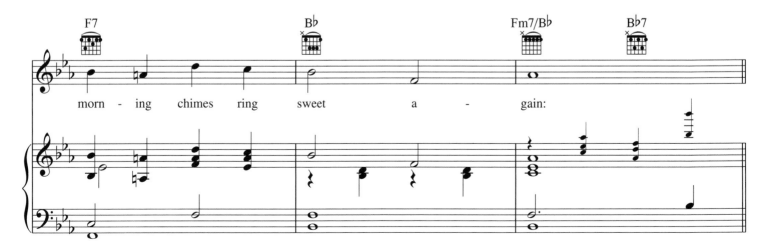

Slowly

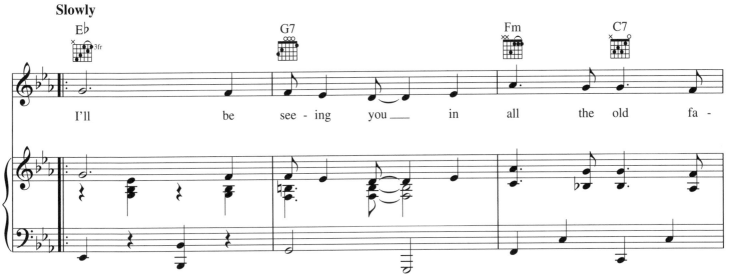

I'll be see - ing you ___ in all the old fa -

mil - iar plac - es that this heart of mine em - brac - es

all day thru: ___ in that

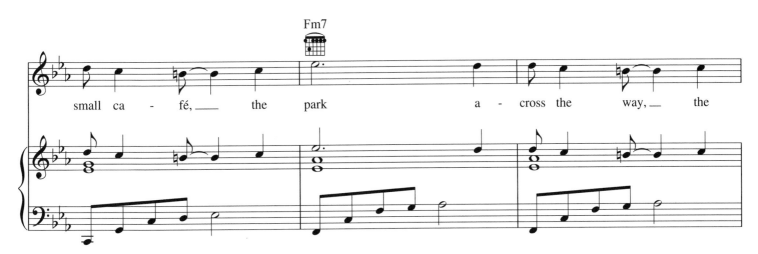

small ca - fé, ___ the park a - cross the way, ___ the

124

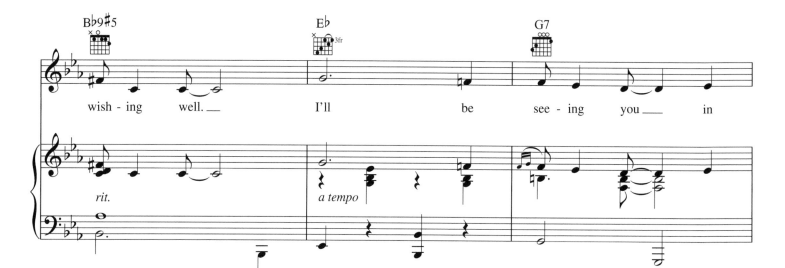

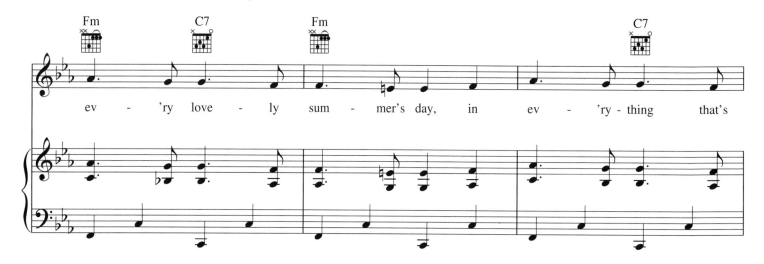

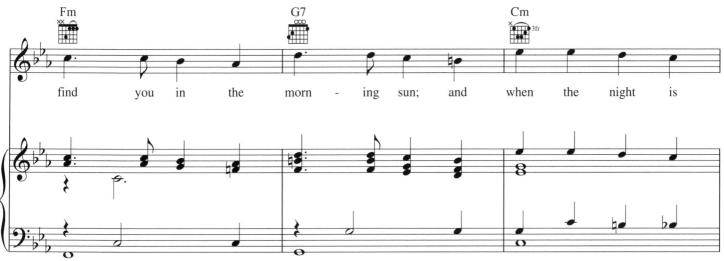

find you in the morn - ing sun; and when the night is

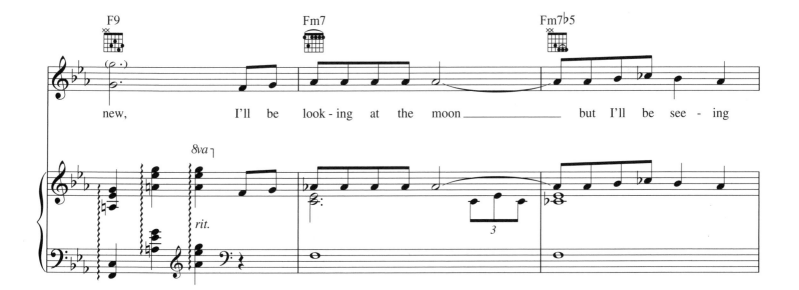

new, I'll be look-ing at the moon _____ but I'll be see - ing

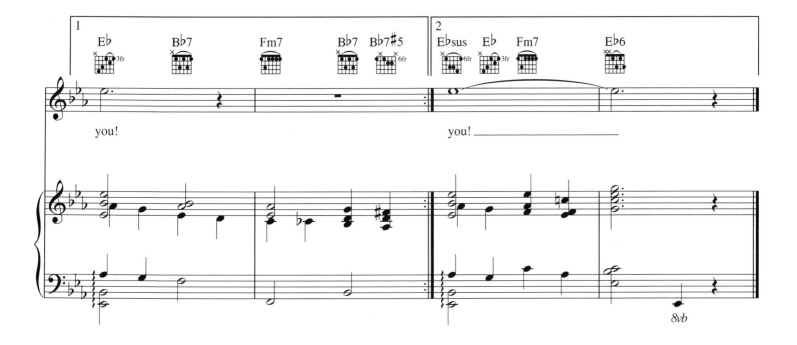

you!

you! _____

I'M IN THE MOOD FOR LOVE

from EVERY NIGHT AT EIGHT

Words and Music by JIMMY McHUGH
and DOROTHY FIELDS

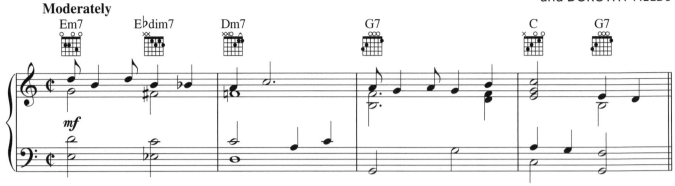

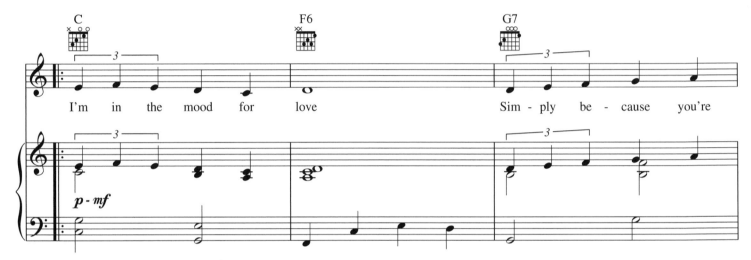

I'm in the mood for love Sim - ply be - cause you're

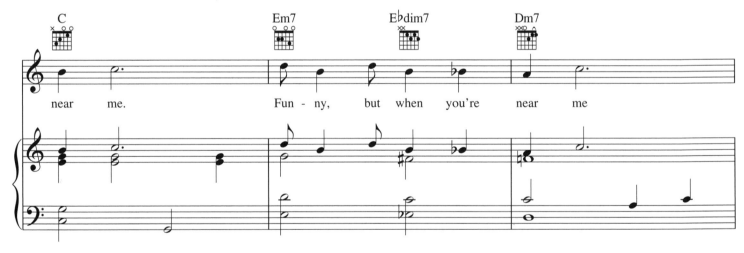

near me. Fun - ny, but when you're near me

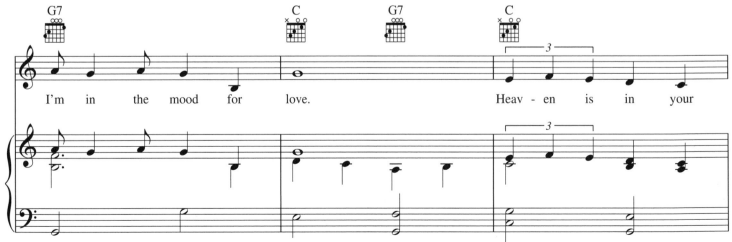

I'm in the mood for love. Heav - en is in your

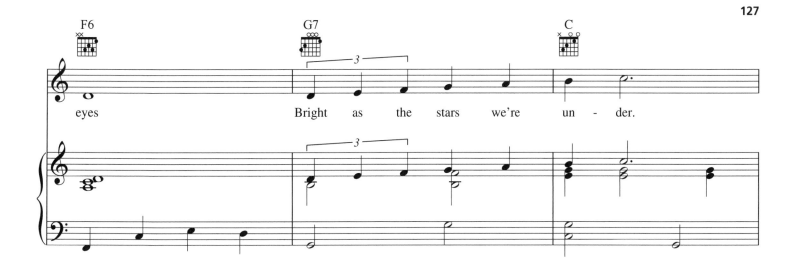

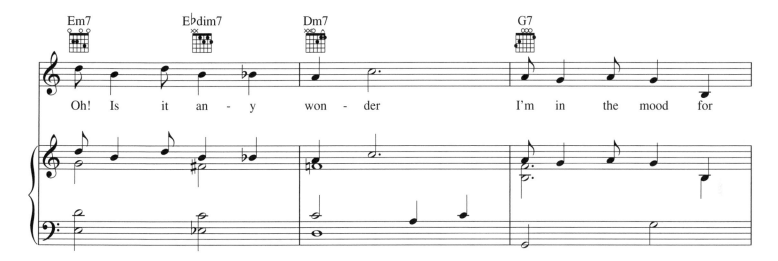

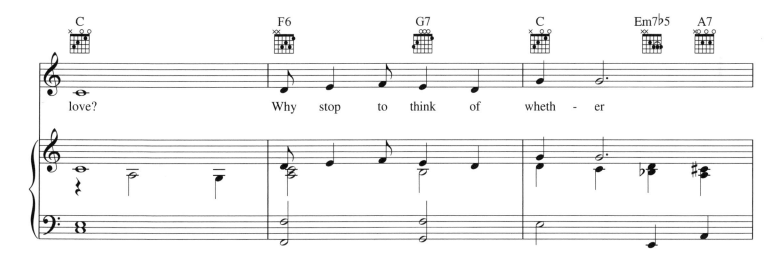

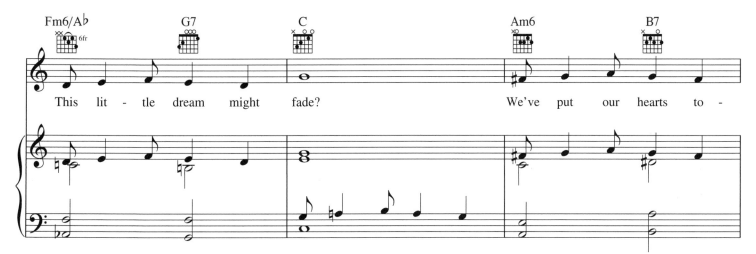

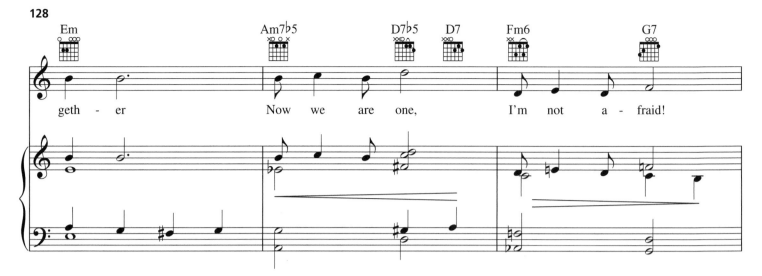

geth - er   Now we are one,   I'm not a - fraid!

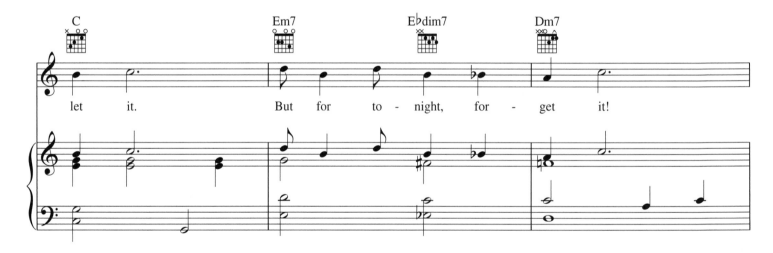

If there's a cloud a - bove,   If it should rain we'll

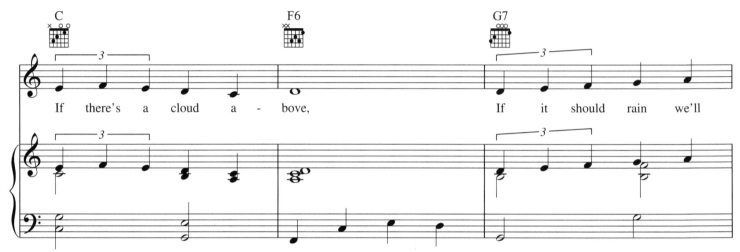

let it.   But for to - night, for - get it!

I'm in the mood for love.   I'm in the mood for love.

I'M YOURS

Words and Music by
JASON MRAZ

Moderately slow, with a Reggae feel

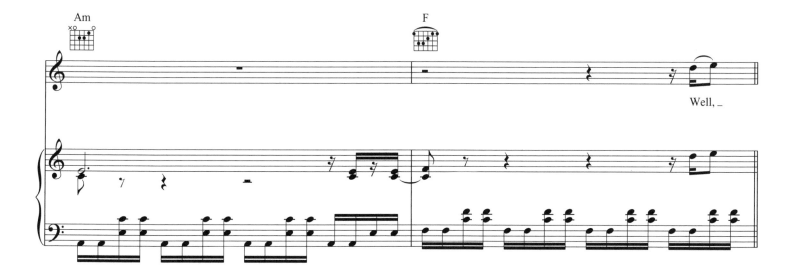

you done done me in; you bet I felt it. I tried to be chill, but you're so hot that I melt ed. I

*Recorded a half step lower.

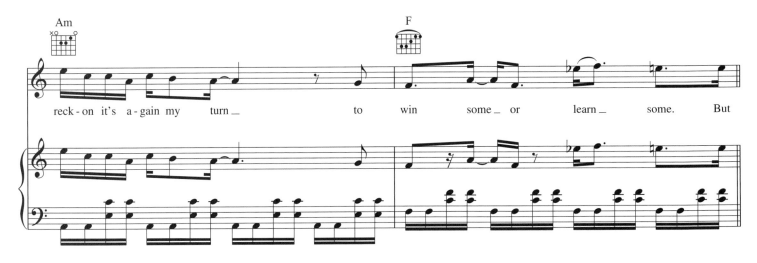

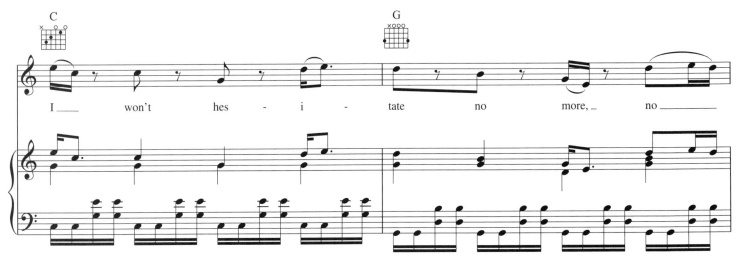

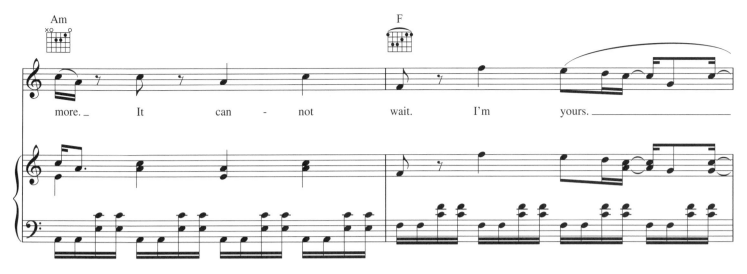

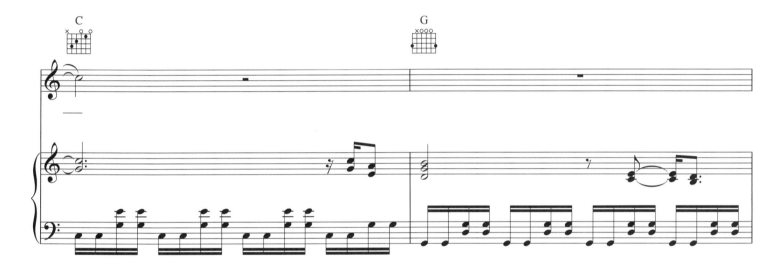

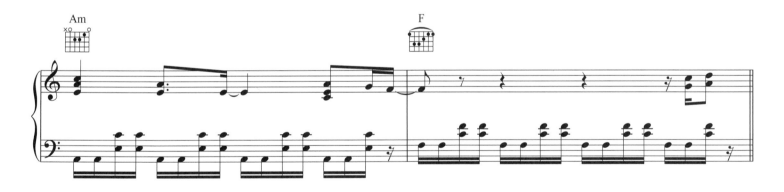

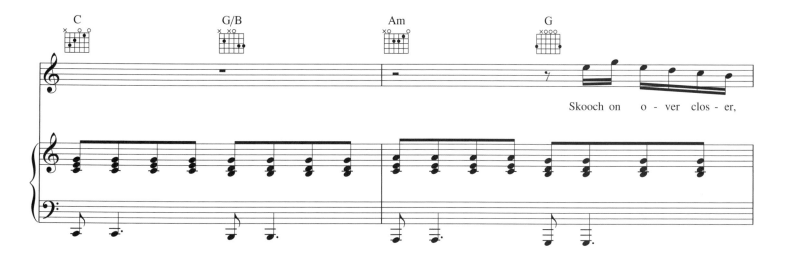

dear,   and I will nib - ble your ear. _____ *Scat sing...*

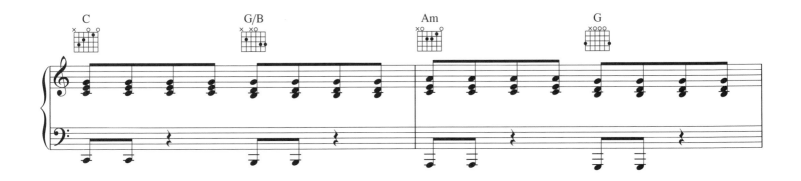

I've been spend - ing

way too long _ check-ing my tongue in the mir - ror   and bend-ing o - ver back-wards just to try to see it clear- er. But

my breath fogged_ up the glass, _ and so I drew a new face_ and I laughed._____ I

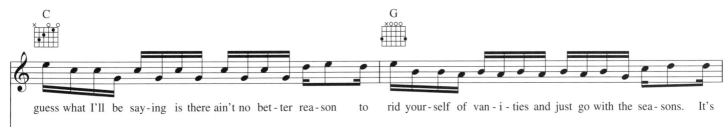

guess what I'll be say-ing is there ain't no bet-ter rea-son   to   rid your-self of van-i-ties and just go with the sea-sons.   It's

what   we aim   to do.   Our____ name   is__ our   vir - tue.   But

I____   won't   hes - i - tate   no   more, _   no_____

more. ___ It can - not wait. I'm yours. _____

O - pen up your mind ___ and see like me. ___ O - pen up your plans ___ and, damn, _ you're _ free. _

(I won't hes - i - tate no more, no

___ Look in - to your heart _ and you'll _ find _ that the sky _ is yours. _____ So

more. It can - not wait. I'm sure. _____ No

please don't, please don't, please don't... There's no need to com - pli - cate 'cause our time
need to com - pli - cate. Our time is

is short. This is, this is, this is our fate. I'm yours. Scat sing...
short. This is our fate. I'm yours.)

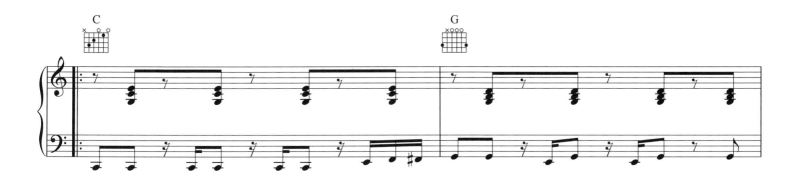

Repeat and fade

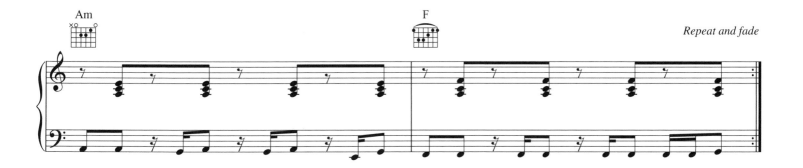

IF I AIN'T GOT YOU

Words and Music by
ALICIA KEYS

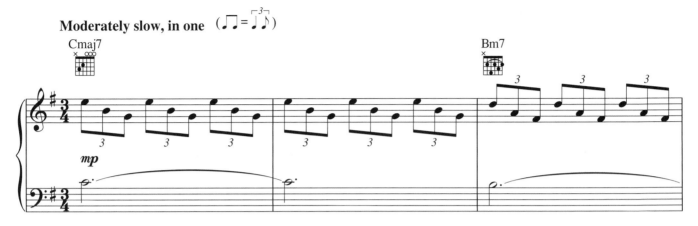

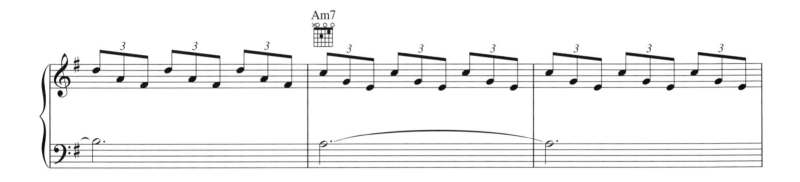

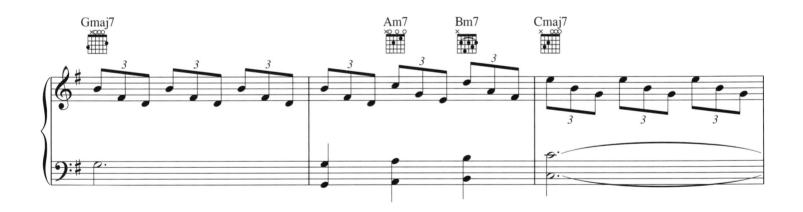

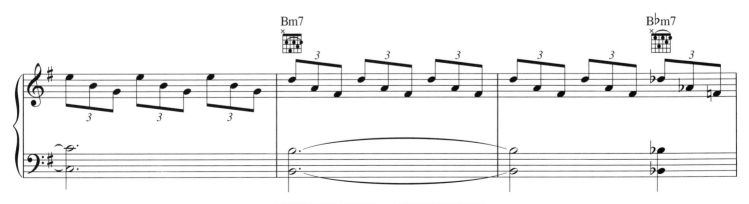

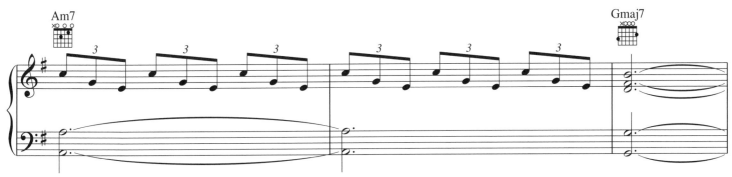

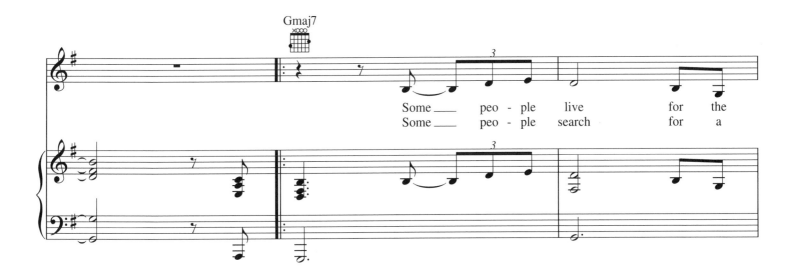

Some ___ peo - ple live ___ for the
Some ___ peo - ple search for a

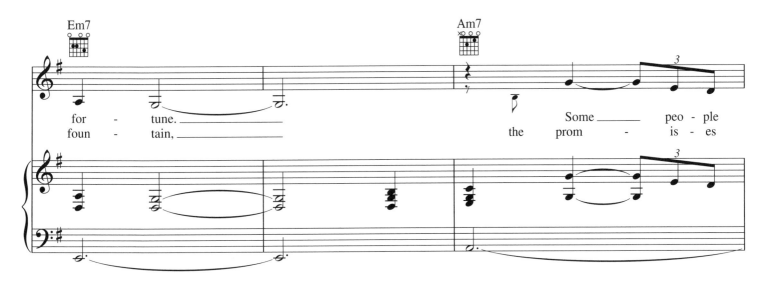

for - tune. ___
foun - tain, ___
Some ___ peo - ple
the prom - is - es

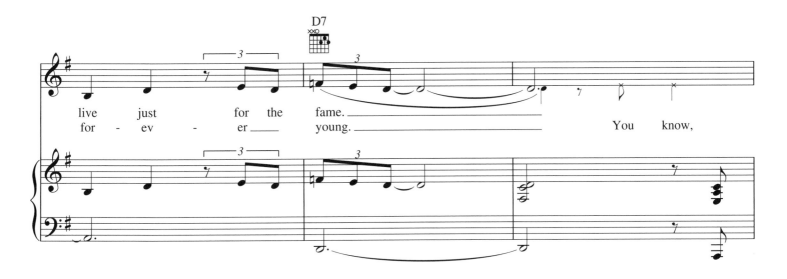

live just for the fame. ___
for - ev - er ___ young. ___ You know,

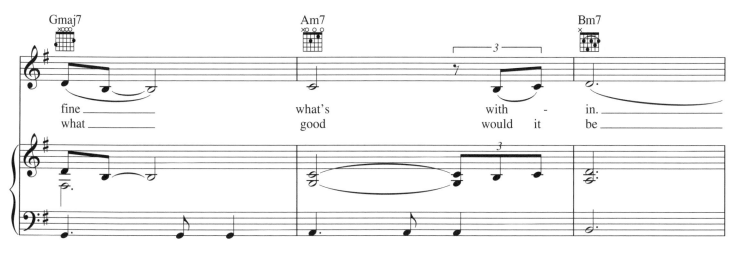

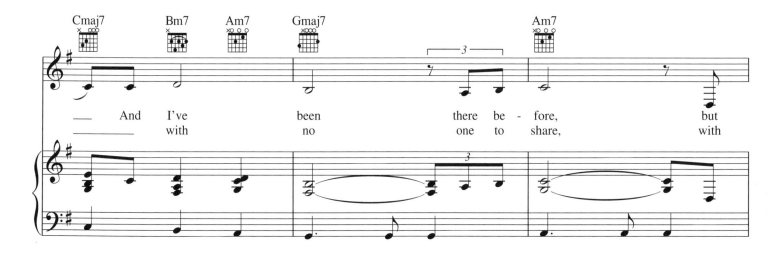

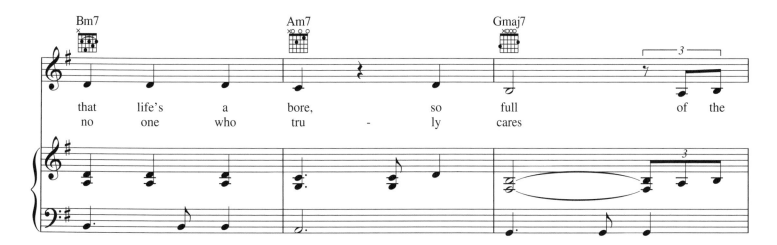

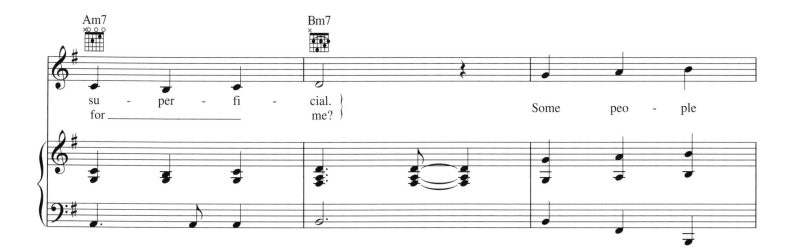

want it all, but I don't want noth-in' at all

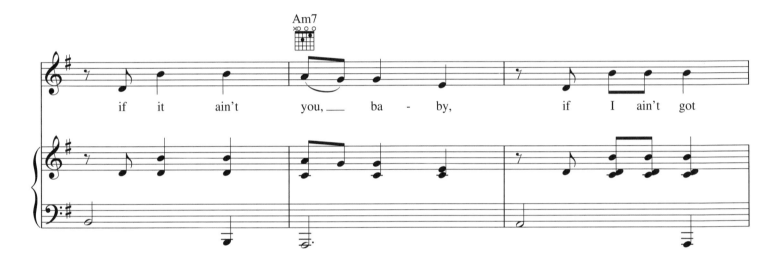

if it ain't you, __ ba - by, if I ain't got

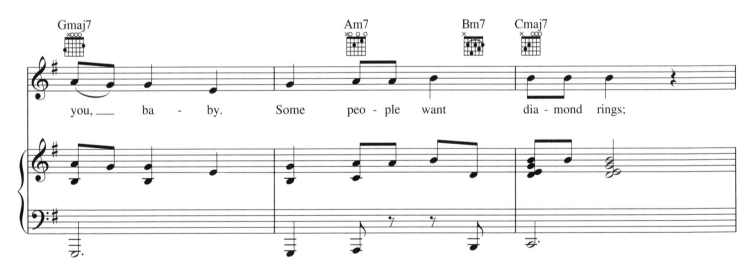

you, __ ba - by. Some peo-ple want dia-mond rings;

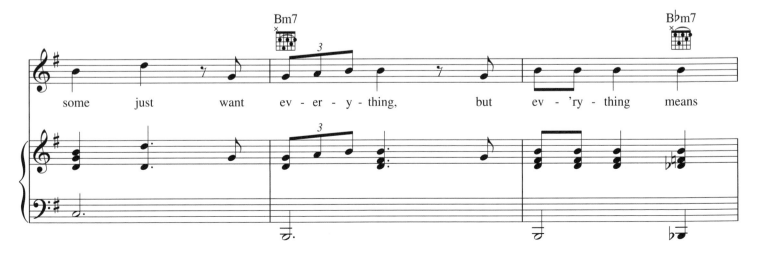

some just want ev-er-y-thing, but ev-'ry-thing means

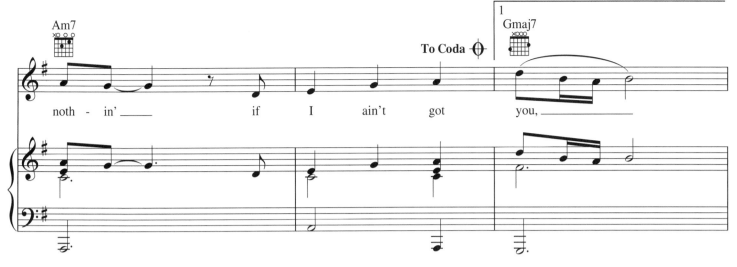

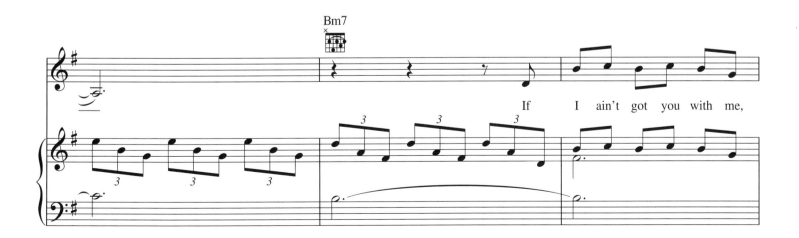

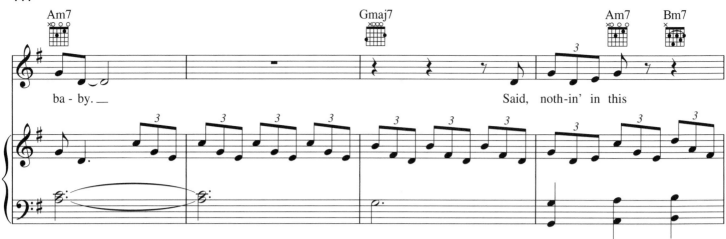

ba - by. ___

Said, noth-in' in this

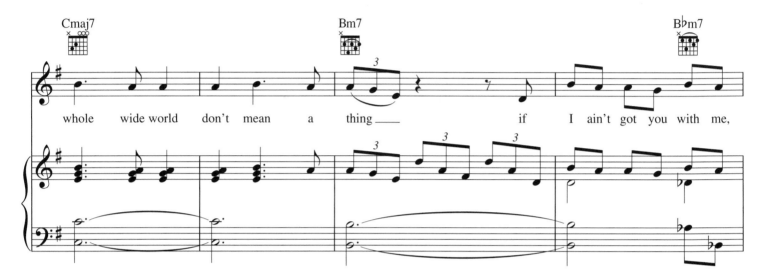

whole wide world don't mean a thing ___ if I ain't got you with me,

ba - by. ___

rit.

Freely

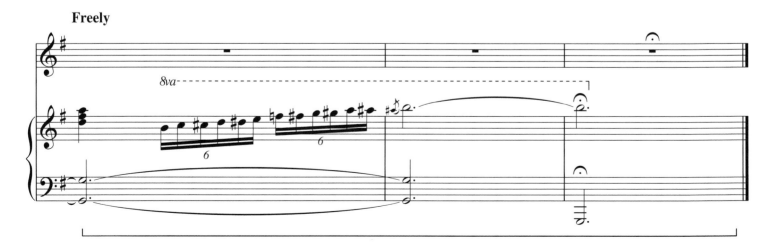

JUST IN TIME

from BELLS ARE RINGING

Words by BETTY COMDEN and ADOLPH GREEN
Music by JULE STYNE

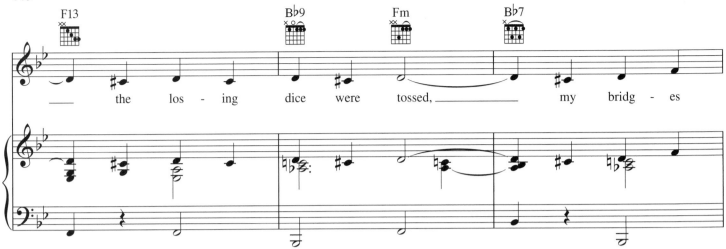

the los - ing dice were tossed, _____ my bridg - es

all were crossed, _____ no - where to go. _____

_____ Now you're here, _____ and now I

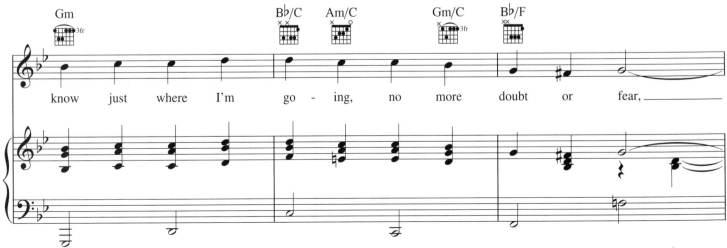

know just where I'm go - ing, no more doubt or fear, _____

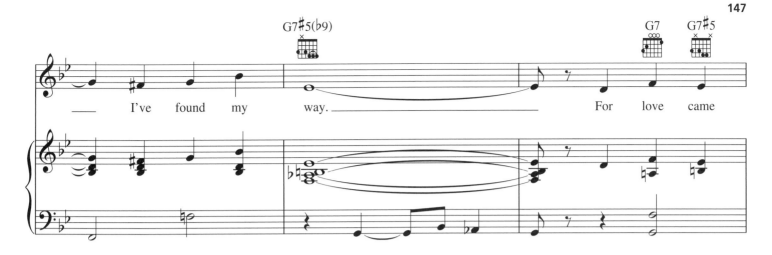

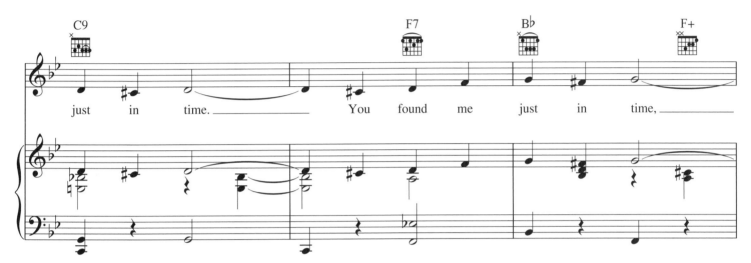

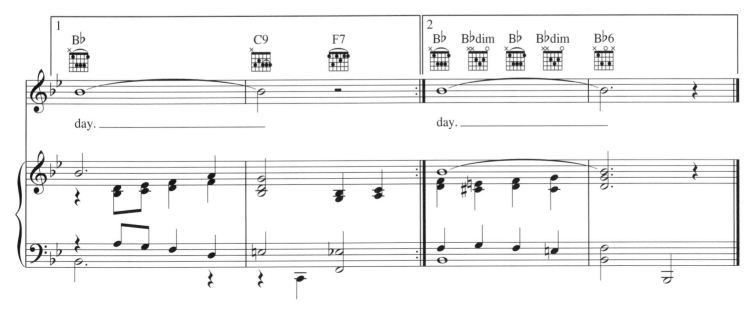

JUST THE WAY YOU ARE

Words and Music by
BILLY JOEL

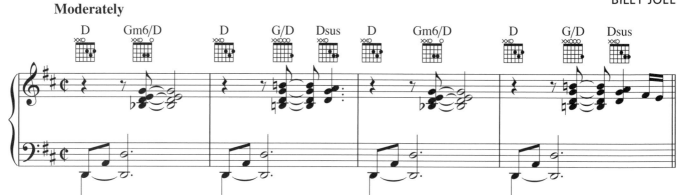

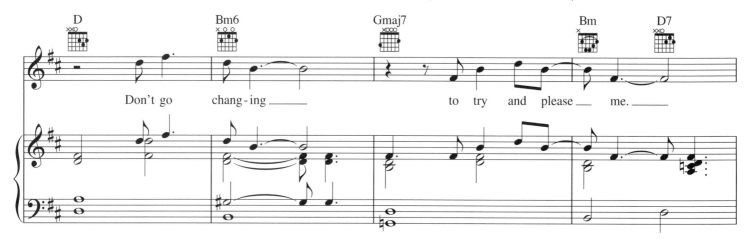

Don't go chang-ing _____ to try and please _ me. _____

You nev - er let me down _ be - fore. _____ Mm, _____ mm. ____

_____ Don't i-mag - ine _____ you're too fa - mil - iar. _____

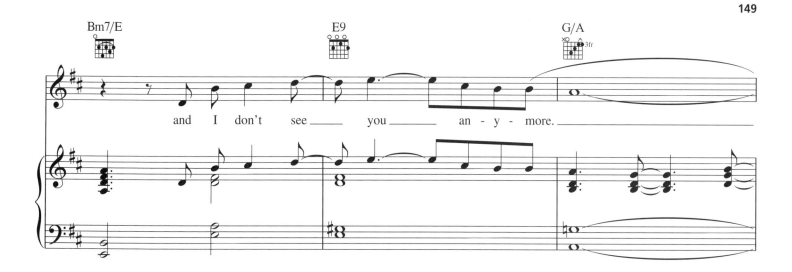

and I don't see ___ you ___ an - y - more. ___

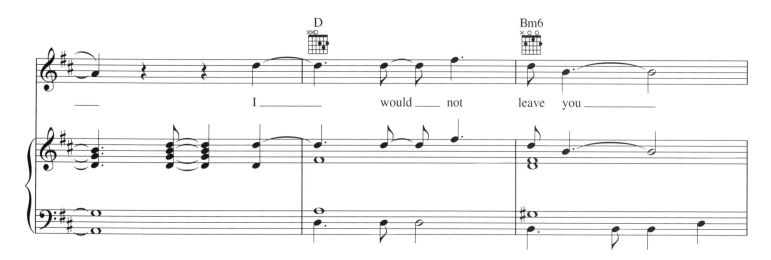

___ I ___ would ___ not leave you ___

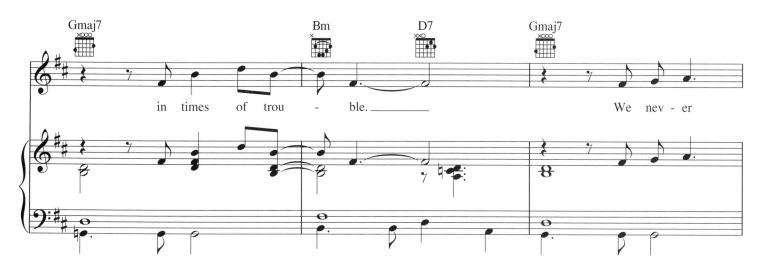

in times of trou - ble. ___ We nev - er

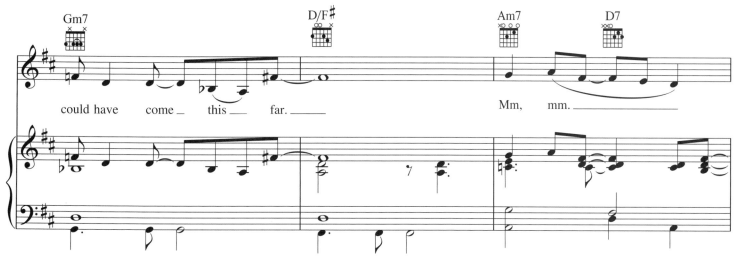

could have come ___ this ___ far. ___ Mm, mm. ___

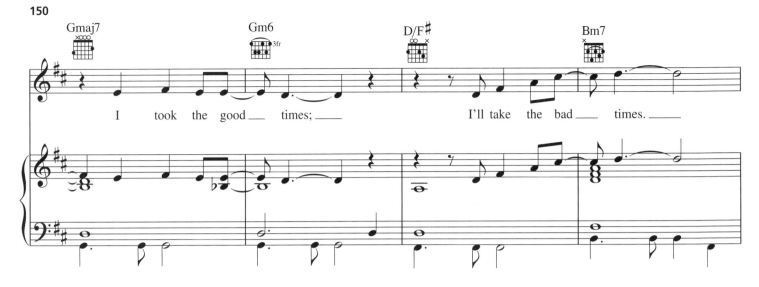

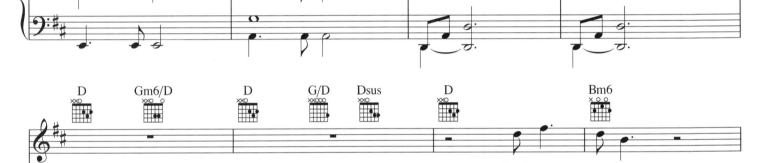

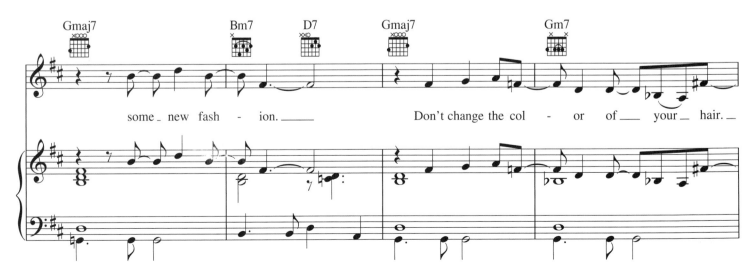

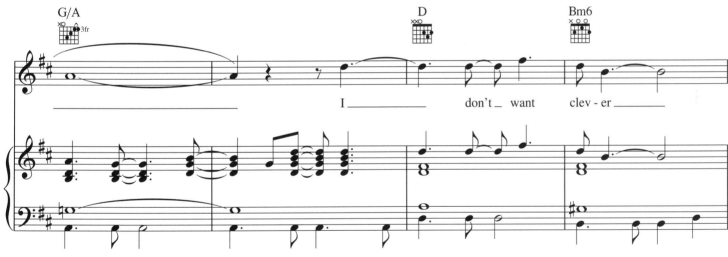

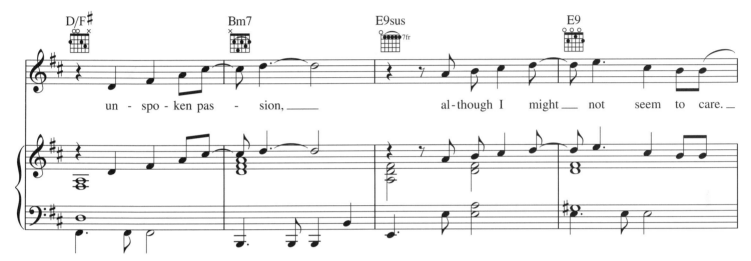

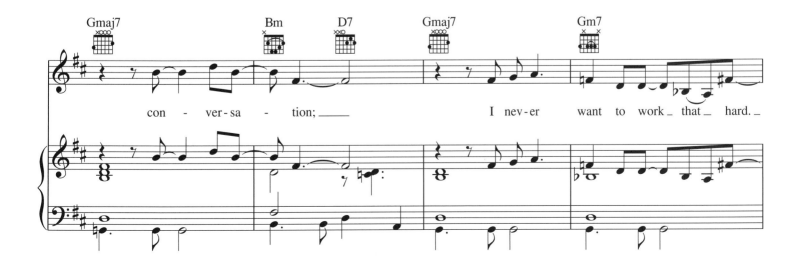

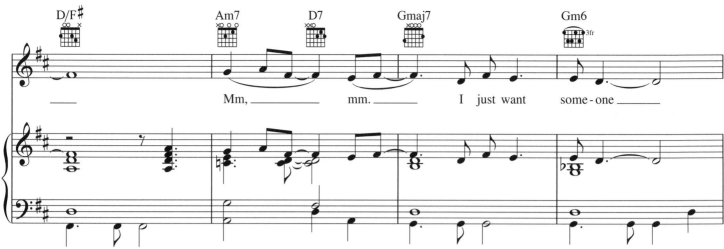

Mm, _____ mm. _____ I just want some-one _____

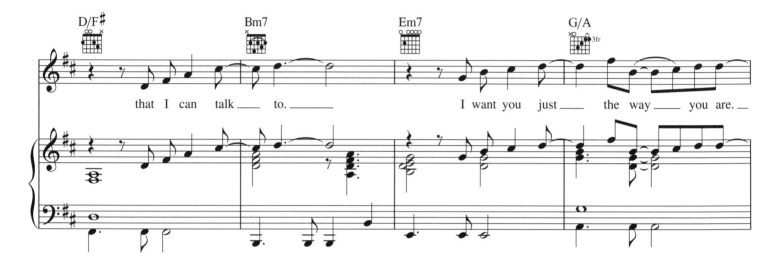

that I can talk ____ to. _____ I want you just ____ the way ____ you are. ____

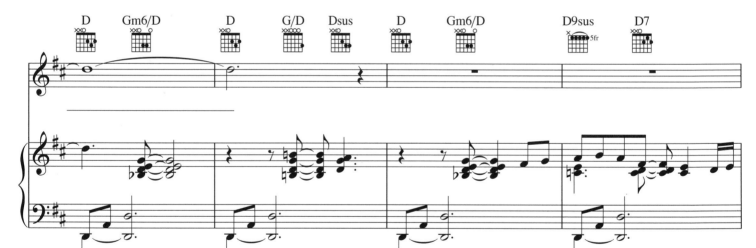

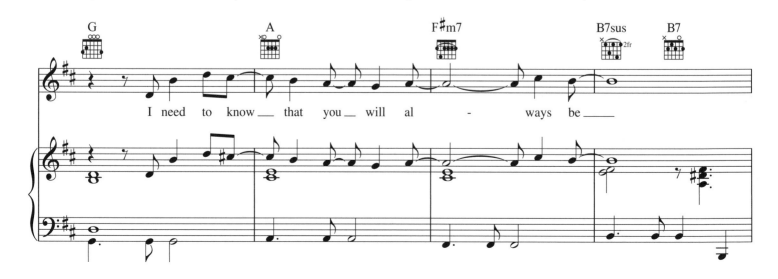

I need to know ____ that you ____ will al - ways be _____

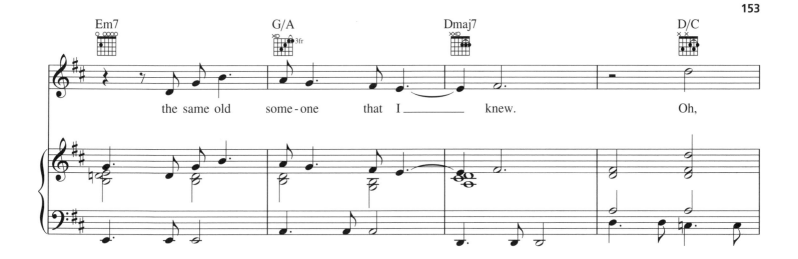

the same old some-one that I _____ knew. Oh,

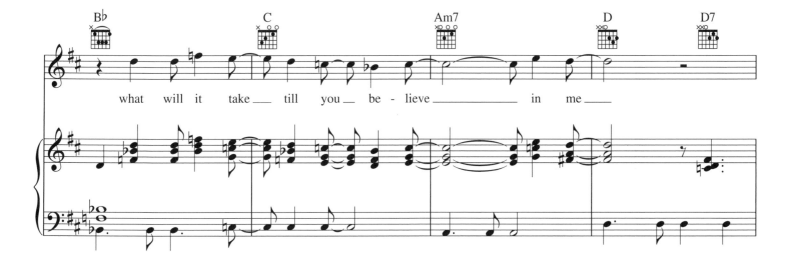

what will it take ___ till you ___ be-lieve _____ in me ____

the way that I ____ be-lieve ___ in you? _____ I _____

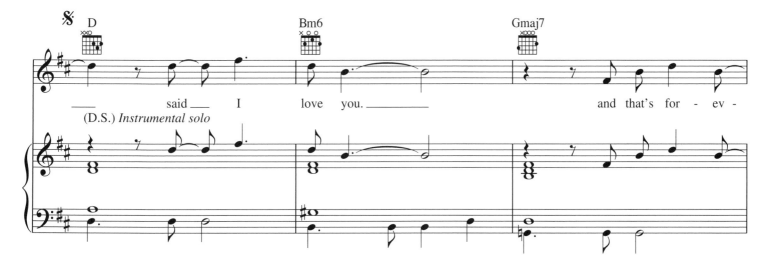

_____ said ___ I love you. _____ and that's for-ev-

(D.S.) *Instrumental solo*

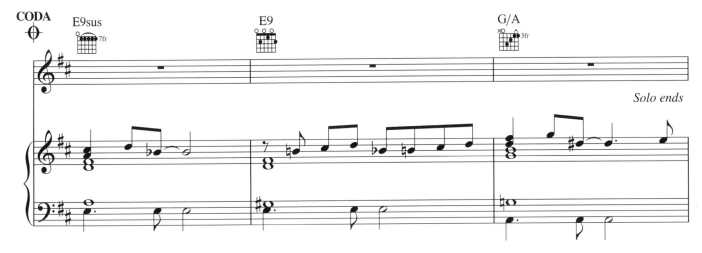

Solo ends

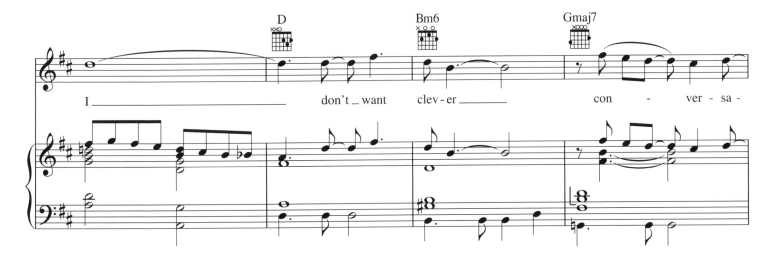

I _____ don't _ want clev-er _____ con - ver-sa-

-tion; I nev-er want_ to work_ that_ hard._

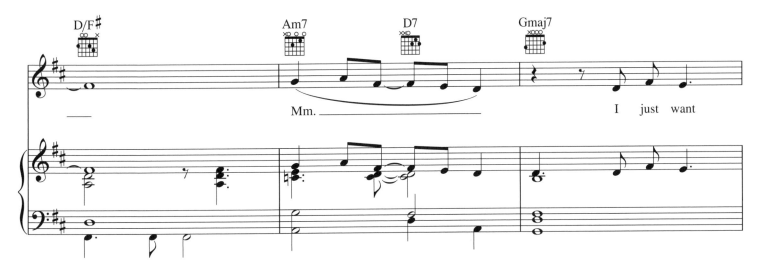

Mm. _____ I just want

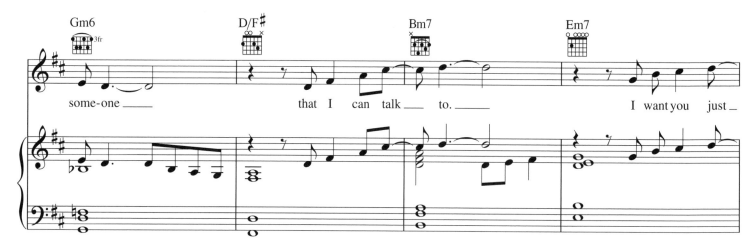

some-one ____ that I can talk ____ to. ____ I want you just ____

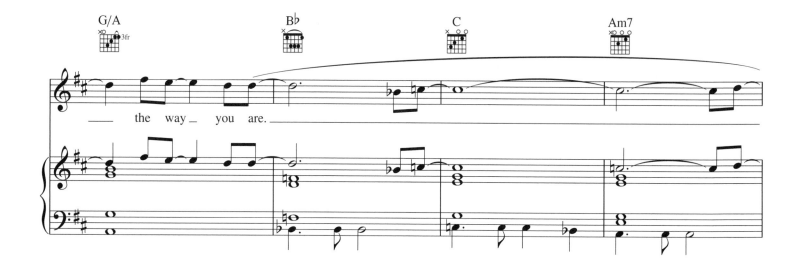

____ the way ____ you are. ____

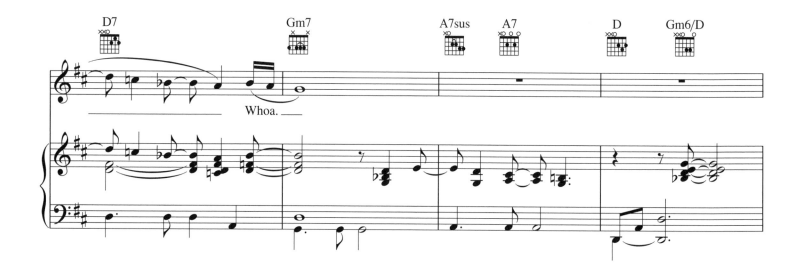

_____ Whoa. ____

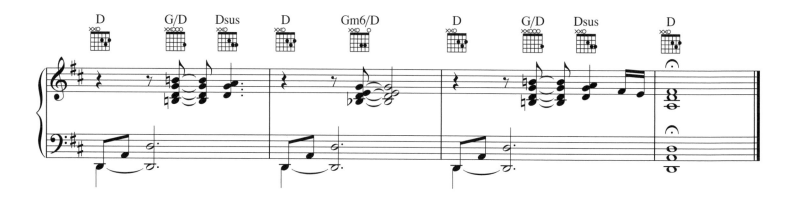

MOON RIVER

from the Paramount Picture BREAKFAST AT TIFFANY'S

Words by JOHNNY MERCER
Music by HENRY MANCINI

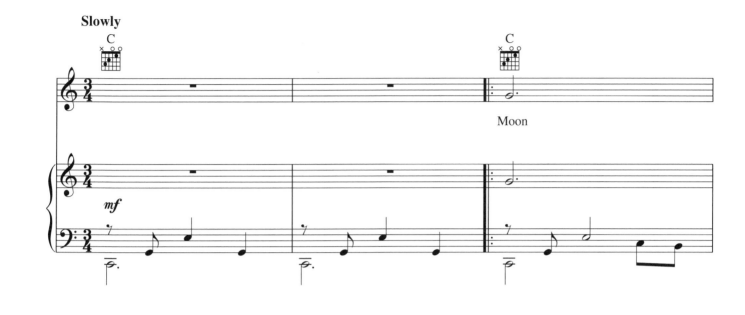

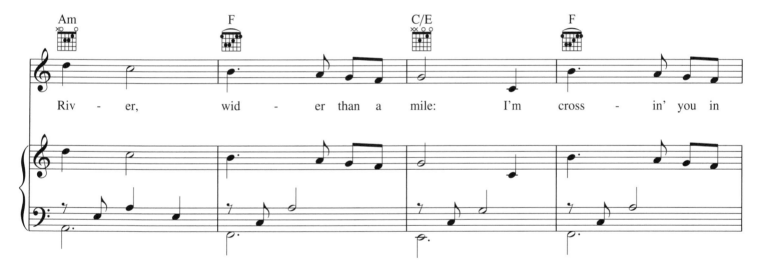

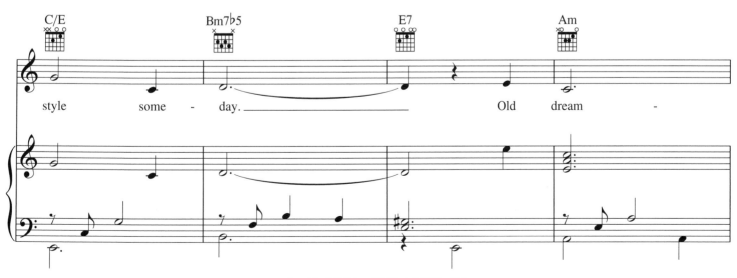

LIKE A VIRGIN

Words and Music by BILLY STEINBERG
and TOM KELLY

ver - y first time.   Like a vir -   gin, _____

_____ when your heart   beats   next to ___ mine. Gon - na give you
with your heart - beat
with your heart - beat

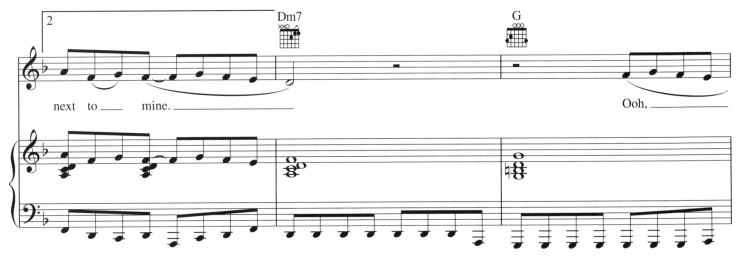

next to ___ mine. _____   Ooh, _____

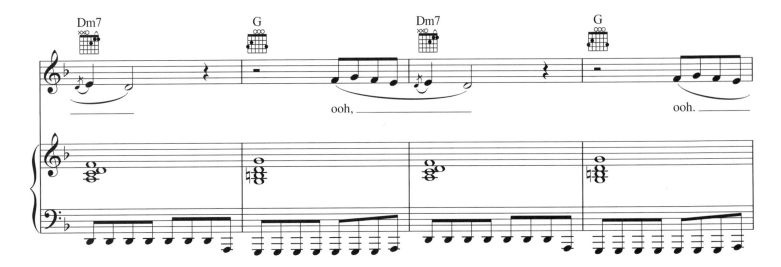

_____   ooh, _____   ooh. _____

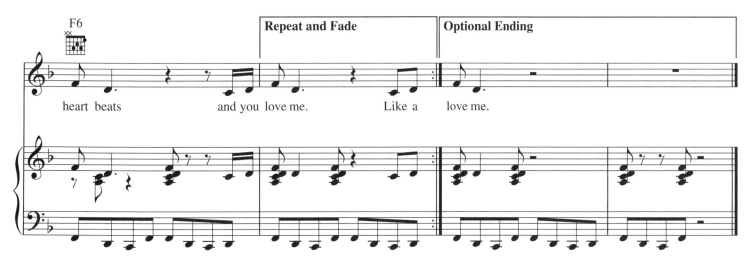

LIVIN' ON A PRAYER

Words and Music by JON BON JOVI,
DESMOND CHILD and RICHIE SAMBORA

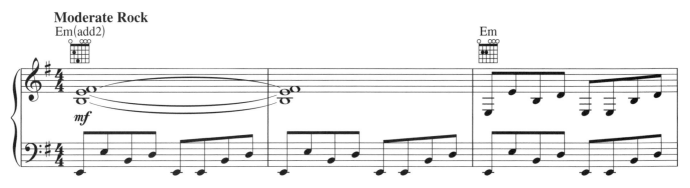

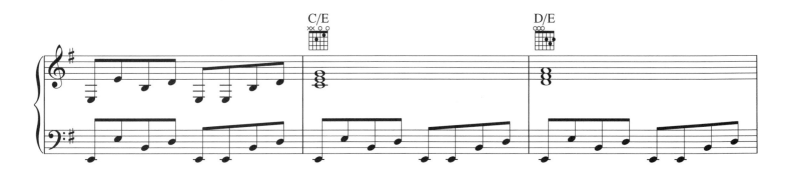

(Spoken:) Once upon a time,

not so long ago...

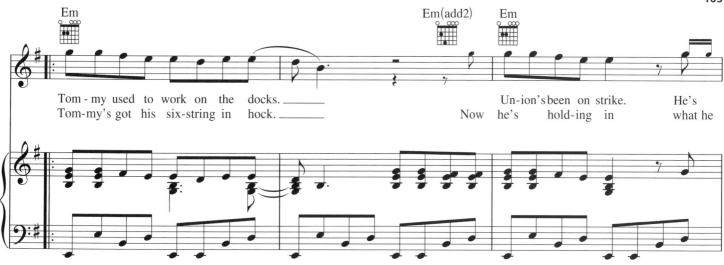

Tom - my used to work on the docks. _____ Un-ion's been on strike. He's
Tom-my's got his six-string in hock. _____ Now he's hold-ing in what he

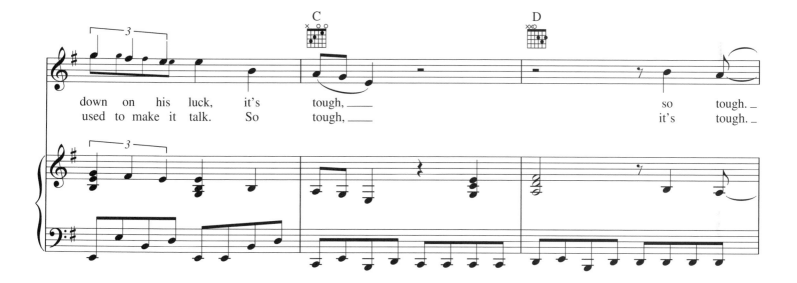

down on his luck, it's tough, _____ so tough. _
used to make it talk. So tough, _____ it's tough. _

_____ Gi - na works the din - er all day. _
_____ Gi - na dreams of run-ning a - way. _

Work-ing for her man, she brings home her pay for
When she cries in the night, Tom-my whis-pers: Ba - by, it's

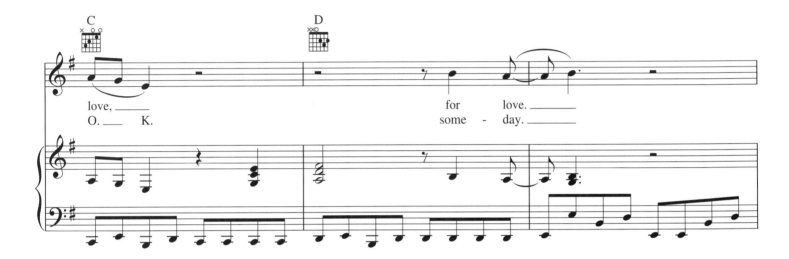

love, _____
O. ___ K.

for love. _____
some - day. _____

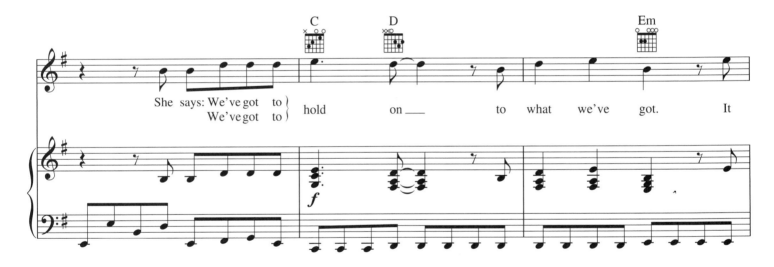

She says: We've got to } hold on _____ to what we've got. It
We've got to }

does-n't make a dif-f'rence if we make it or not. We've got each oth - er and

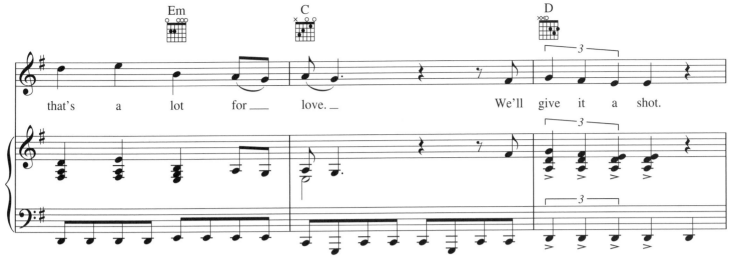

that's a lot for ___ love. ___ We'll give it a shot.

Whoa, _____ we're half - way there. ____ Whoa, _____ liv -

- in' on a prayer. ___ Take my ___ hand, ___ we'll make it, I swear. ___

Whoa, _____ liv - in' on a prayer. ___

Liv - in' on ___ a prayer. ___

Instrumental

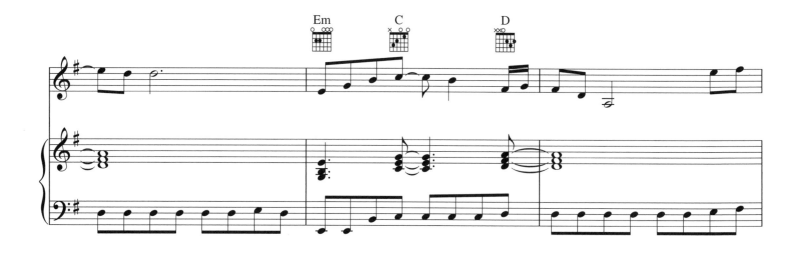

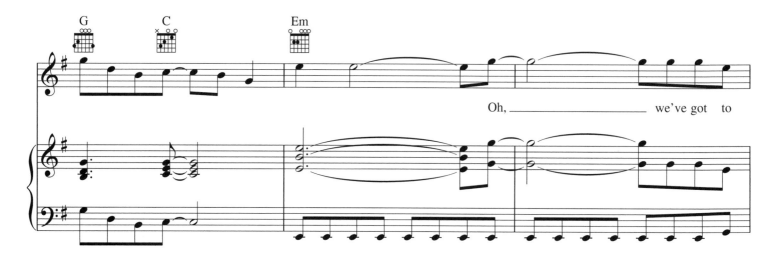

Oh, ___ we've got to

LOCKED OUT OF HEAVEN

Words and Music by BRUNO MARS,
ARI LEVINE and PHILIP LAWRENCE

Oh, yeah, _ yeah, oh, yeah, _ yeah, yeah, _ yeah.

Nev- er had much faith _ in love _ or mi- tes -
You bring me to my knees, _ you make _ me tes -

-it - ual; _____
_____ the light. _____

I'm born a-gain ev-'ry time _____ you spend _____ the night, _____ ee -
And right _____ there is _____ where _____ I want _____ to stay, _____ ee -

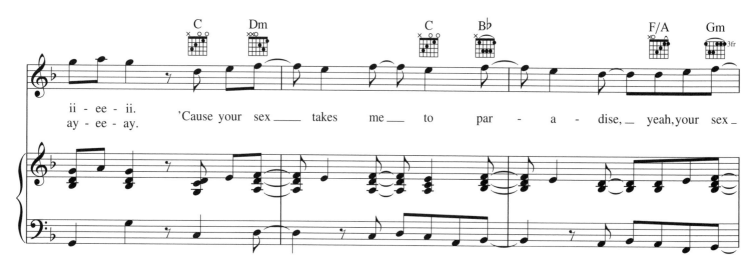

ii - ee - ii.   'Cause your sex _____ takes me _____ to par - a - dise, _____ yeah, your sex _____
ay - ee - ay.

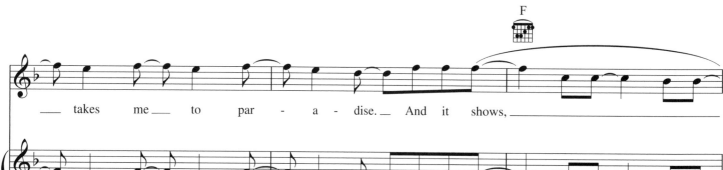

_____ takes me _____ to par - a - dise. _____ And it shows, _____

yeah, ____ yeah, ____ yeah. ____ 'Cause you make me

feel ____ like ____ I've been locked out of heav - en ____

for too long, _____ for too

long. _____ Yeah, you ___ make me feel ____ like ____

D.S. al Coda

yeah,   oh,   yeah,   yeah,   yeah,   yeah.

CODA

Oh,

yeah.   Can   I   just   stay   here,

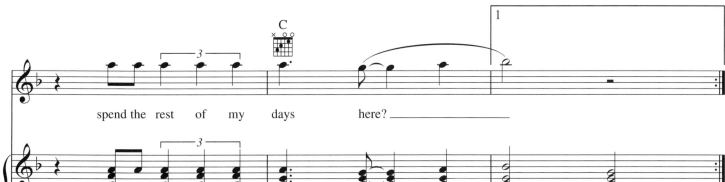

spend   the   rest   of   my   days   here?

'Cause you make me feel ____ like ____ I've been locked out of heav-

-en ____ for too long, _____ for too

long. _____ Yeah, you make me feel ____ like ____

I've been locked out of heav - en ____ for too

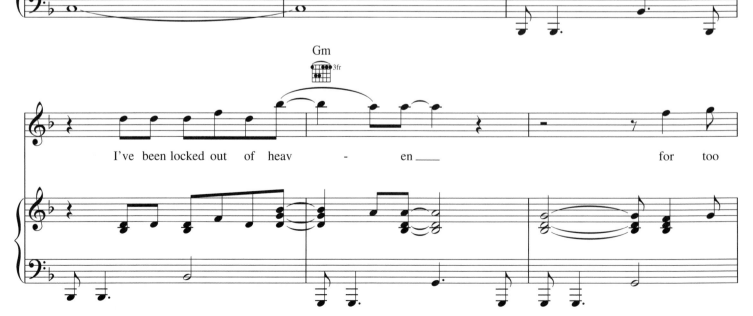

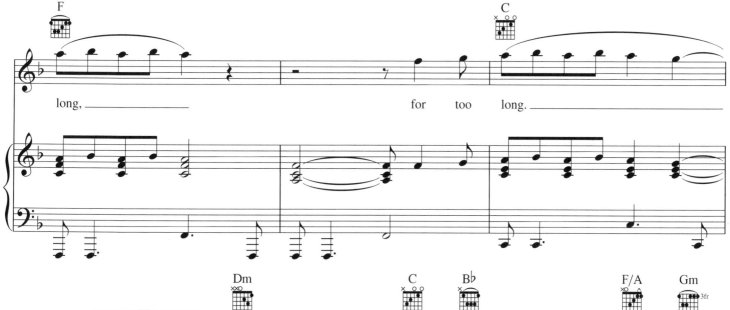

long, _____   for too long. _____

Oh,   yeah, _

_ yeah,   yeah, _ yeah.   Oh,   yeah, _

_ yeah,   oh,   yeah, ___ yeah,   yeah, _ yeah.

MY FUNNY VALENTINE
from BABES IN ARMS

Words by LORENZ HART
Music by RICHARD RODGERS

tent. Thou no - ble, up - right, truth - ful, sin - cere and slight - ly dop - ey

Slowly, with much expression

gent, you're My fun - ny Val - en - tine, Sweet com - ic

Val - en - tine, You make me smile with my

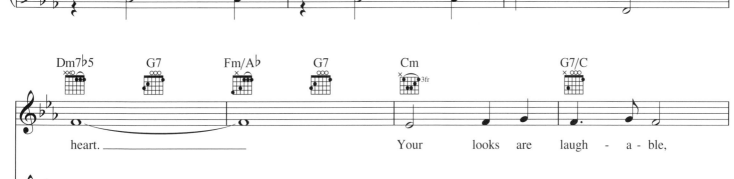

heart. _____ Your looks are laugh - a - ble,

MY GIRL

Words and Music by WILLIAM "SMOKEY" ROBINSON
and RONALD WHITE

Moderately

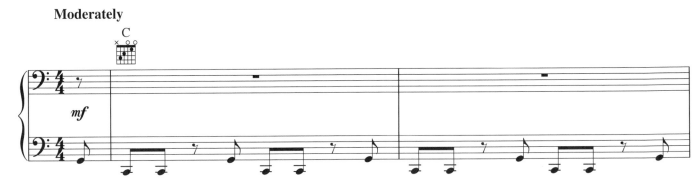

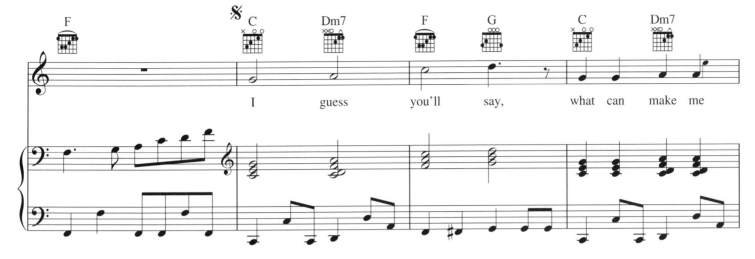

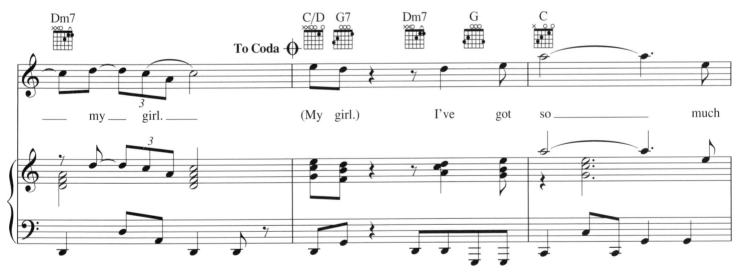

sweet-er song ____ than the birds in the trees.

D.S. al Coda

Well, _

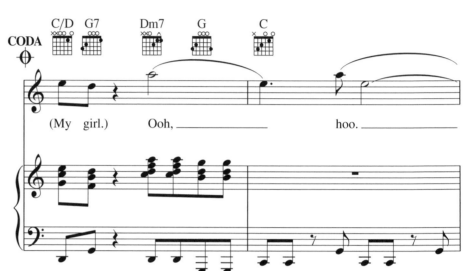

CODA

(My girl.) Ooh, _____ hoo. _____

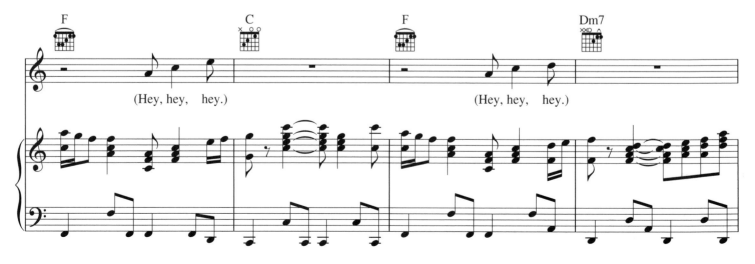

(Hey, hey, hey.) (Hey, hey, hey.)

Ooh, _____ hoo, _____ yeah. ___ I don't

need no ____ mon - ey, ___ for - tune

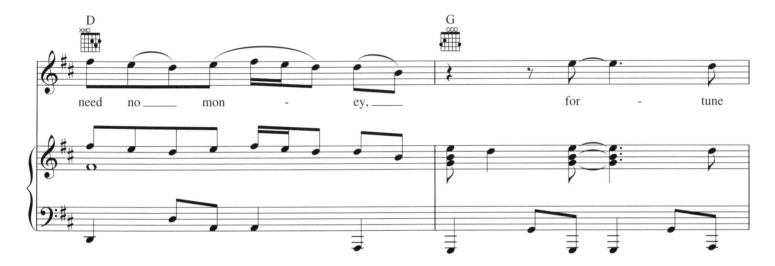

or fame. _____ I've got all ___ the rich - es, ba - by,

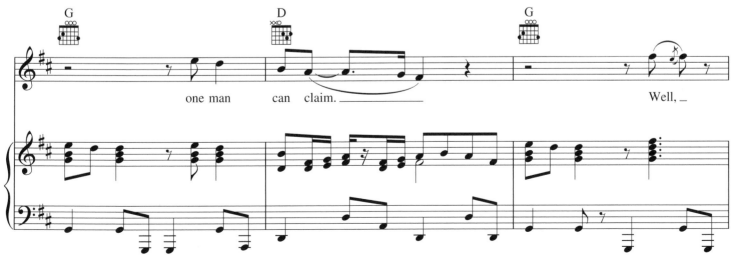

one man can claim. _____ Well, _

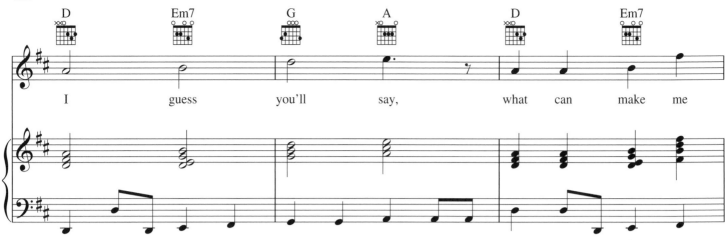

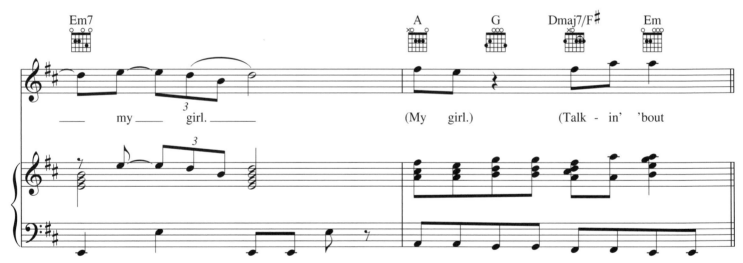

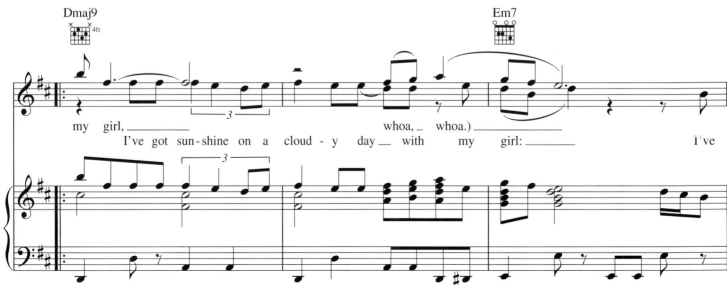

(Talk - in' 'bout   my   girl,   my   girl,

e - ven got the month __ of   May with   my   girl. _____

my girl,   whoa, __   whoa.) _____

Talk - in' 'bout, __   talk - in' 'bout,   talk - in' 'bout __   my ____   girl. _____

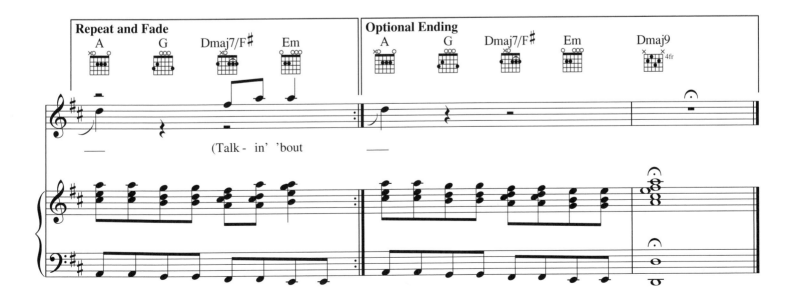

Repeat and Fade

Optional Ending

__   (Talk - in' 'bout   __

NIGHT AND DAY

from GAY DIVORCE

Words and Music by
COLE PORTER

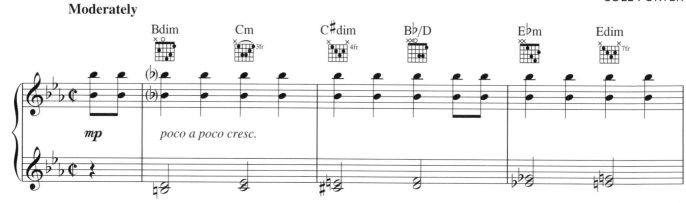

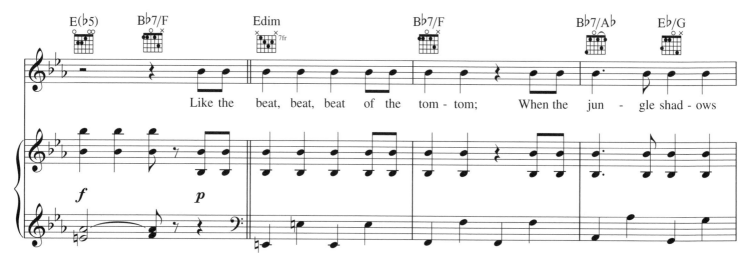

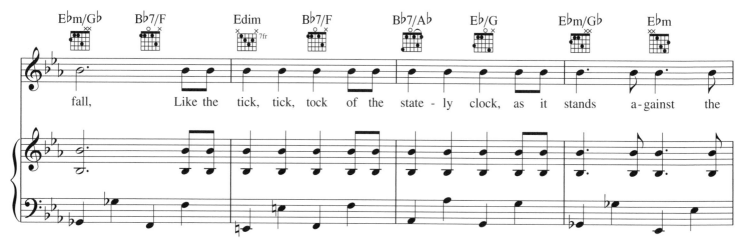

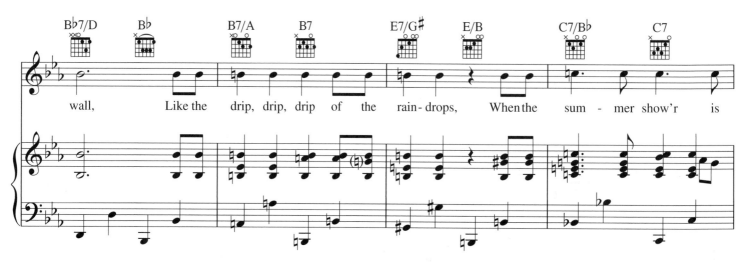

Like the beat, beat, beat of the tom-tom; When the jun - gle shad - ows fall, Like the tick, tick, tock of the state - ly clock, as it stands a - gainst the wall, Like the drip, drip, drip of the rain - drops, When the sum - mer show'r is

NOTHING COMPARES 2 U

Words and Music by
PRINCE

since you took your love a - way. ___

Since you been gone I can do what - ev - er I want, ___

I can see whom - ev - er I choose. ___

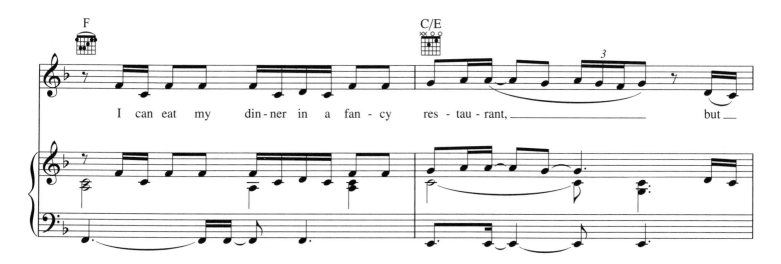

I can eat my din - ner in a fan - cy res - tau - rant, ___ but ___

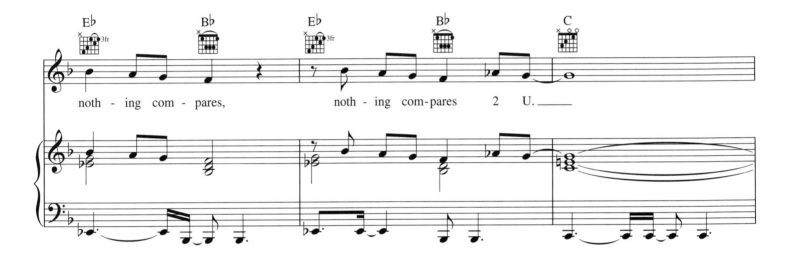

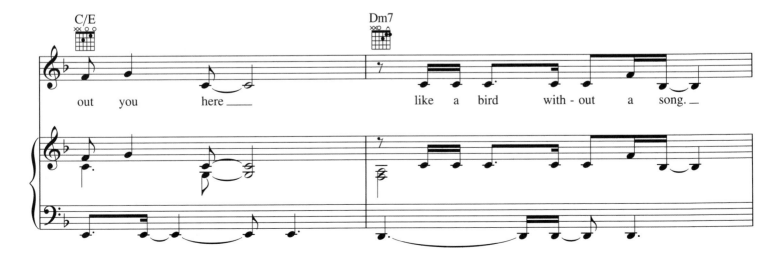

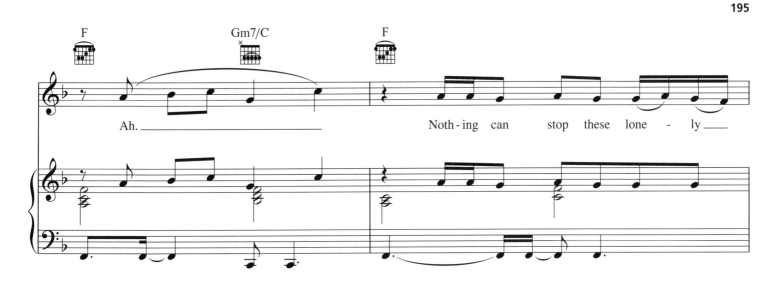

Ah. _____ Noth-ing can stop these lone - ly _____

tears from fall - ing, tell me ba - by, _____ where did I go

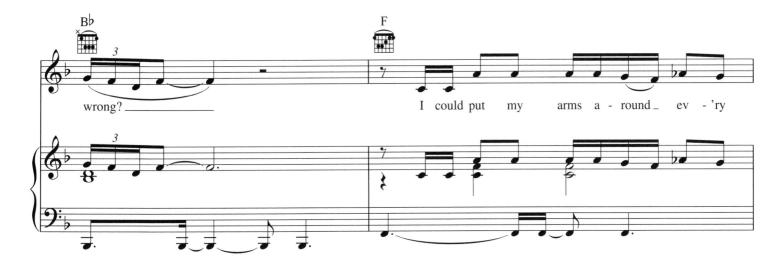

wrong? _____ I could put my arms a - round _ ev - 'ry

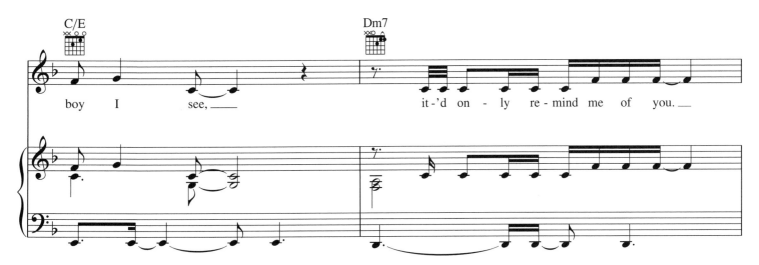

boy I see, _____ it-'d on - ly re - mind me of you. _

196

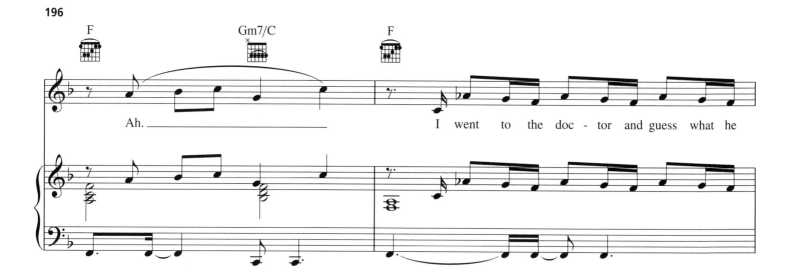

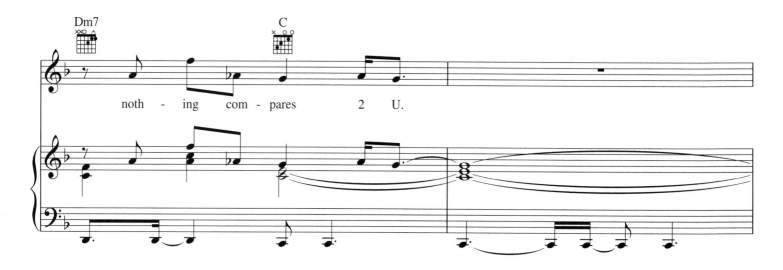

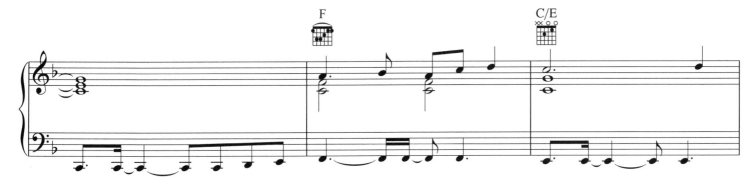

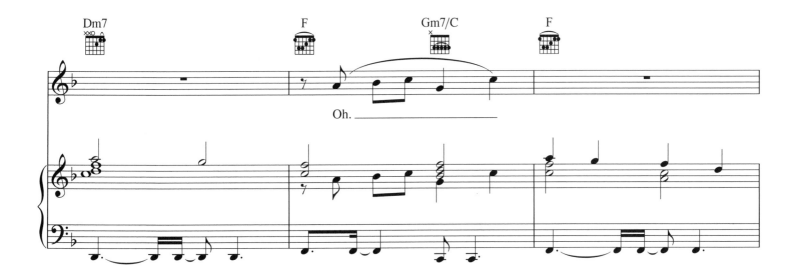

Oh. _____

All the flow - ers that you plant-ed, ma-ma, in the back yard _____

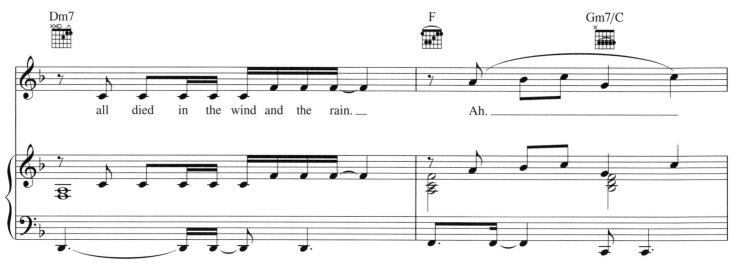

all died in the wind and the rain. ___ Ah. _____

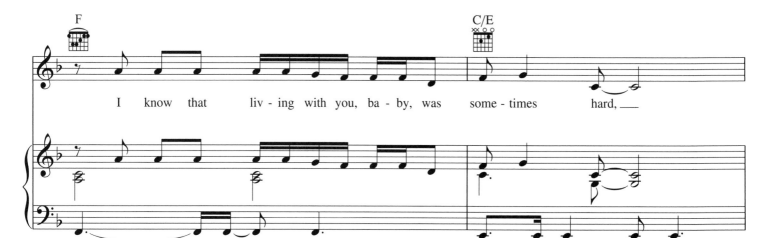

I know that liv - ing with you, ba - by, was some - times hard, ___

but I'm will - ing to give it an - oth - er try. _____

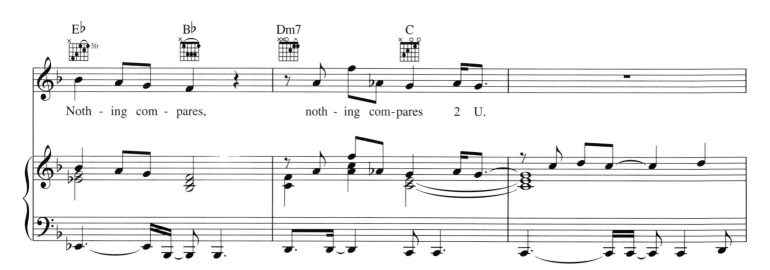

Noth - ing com - pares, noth - ing com - pares 2 U.

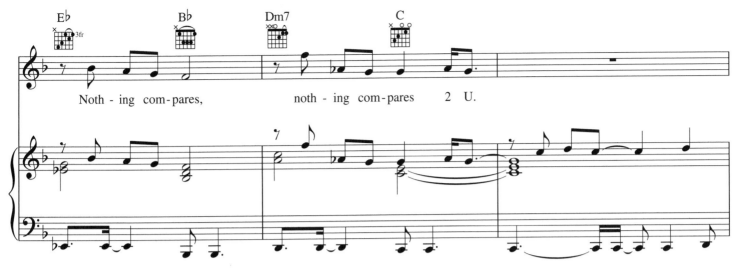

Noth - ing com - pares, noth - ing com - pares 2 U.

Noth - ing com - pares, __ noth - ing com - pares 2 U.

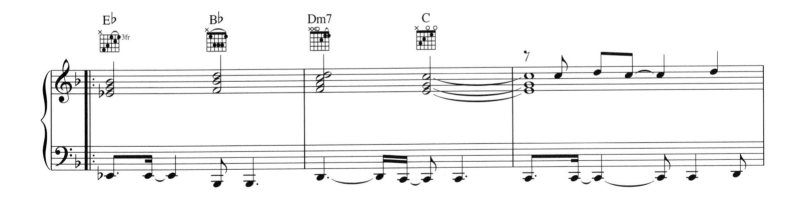

Repeat and Fade

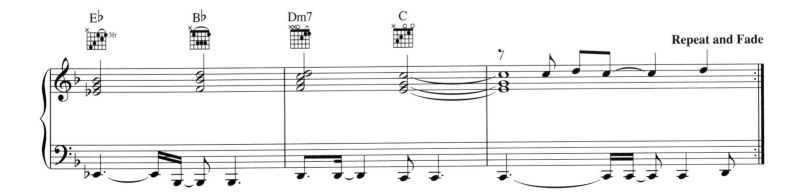

OL' MAN RIVER
from SHOW BOAT

Lyrics by OSCAR HAMMERSTEIN II
Music by JEROME KERN

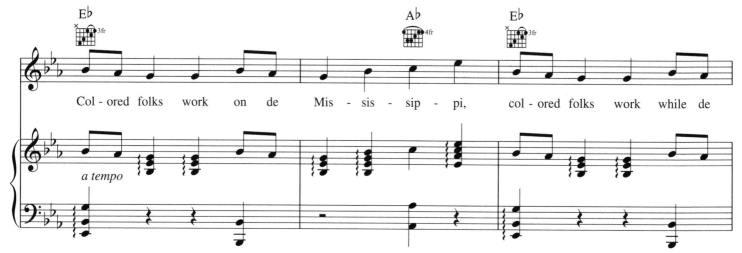

Col - ored folks work on de Mis - sis - sip - pi, col - ored folks work while de

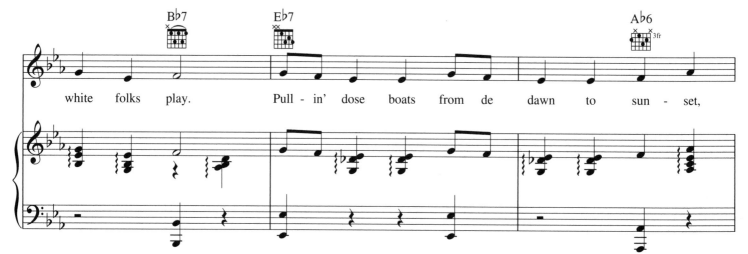

white folks play. Pull - in' dose boats from de dawn to sun - set,

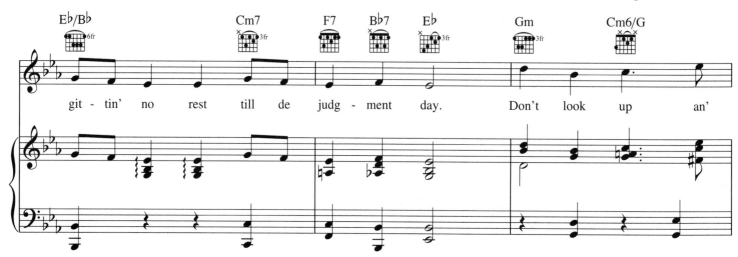

git - tin' no rest till de judg - ment day. Don't look up an'

don't look down, you don't dast make de white boss frown.

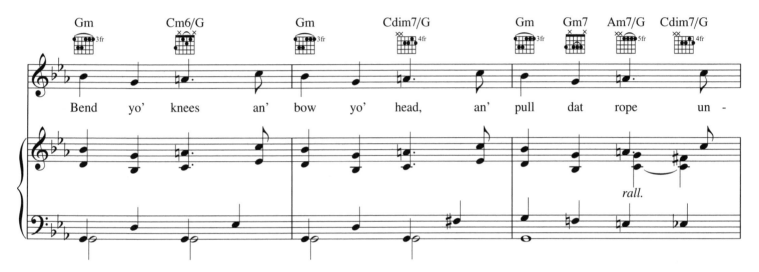

Bend yo' knees an' bow yo' head, an' pull dat rope un-

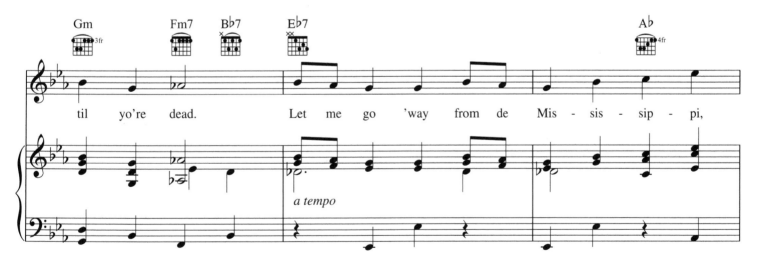

til yo're dead. Let me go 'way from de Mis - sis - sip - pi,

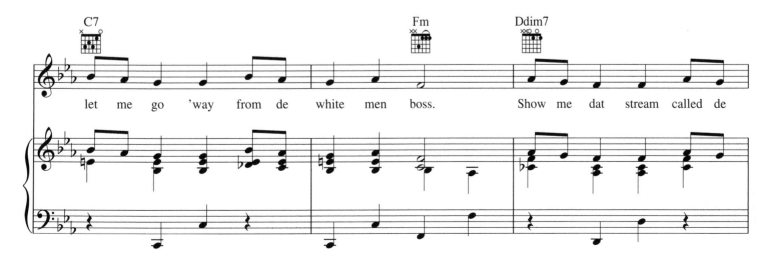

let me go 'way from de white men boss. Show me dat stream called de

riv - er Jor - dan. Dat's de ol' stream dat I long to cross. _____

Slower

Ol' man riv - er, dat ol' man riv - er; he must know sump - in', but

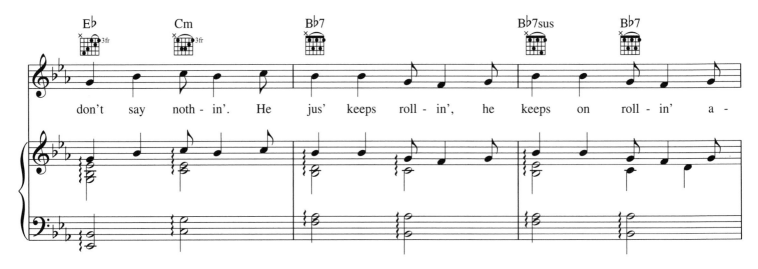

don't say noth - in'. He jus' keeps roll - in', he keeps on roll - in' a -

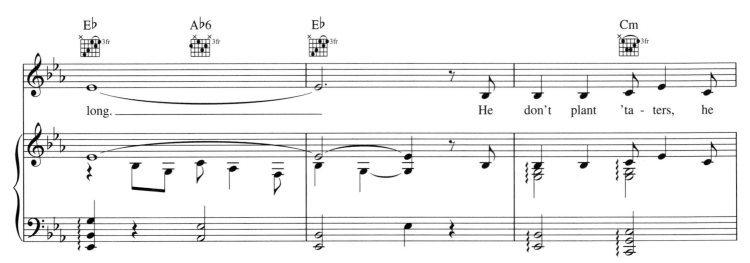

long. _____ He don't plant 'ta - ters, he

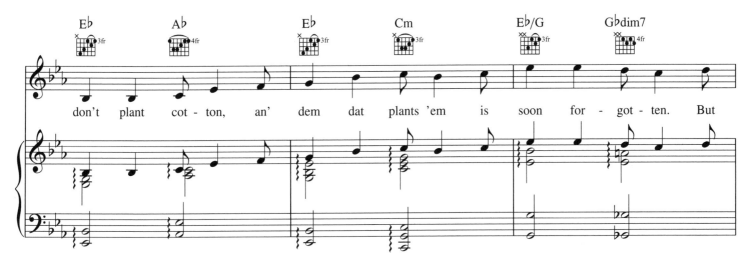

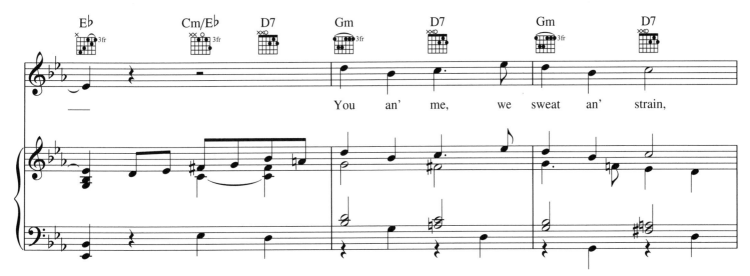

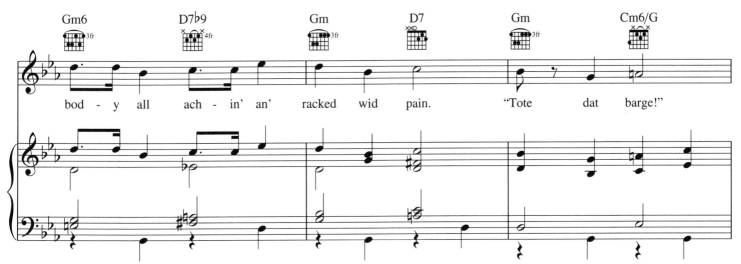

"Lift dat bale," Git a lit - tle drunk an' you land in jail.

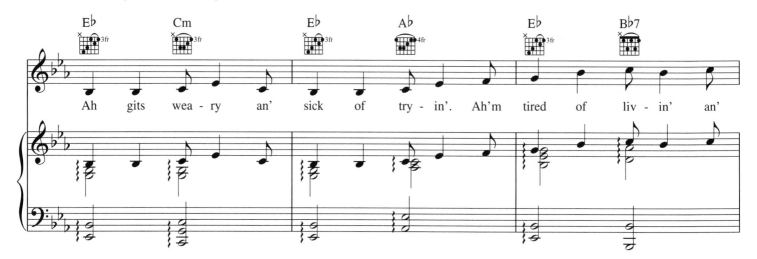

Ah gits wea - ry an' sick of try - in'. Ah'm tired of liv - in' an'

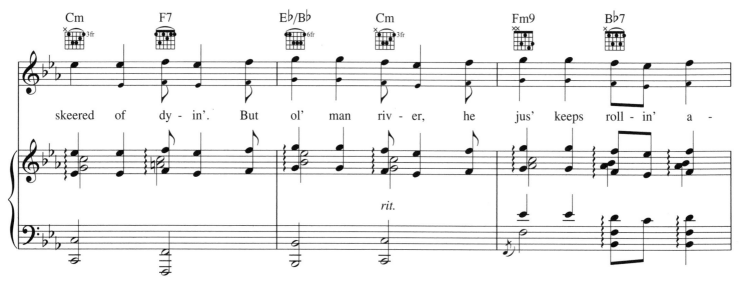

skeered of dy - in'. But ol' man riv - er, he jus' keeps roll - in' a -

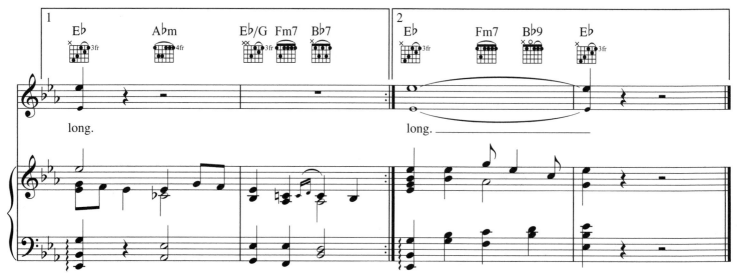

long.   long.

OVER THE RAINBOW
from THE WIZARD OF OZ

Music by HAROLD ARLEN
Lyric by E.Y. "YIP" HARBURG

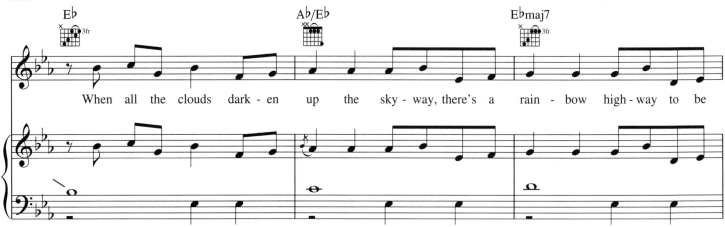

When all the clouds dark-en up the sky-way, there's a rain-bow high-way to be

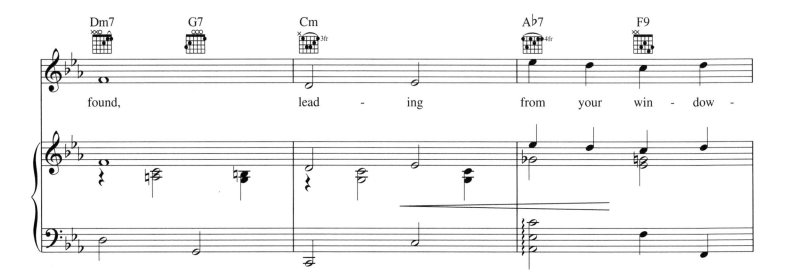

found, lead - ing from your win - dow -

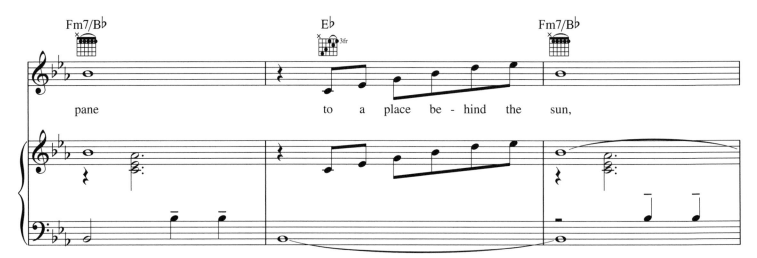

pane to a place be-hind the sun,

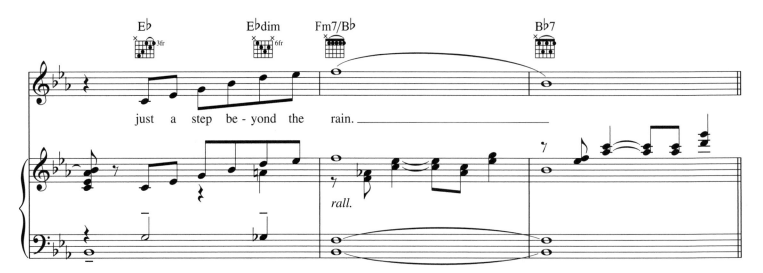

just a step be-yond the rain.

rall.

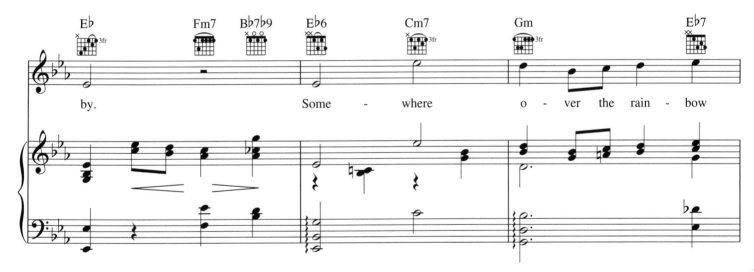

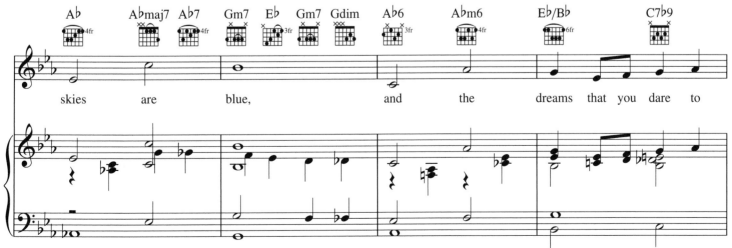

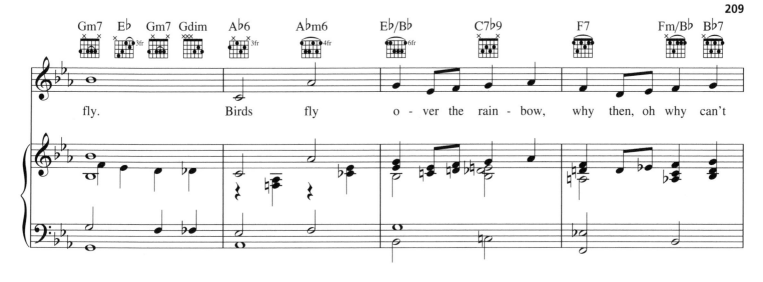

fly. Birds fly o - ver the rain - bow, why then, oh why can't

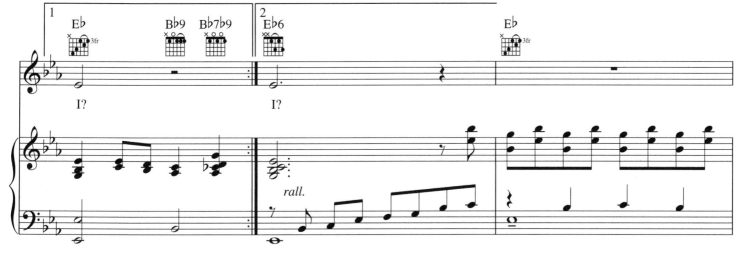

I? I?

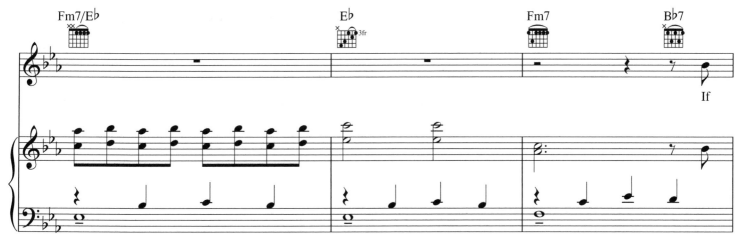

If

hap - py lit - tle blue-birds fly be - yond the rain - bow, why oh why can't I?

OVER THERE

Words and Music by
GEORGE M. COHAN

Moderately fast

John - nie get your gun, get your
John - nie get your gun, get your
John - nie, sac au dos, sac au
John - nie, sac au dos, sac au

gun, get your gun,
gun, get your gun,
dos, sac au dos,
dos, sac au dos,

Take it on the run, on the run, on the
John - nie show the Hun you're a son - of - a
Pars au grand gal - op, au gal - op, au gal -
Cours sus à ces Goths, Os - tro - goths, sal - i -

211

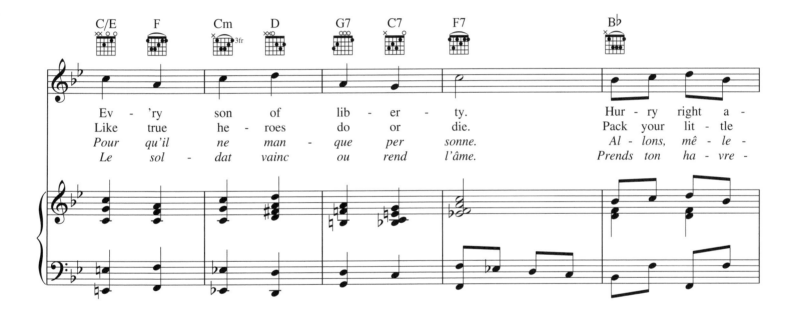

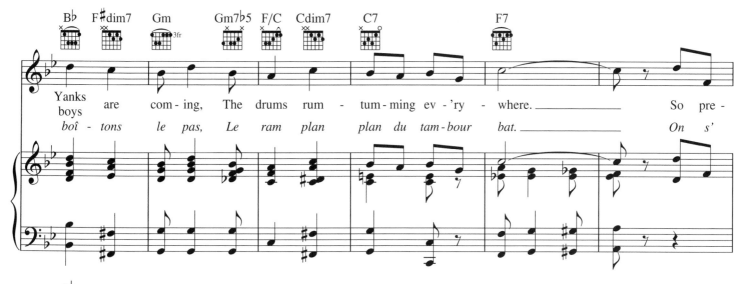

RAINDROPS KEEP FALLIN' ON MY HEAD

from BUTCH CASSIDY AND THE SUNDANCE KID

Lyric by HAL DAVID
Music by BURT BACHARACH

sun. And I said I did-n't like the way he got things done. Sleep-in'on the

job. Those rain - drops are fall - in'on my head. They keep fall - in'! But there's one

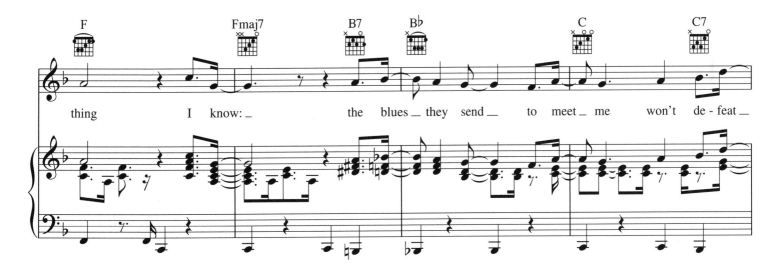

thing I know: _ the blues _ they send _ to meet _ me won't de-feat _

___ me. It won't be long _ till hap-pi-ness _ steps up _

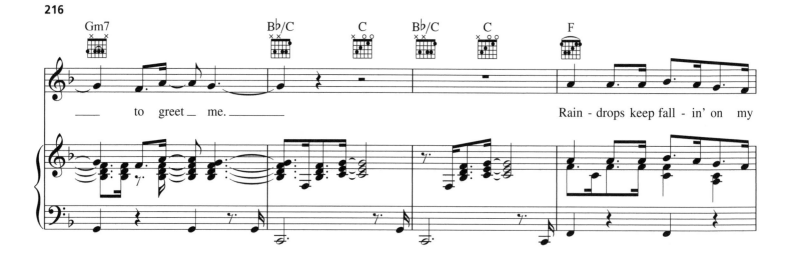

to greet me. Rain - drops keep fall - in' on my

head, but that does-n't mean my eyes will soon be turn - in' red. Cry-in's not for

me 'cause I'm nev - er gon - na stop the rain by com-plain - in'.

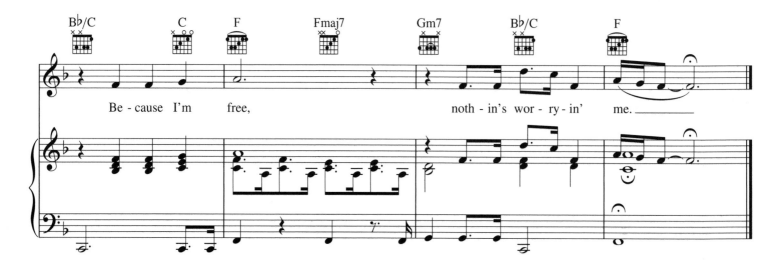

Be - cause I'm free, noth - in's wor - ry - in' me.

ST. LOUIS BLUES

from BIRTH OF THE BLUES

Words and Music by
W.C. HANDY

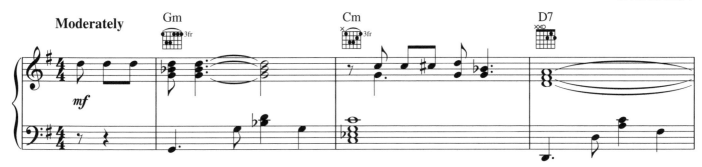

I hate to see _____ de eve-nin' sun go
Been to de Gyp-sy to get ma for-tune
You ought to see _____ dat stove-pipe brown of

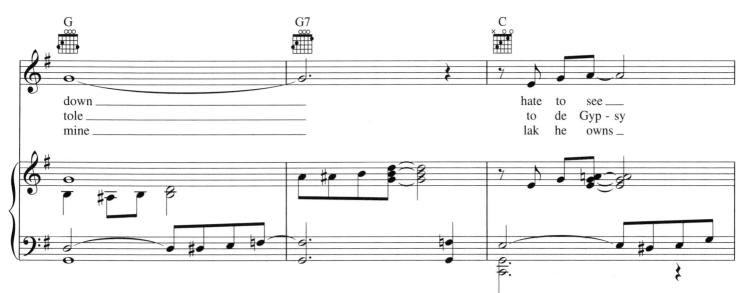

down _____ hate to see _____
tole _____ to de Gyp-sy
mine _____ lak he owns _____

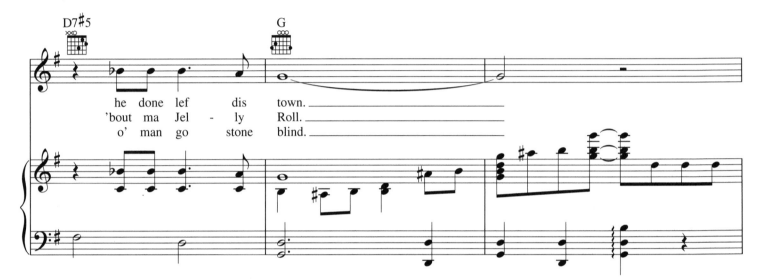

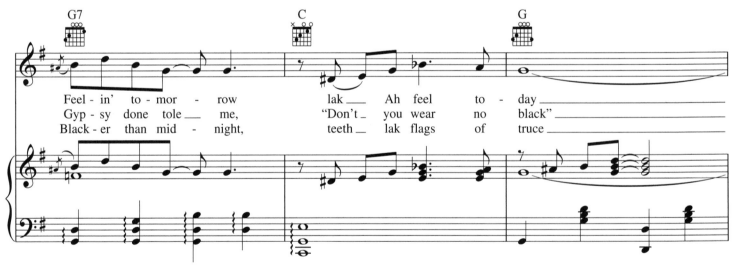

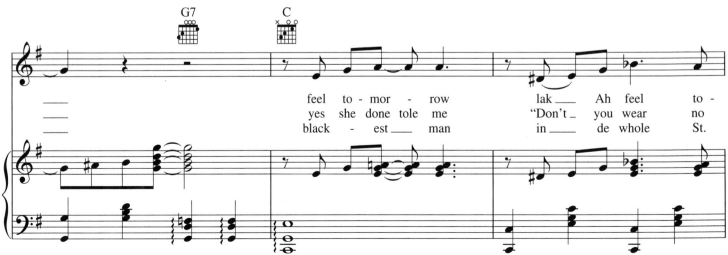

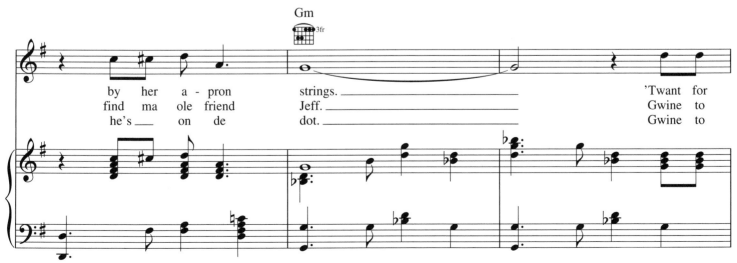

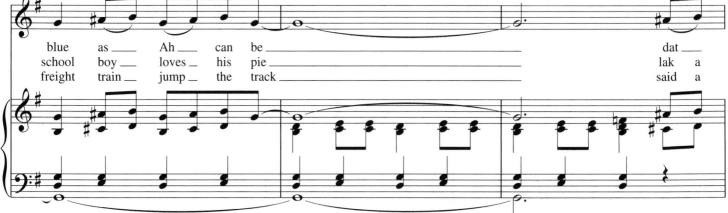

man got a heart lak a rook cast __ in the __ sea _____
Ken - tuck - y Col' - nel __ loves his __ mint an' __ rye _____
black - head - ed gal make a freight train __ jump the __ track _____

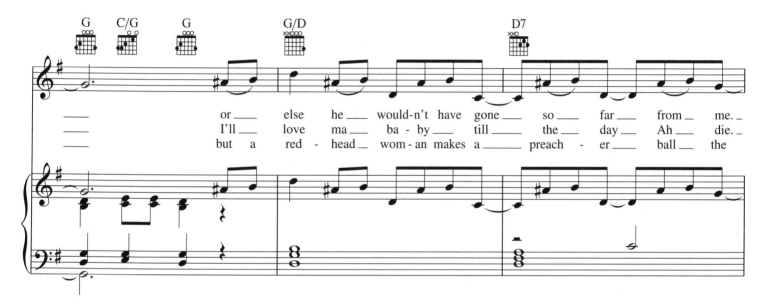

__ or __ else he __ would-n't have gone __ so __ far __ from __ me. __
__ I'll __ love ma ba - by __ till __ the __ day Ah __ die. __
__ but a red - head wom - an makes a __ preach - er ball __ the

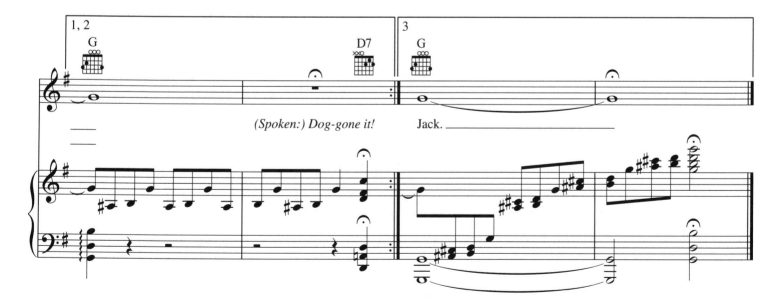

(Spoken:) Dog-gone it!   Jack. _____

Extra Choruses (optional)

Lawd, a blonde-headed woman makes a good man leave the town,
I said a blonde-headed woman makes a good man leave the town,
But a red-head woman makes a boy slap his papa down.

O ashes to ashes and dust to dust,
I said ashes to ashes and dust to dust,
If my blues don't get you my jazzing must.

ROCK AROUND THE CLOCK

Words and Music by MAX C. FREEDMAN
and JIMMY DeKNIGHT

Swing Shuffle

One, two, three o'-clock, four o'-clock rock. Five, six, sev-en o' clock,
eight o'-clock rock. Nine, ten, e-lev-en o'-clock,
twelve o'-clock rock, we're gon-na rock a-round the clock to-night. _ 1. Put your

glad rags on and join me, Hon. _ We'll have some fun when the
clock strikes two and three and four, _ if the band slows down we'll _
chimes ring five and six and seven, _ we'll be rock-in' up in _
eight, nine, ten e-lev-en, too, _ I'll be go-in' strong and _
clock strikes twelve, we'll cool off, then, _ start a rock-in' 'round the _

clock strikes one. __
yell for more. __
sev - enth heav'n. __ We're gon - na rock a - round the clock to - night, __ we're gon - na
so will you. __
clock a - gain. __

rock, rock, rock, 'til broad day - light. __ We're gon - na rock, gon - na rock a - round __

__ the clock __ to - night. _____

When the
When the
When it's
When the

SECRETS

Words and Music by
RYAN TEDDER

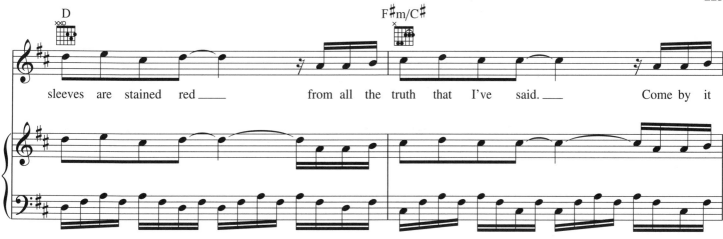

sleeves are stained red ____ from all the truth that I've said. ____ Come by it

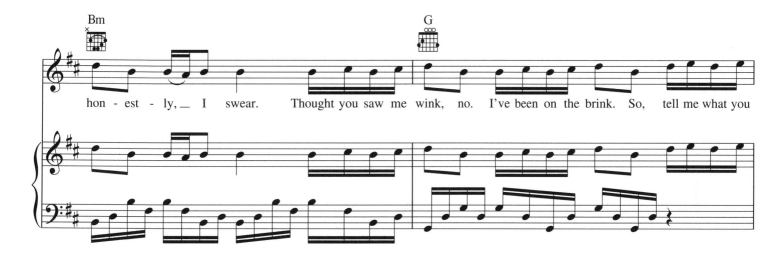

hon - est - ly, __ I swear. Thought you saw me wink, no. I've been on the brink. So, tell me what you

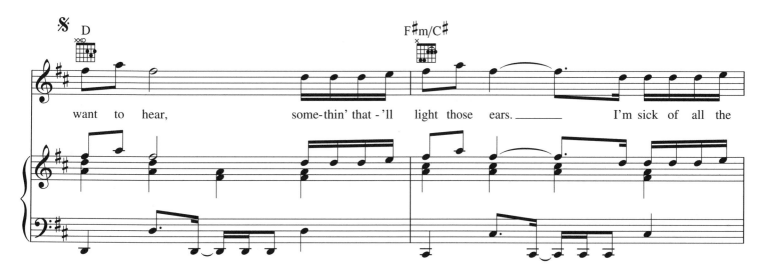

want to hear, some-thin' that - 'll light those ears. _____ I'm sick of all the

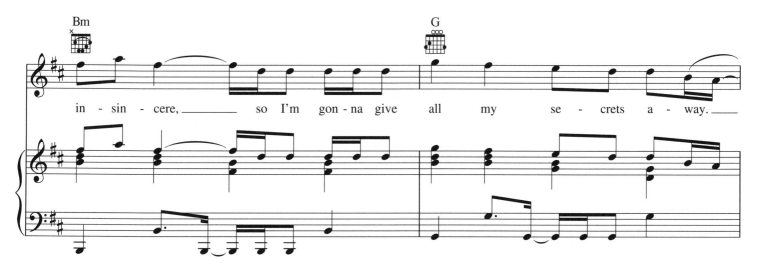

in - sin - cere, _____ so I'm gon - na give all my se - crets a - way. ____

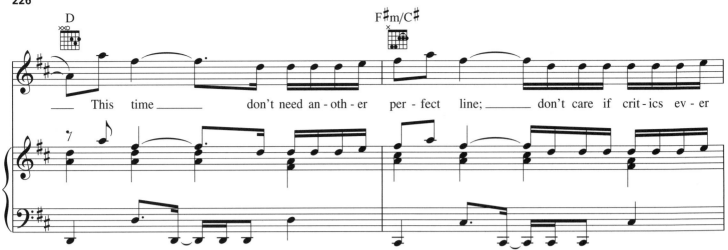

This time ____ don't need an-oth-er per-fect line; ____ don't care if crit-ics ev-er

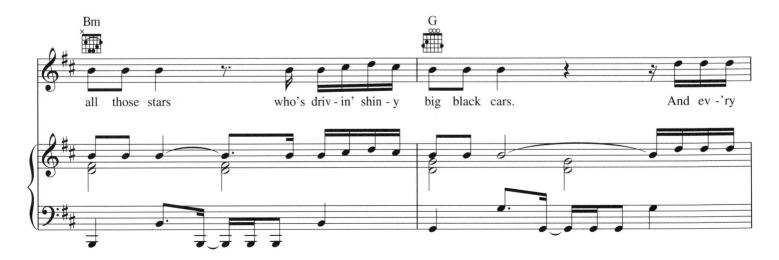

jump in line. ____ I'm gon-na give all my se-crets a-way. ____

____ My God, a-maz-ing how we got this far. It's like we're chas-in'

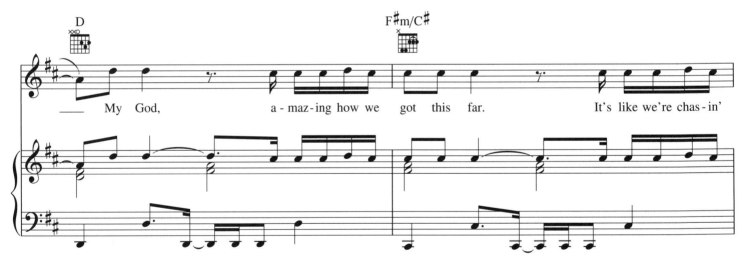

all those stars who's driv-in' shin-y big black cars. And ev-'ry

D

day I see the news, all the prob-lems that we could solve. And when a

F#m/C#   **Bm**

sit-u-a-tion ris-es, just write it in-to an al-bum. Send it straight to go, _____ but I don't real-ly

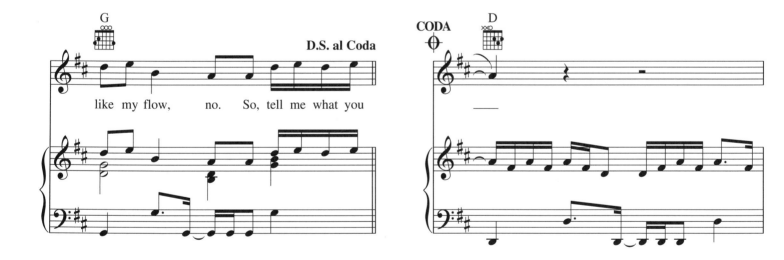

G   *D.S. al Coda*   **CODA**   **D**

like my flow, no. So, tell me what you

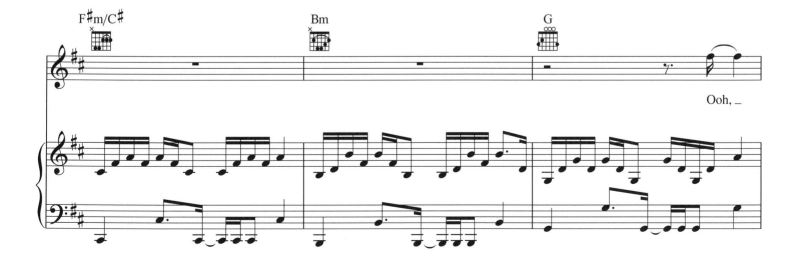

F#m/C#   **Bm**   **G**

Ooh, _

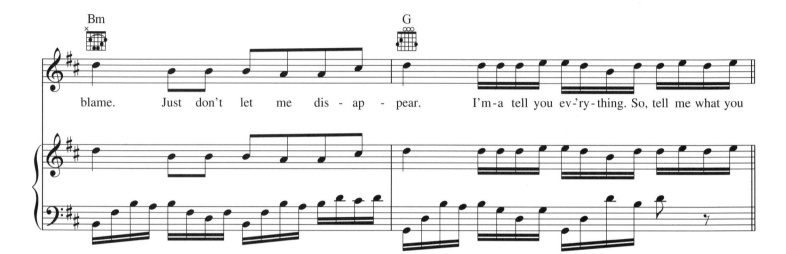

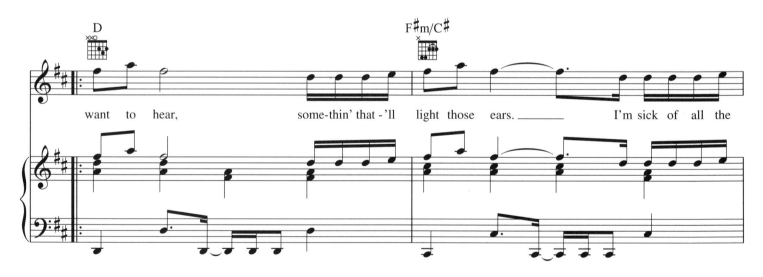

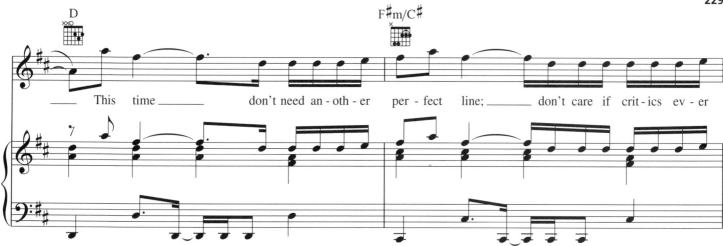

This time _____ don't need an-oth-er per-fect line; _____ don't care if crit-ics ev-er

jump in line. _____ I'm gon-na give all my se-crets a - way. _____ So, tell me what you

all my se - crets a - way. _____

All my se - crets a - way. _____

THE SHADOW OF YOUR SMILE
Love Theme from THE SANDPIPER

Music by JOHNNY MANDEL
Words by PAUL FRANCIS WEBSTER

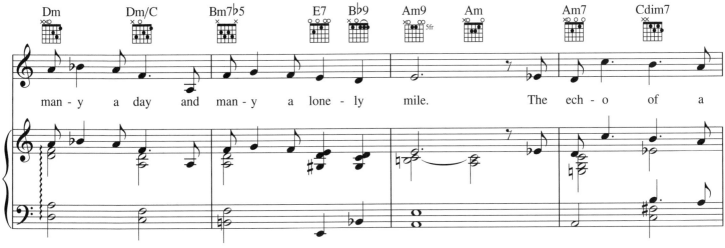

man - y a day and man - y a lone - ly mile. The ech - o of a

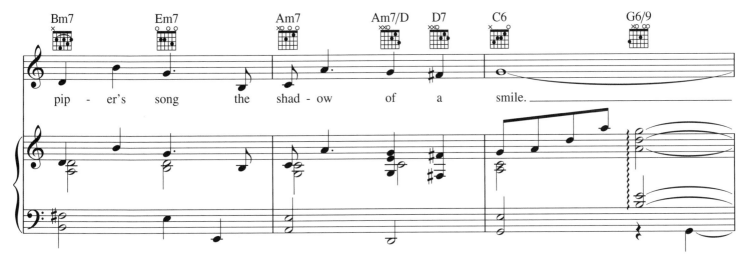

pip - er's song the shad - ow of a smile.

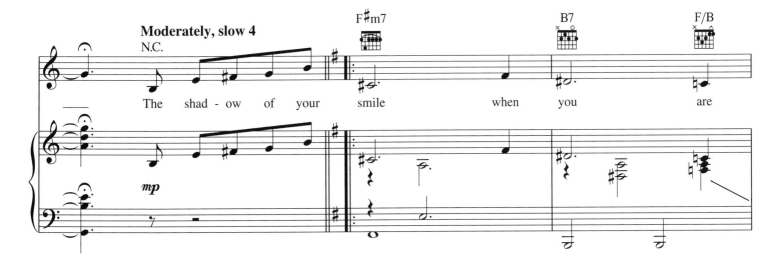

Moderately, slow 4

N.C.

The shad - ow of your smile when you are

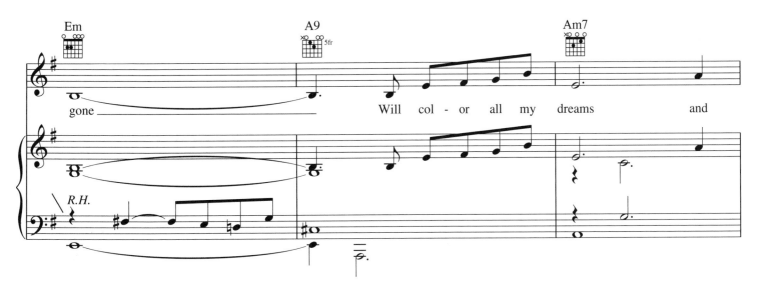

gone Will col - or all my dreams and

SINGLE LADIES
(Put a Ring on It)

Words and Music by BEYONCÉ KNOWLES,
THADDIS HARRIS, CHRISTOPHER STEWART
and TERIUS NASH

do - in' my own lit - tle thing. You de - cid - ed to dip and now you wan - na trip 'cause an -
tight - er than my De - re - on __ jeans. Act - in' __ up, __ drink __ in my cup, __

oth - er broth - er no - ticed me. I'm up on him, he up on me. Don't
I can care __ less what you think. I need no per - mis - sion. Did I men - tion? Don't

pay him an - y at - ten - tion. __ Just cried my tears for three good years, you
pay him an - y at - ten - tion. __ 'Cause you had your turn and now you gon' learn what it

E5

can't be mad at me. } 'Cause if you like it then you should have put a ring on it. __ If you
real - ly feels __ like to miss __ me. __

236

___ is what ___ I pre-fer, ___ what ___ I de-serve. _____ Here's a man ___ that makes ___

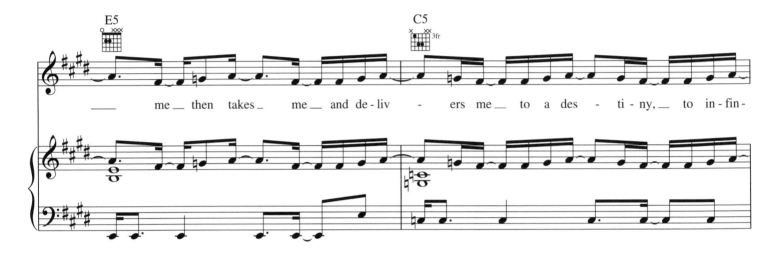

___ me ___ then takes ___ me ___ and de-liv - ers me to a des - ti-ny, ___ to in-fin-

- i-ty ___ and be - yond. ___ Pull me in - to your arms, ___ say I'm ___

___ the one ___ you want. ___ If you don't, ___ you'll be a - lone ___ and like a ghost ___

SMALL TOWN

Words and Music by
JOHN MELLENCAMP

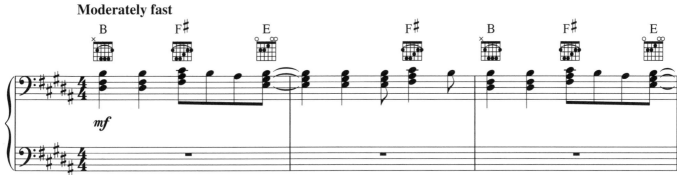

No, I can-not for-get ___ where it is ___ that I ___ come from, I

can-not for-get the peo-ple who love ___ me. Yeah, I can be my-self ___ here in

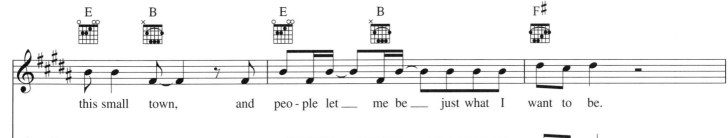

this small town, and peo-ple let ___ me be ___ just what I want to be.

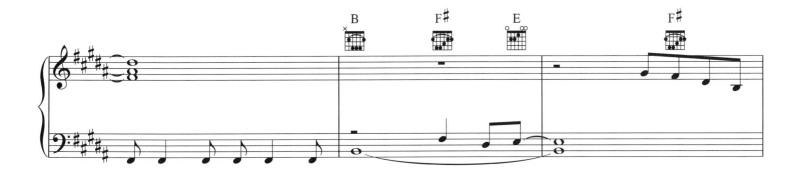

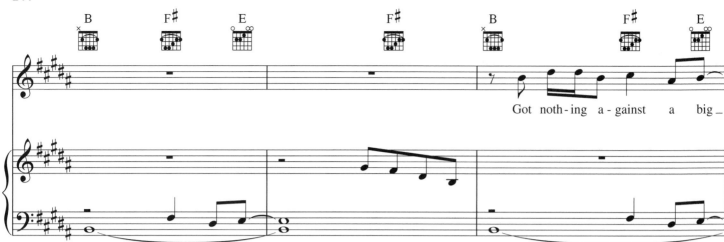

Got noth-ing a-gainst a big _

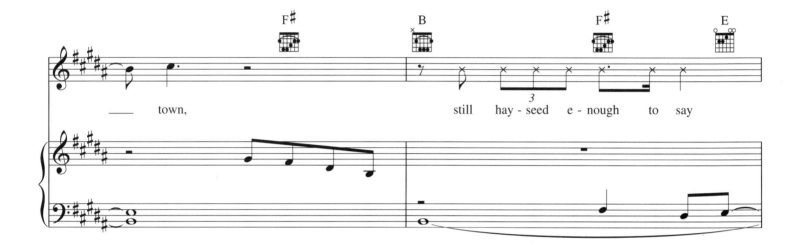

_ town, still hay-seed e-nough to say

"Look who's in the big town." But my bed _ is in a small _ town; oh, and that's

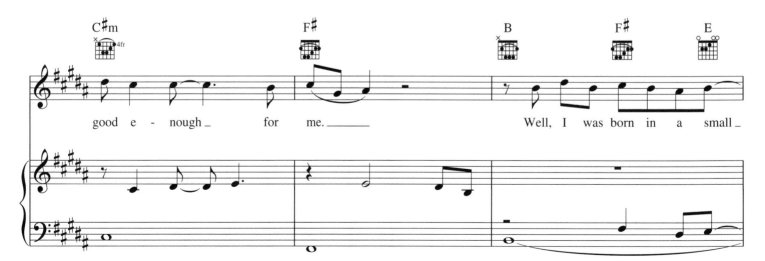

good e-nough _ for me. _ Well, I was born in a small _

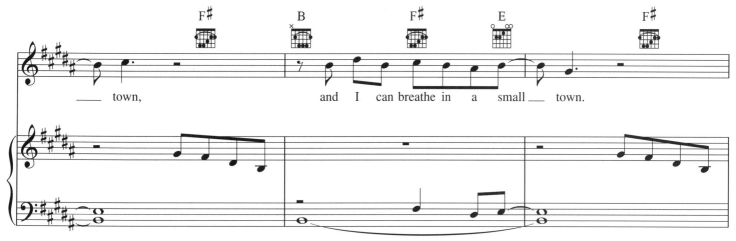

town,   and I can breathe in a small ___ town.

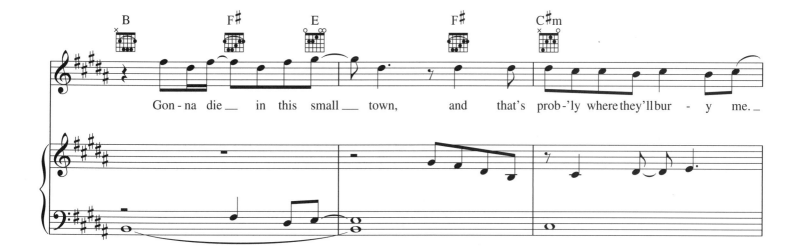

Gon - na die ___ in this small ___ town,   and   that's prob-'ly where they'll bur - y me. ___

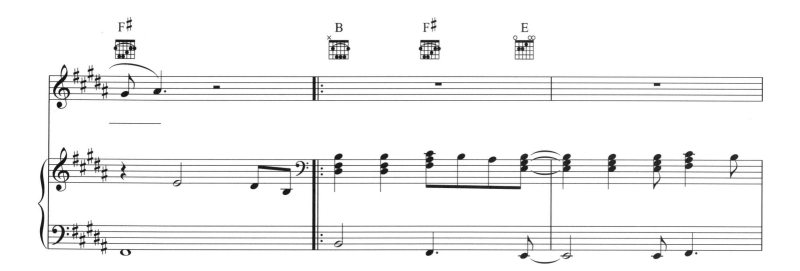

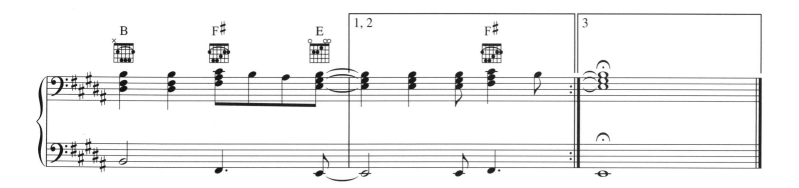

SOMEONE TO WATCH OVER ME

from OH, KAY!

Music and Lyrics by GEORGE GERSHWIN
and IRA GERSHWIN

found him yet; He's the big af-fair I can-not for-get.

On - ly man I ev - er Think of with re - gret.

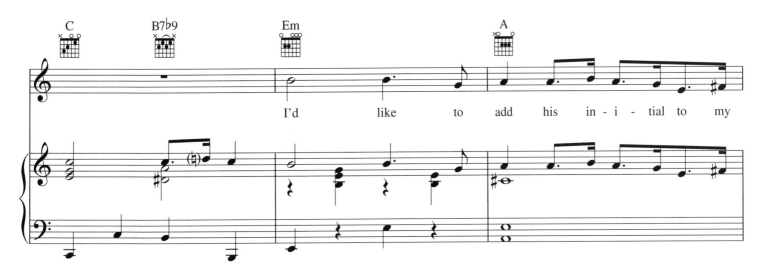

I'd like to add his in-i-tial to my

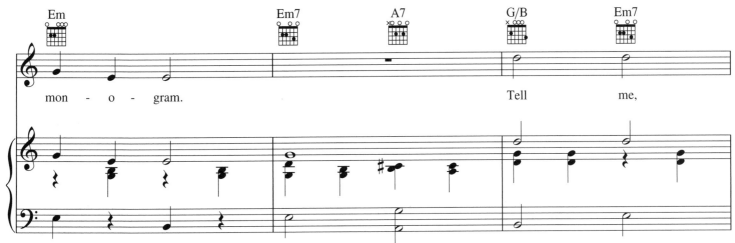

mon - o - gram. Tell me,

248

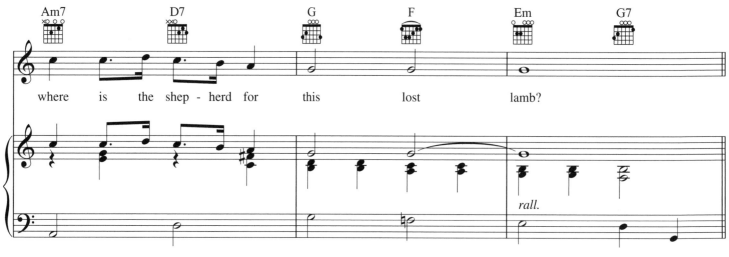

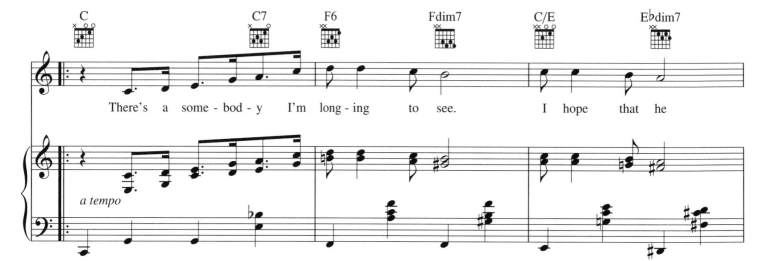

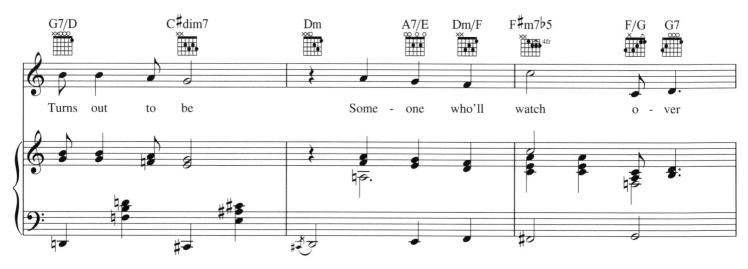

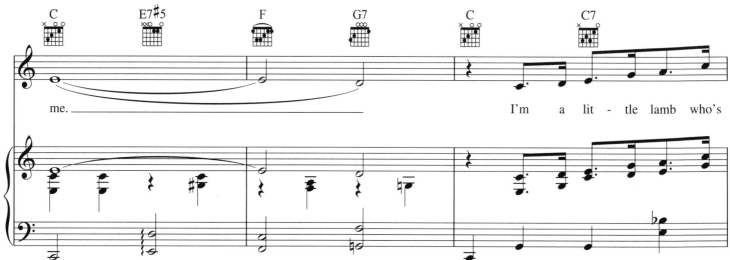

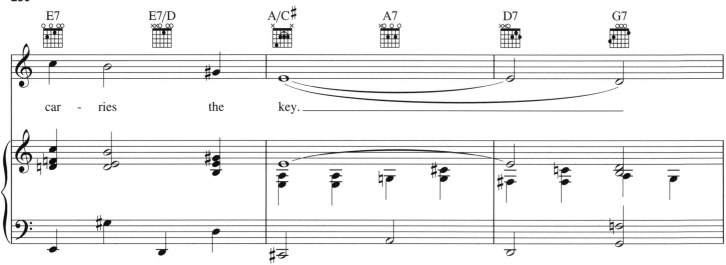

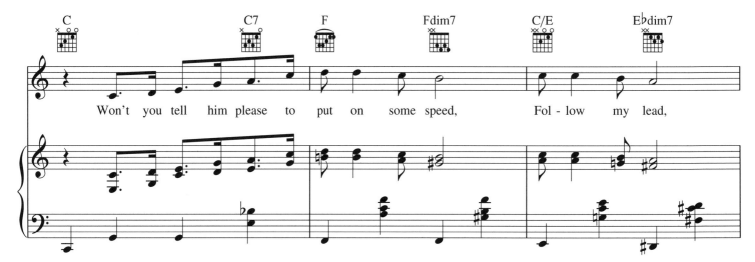

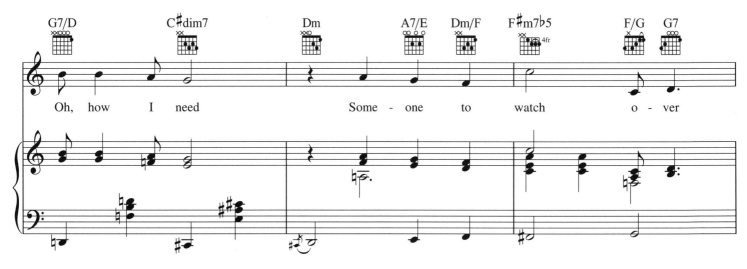

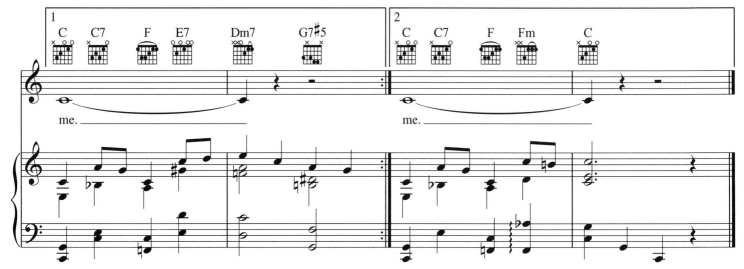

STARDUST

Words by MITCHELL PARISH
Music by HOAGY CARMICHAEL

252

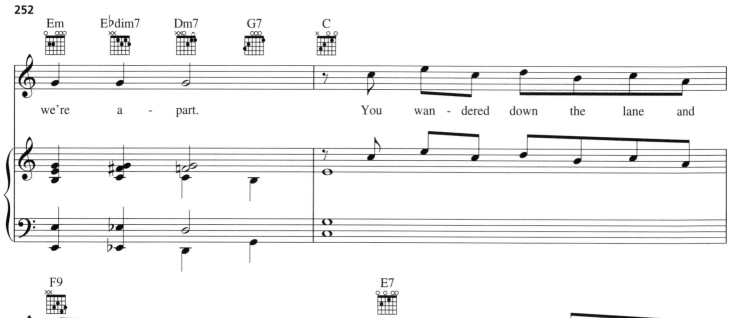

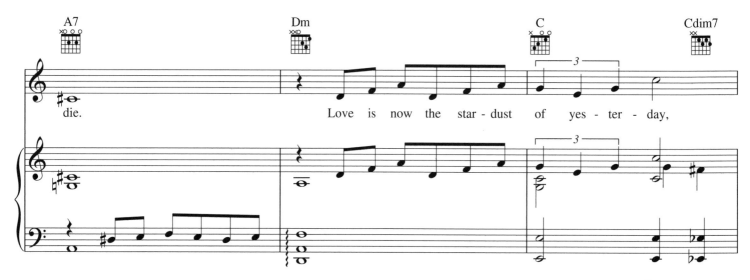

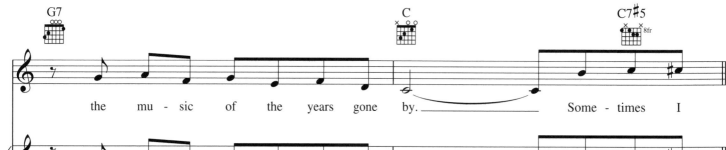

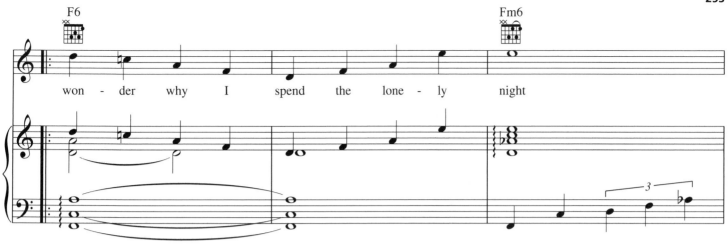

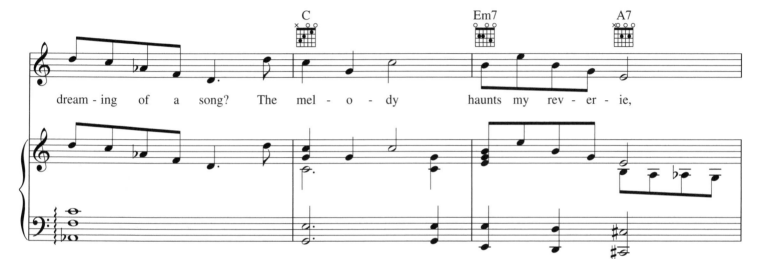

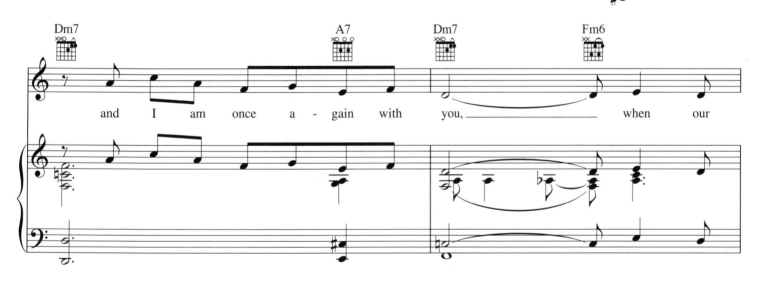

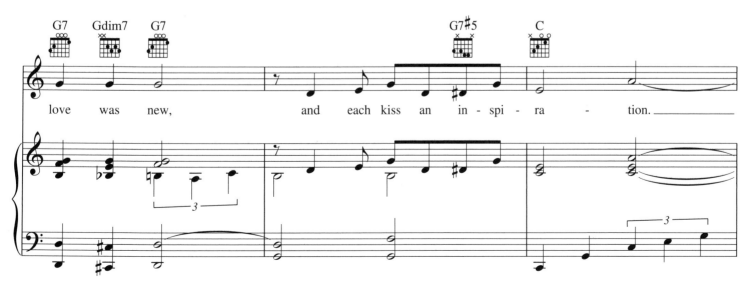

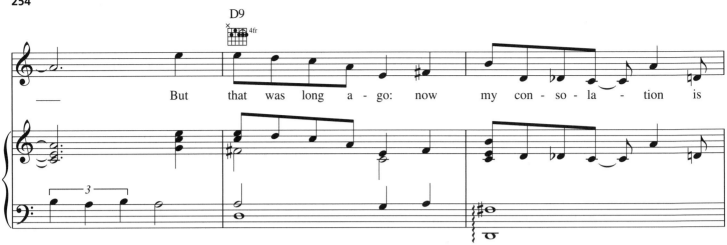

But that was long a-go: now my con-so-la-tion is

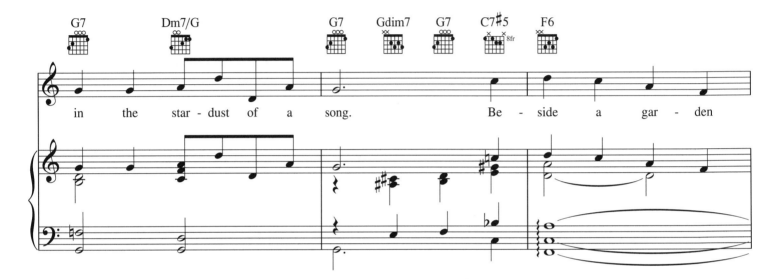

in the star-dust of a song. Be-side a gar-den

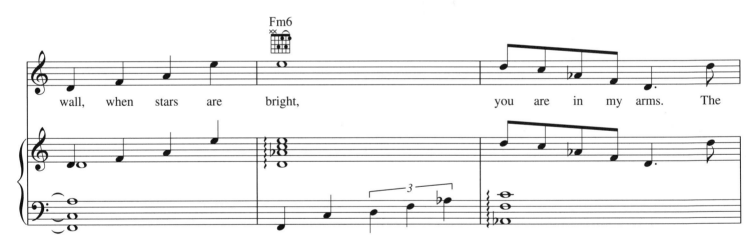

wall, when stars are bright, you are in my arms. The

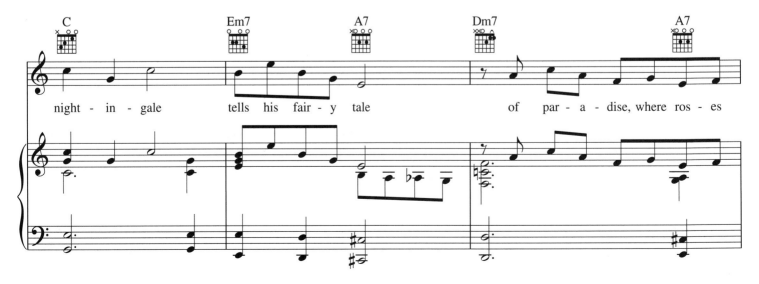

night-in-gale tells his fair-y tale of par-a-dise, where ros-es

SUNNY CAME HOME

Words and Music by SHAWN COLVIN
and JOHN LEVENTHAL

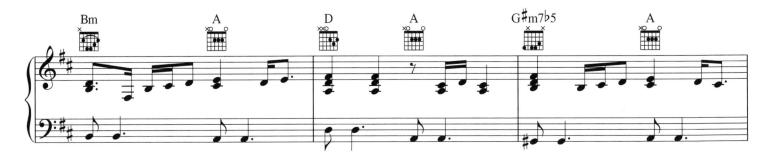

Sun-ny came home to her fa-v'rite room. ___ Sun-ny sat down in the

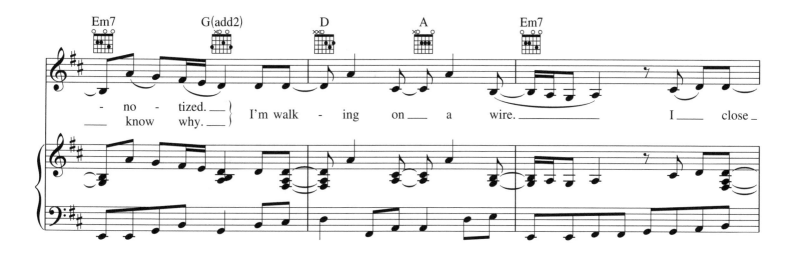

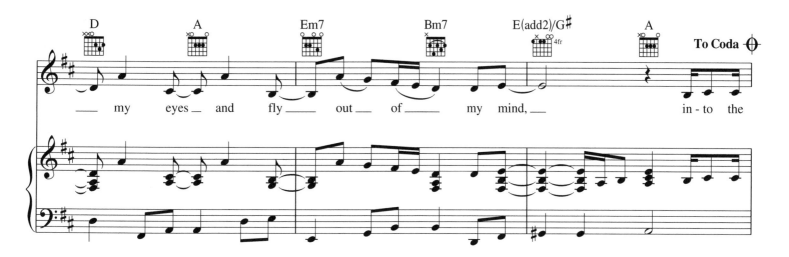

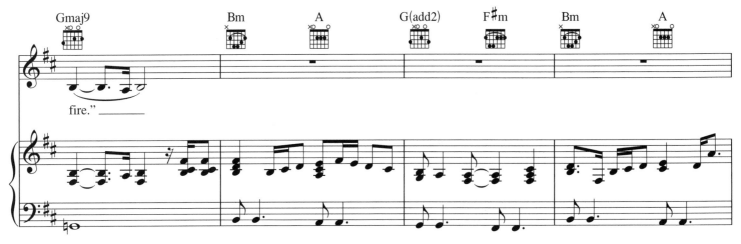

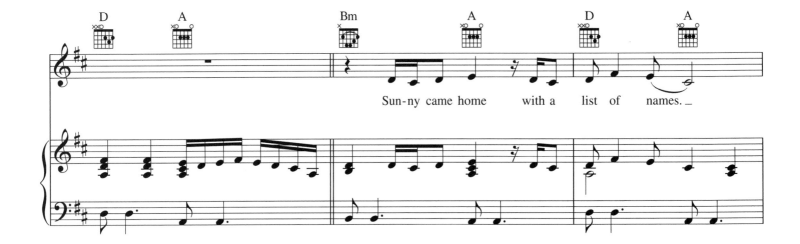

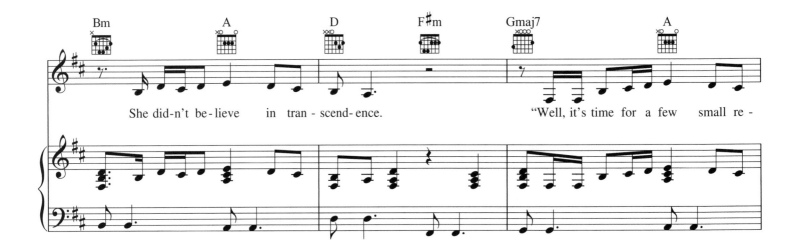

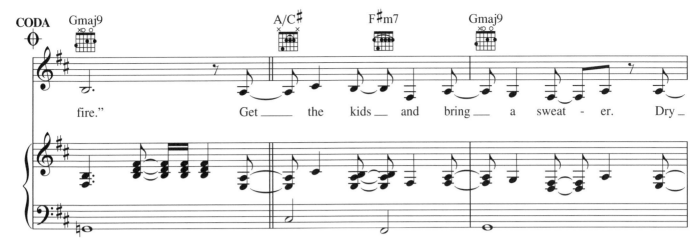

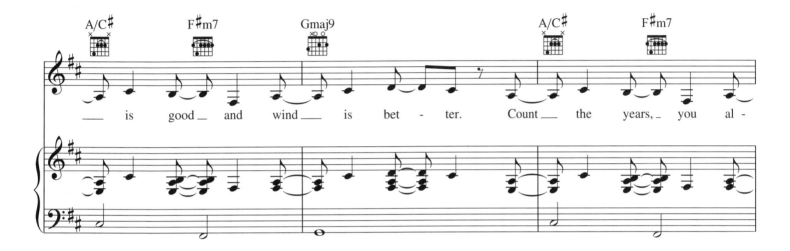

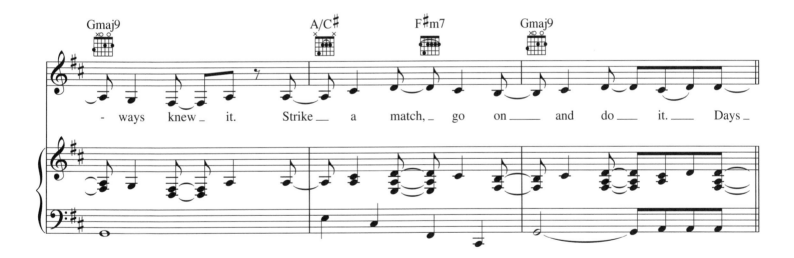

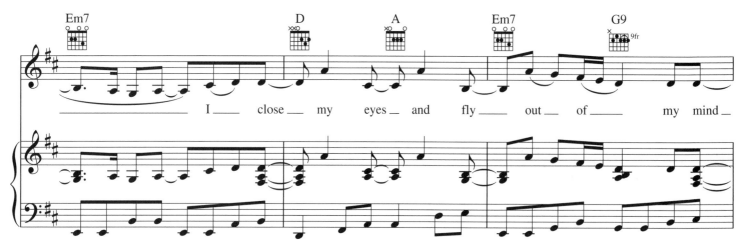

I ___ close ___ my eyes ___ and fly ___ out ___ of ___ my mind ___

___ in - to ___ the fire. ___ Oh, ___ light ___ the ___ sky ___ and ___ hold _

___ on ___ tight. ___ The world ___ is burn - ing down. _____ She's ___ out _

___ there on ___ her own ___ and ___ she's ___ al - right. ___ Sun - ny came

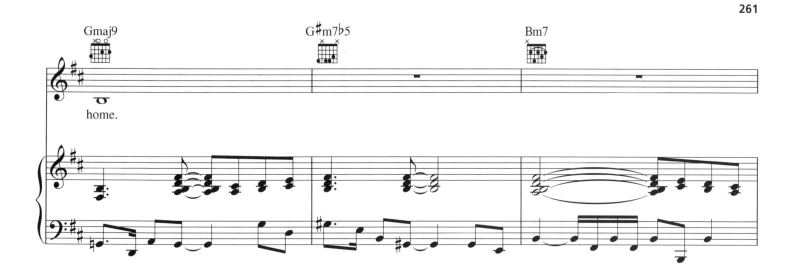

home.

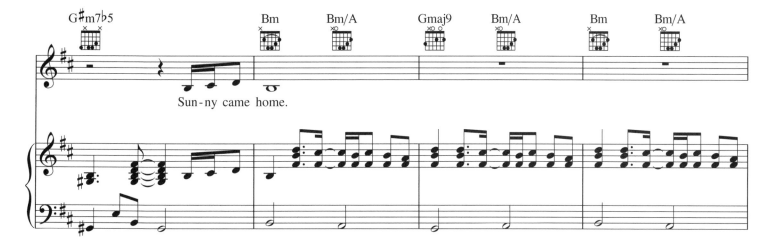

Sun-ny came home.

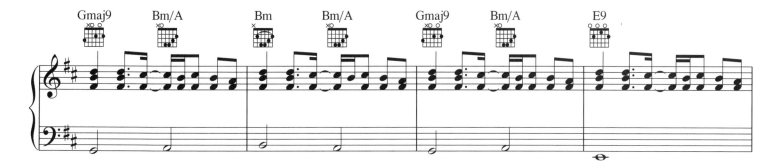

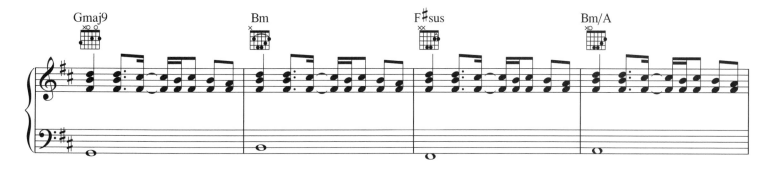

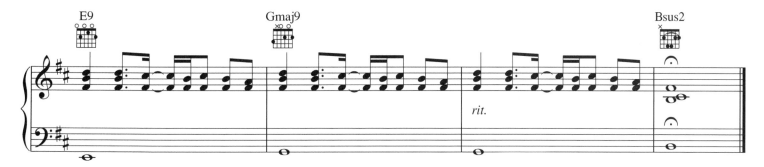

rit.

SWEET GEORGIA BROWN

Words and Music by BEN BERNIE,
MACEO PINKARD and KENNETH CASEY

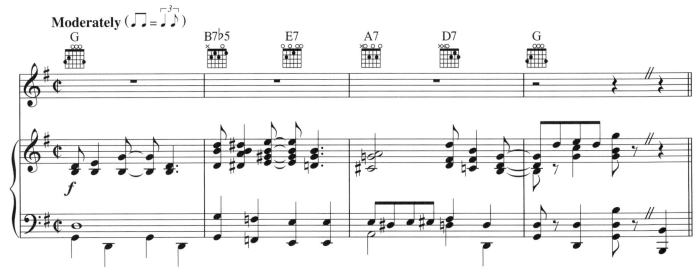

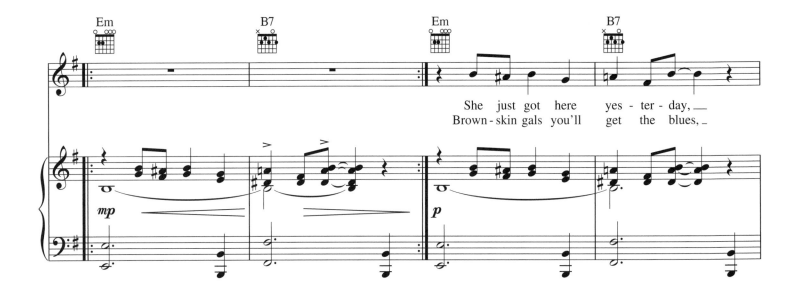

She just got here yes-ter-day, __
Brown-skin gals you'll get the blues, __

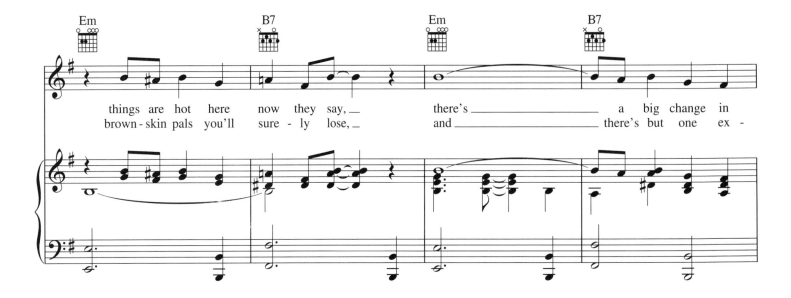

things are hot here now they say, __   there's __ a big change in
brown-skin pals you'll sure-ly lose, __   and __ there's but one ex-

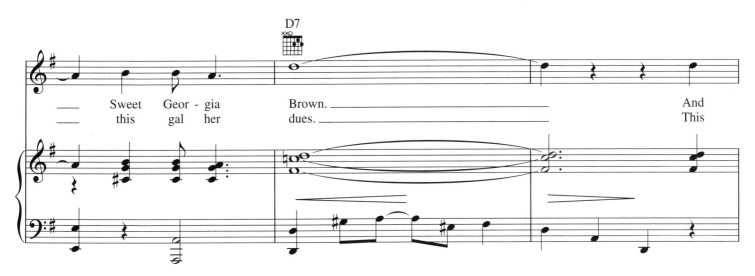

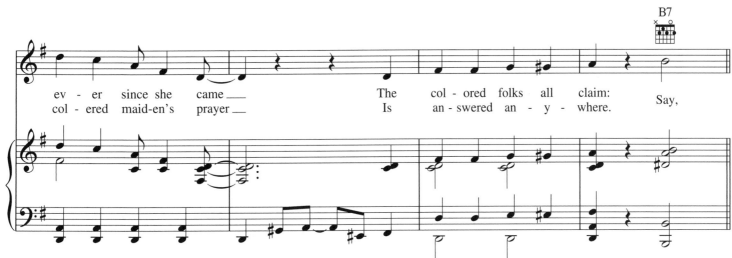

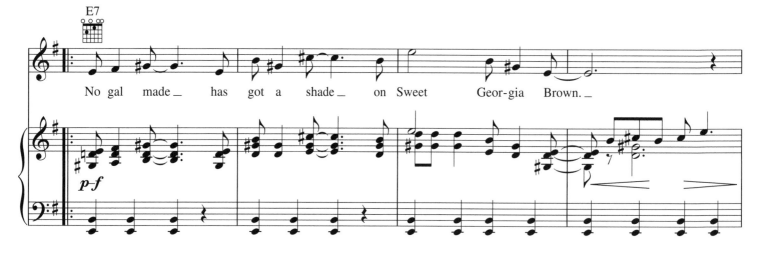

No gal made __ has got a shade __ on Sweet Geor-gia Brown. __

Two left feet, __ but oh so neat, __ has Sweet Geor-gia Brown. __

They all sigh __ and wan-na die __ for Sweet Geor-gia Brown. __ I'll tell __ you just

why, _____ you know __ I don't lie, __ not much!

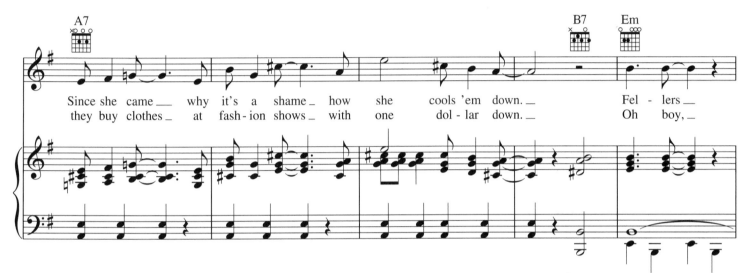

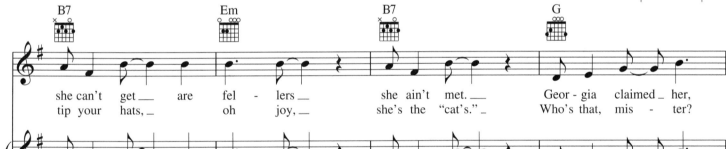

TENDERLY
from TORCH SONG

Lyric by JACK LAWRENCE
Music by WALTER GROSS

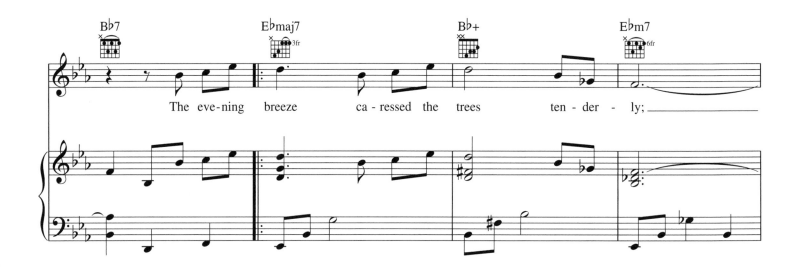

The eve-ning breeze ca-ressed the trees ten-der-ly; ____

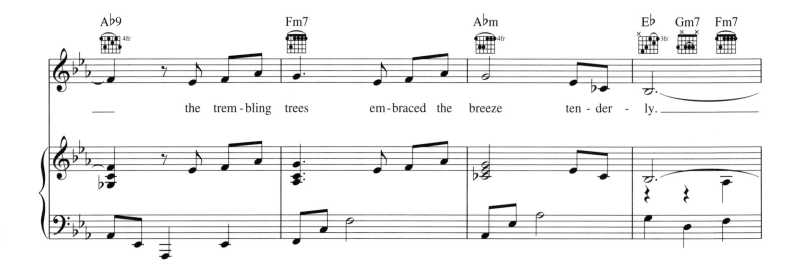

____ the trem-bling trees em-braced the breeze ten-der-ly. ____

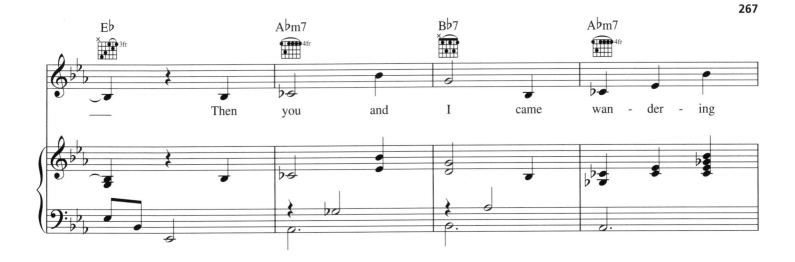

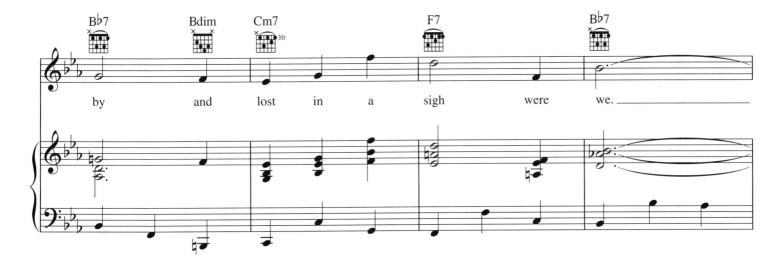

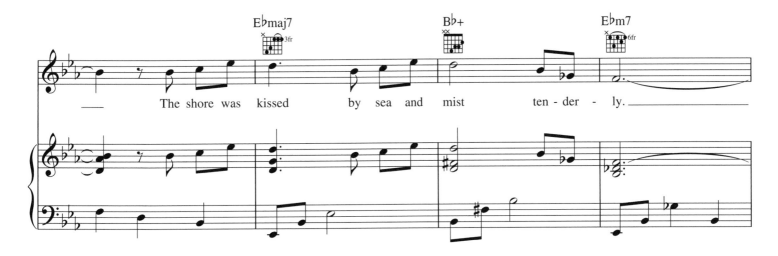

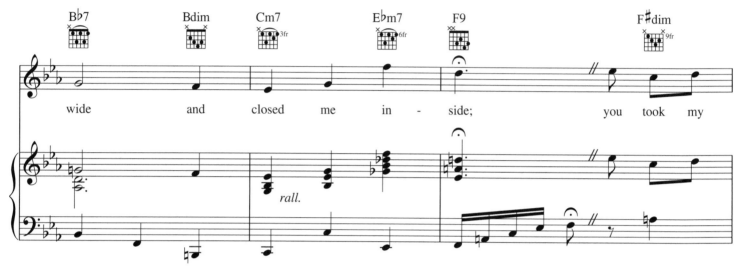

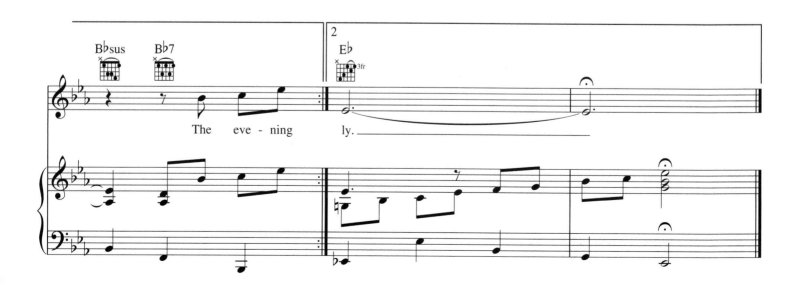

THE WAY WE WERE
from the Motion Picture THE WAY WE WERE

Words by ALAN and MARILYN BERGMAN
Music by MARVIN HAMLISCH

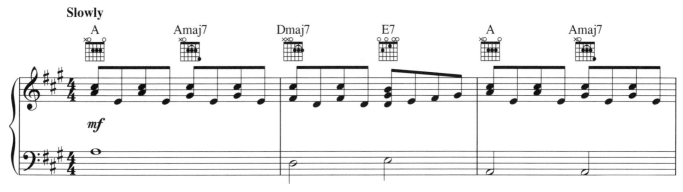

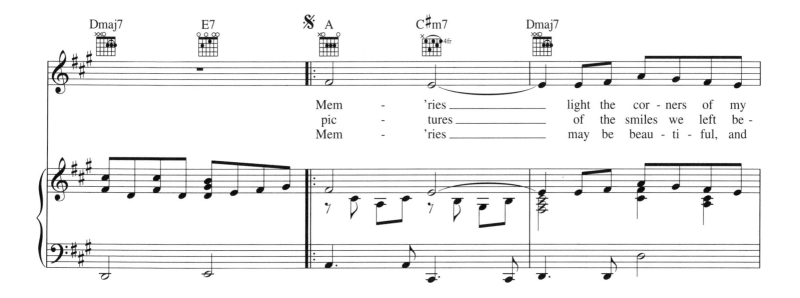

Mem - 'ries _____ light the cor - ners of my
pic - tures _____ of the smiles we left be -
Mem - 'ries _____ may be beau - ti - ful, and

mind.
hind,   Mist - y wa - col - or mem - 'ries _____
yet,   smiles we gave to one an - oth - er _____
         what's too pain - ful to re - mem - ber _____

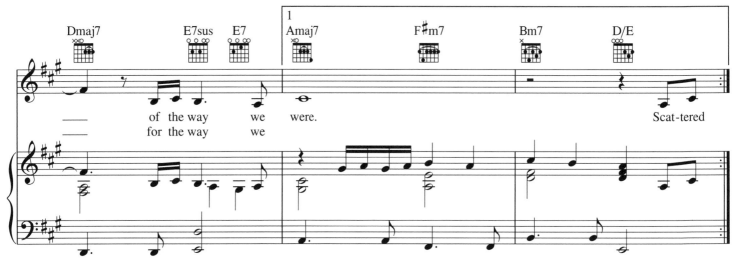

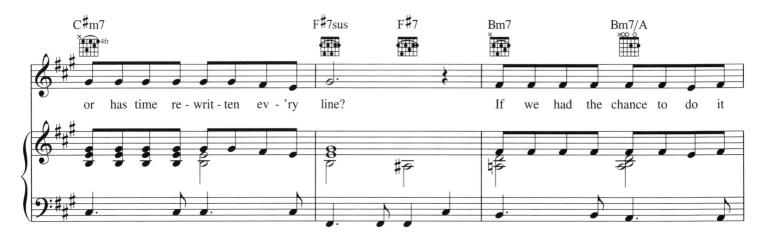

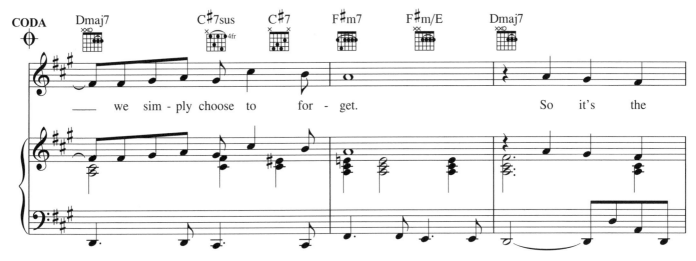

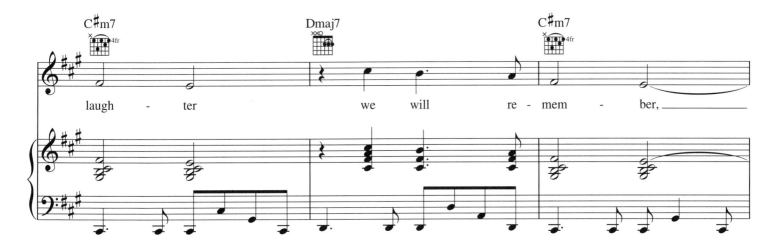

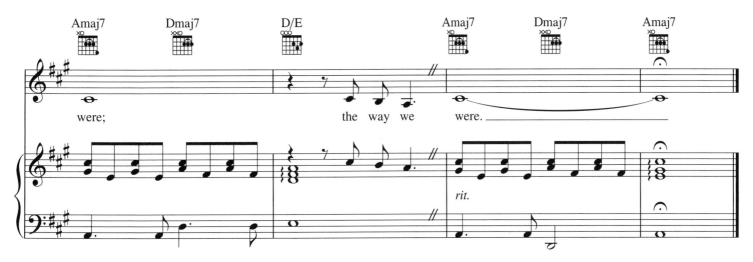

WE'VE ONLY JUST BEGUN

Words and Music by ROGER NICHOLS
and PAUL WILLIAMS

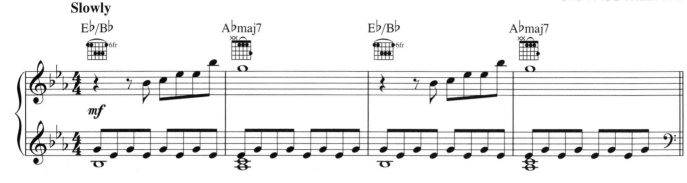

We've on - ly just be - gun _____ to live. _____

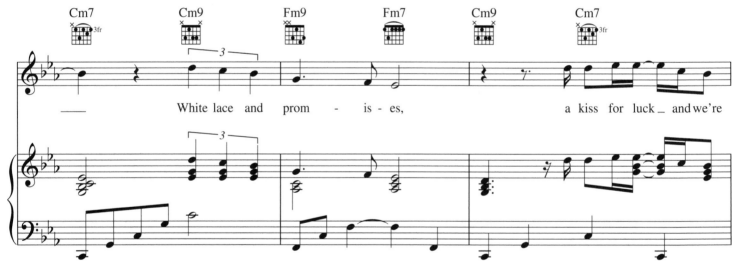

White lace and prom - is - es, _____ a kiss for luck ___ and we're

on our way. _____

(1.) Be - fore the ris - ing
(2., D.S.) And when the eve - ning

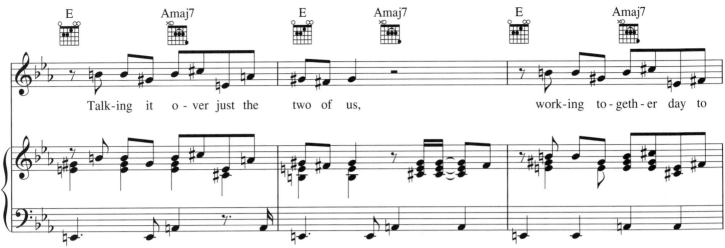

Talk-ing it o-ver just the two of us, work-ing to-geth-er day to

day, to - geth - er. ____ geth - er, _____ to -

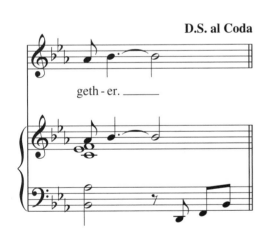

D.S. al Coda

geth - er. ____

CODA And yes, we've just be - gun. _____

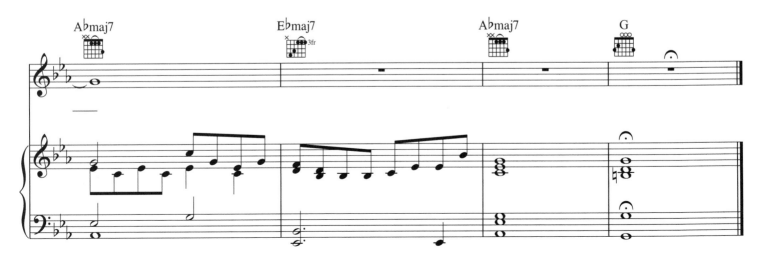

WHEN YOU WISH UPON A STAR

Words by NED WASHINGTON
Music by LEIGH HARLINE

With expression

mf

When a star is born, they pos-sess a gift or two,

one of them is this: They have the pow-er____ to make a wish come true.

rall.

a tempo

When you wish up-on a star, makes no diff-'rence

276

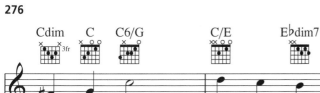

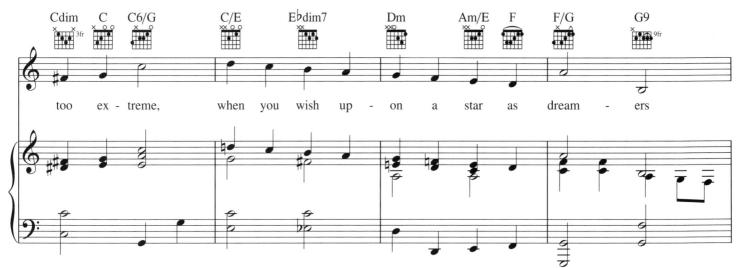
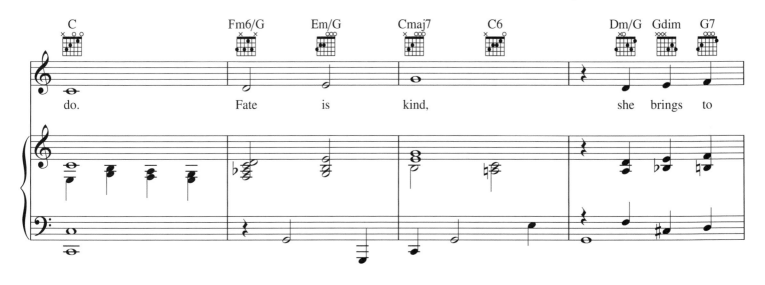

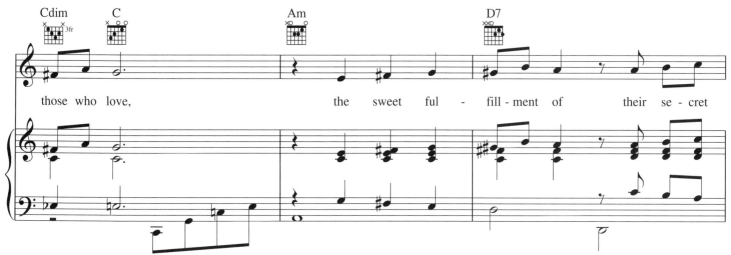

those who love, the sweet ful - fill - ment of their se - cret

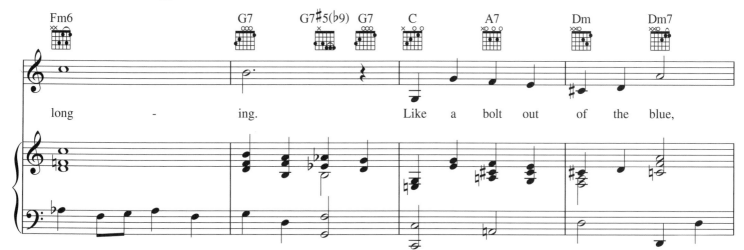

long - ing. Like a bolt out of the blue,

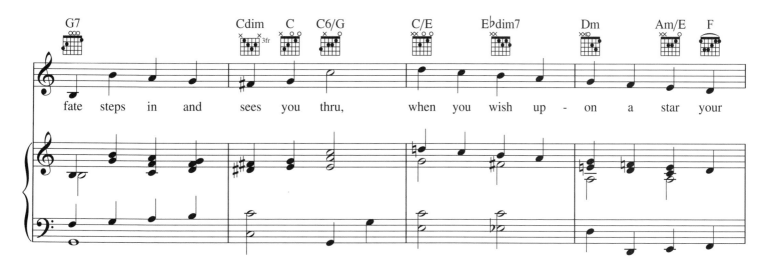

fate steps in and sees you thru, when you wish up - on a star your

dream comes true. dream comes true.

WICHITA LINEMAN

Words and Music by
JIMMY WEBB

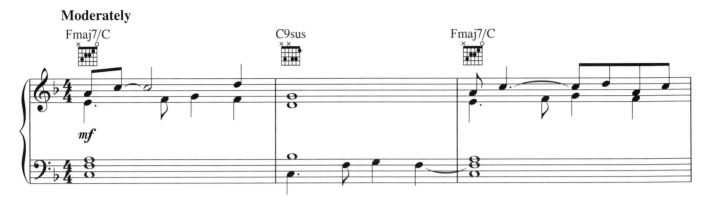

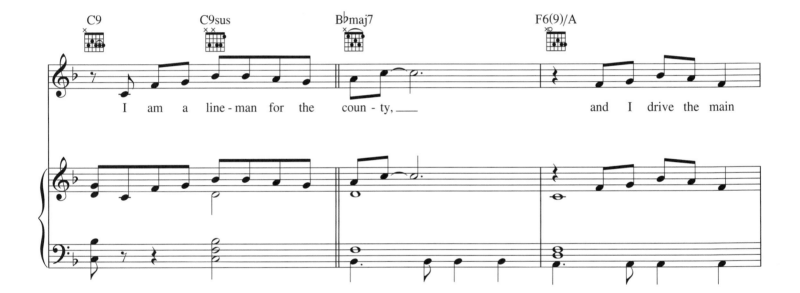

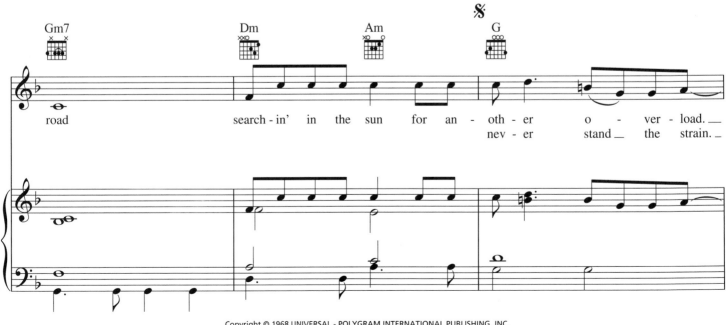

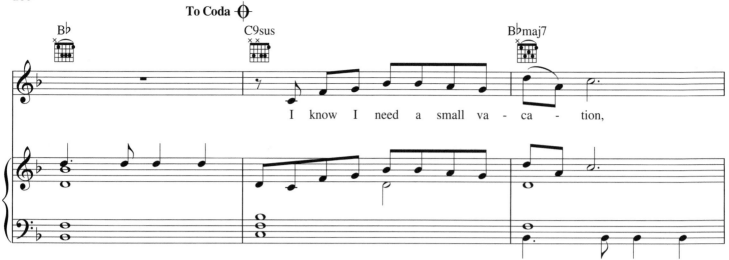

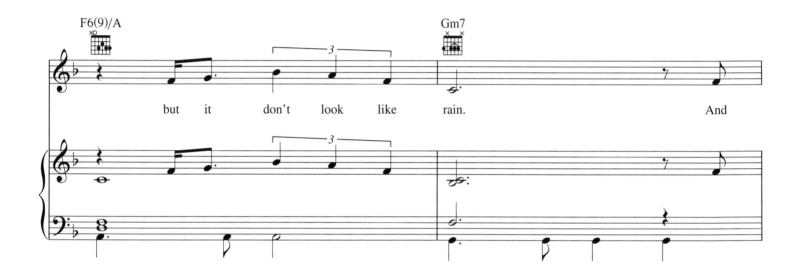

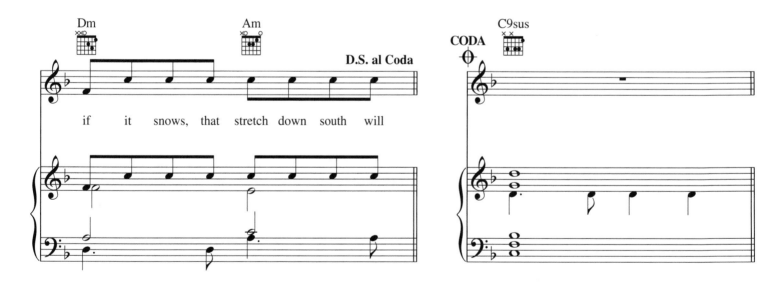

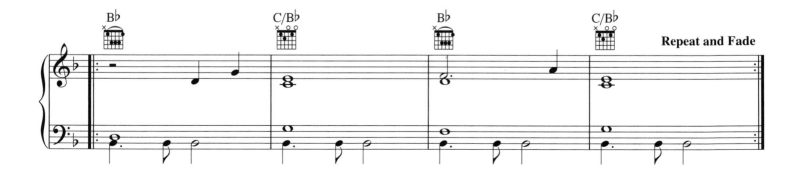

WITCHCRAFT

Music by CY COLEMAN
Lyrics by CAROLYN LEIGH

Medium bounce

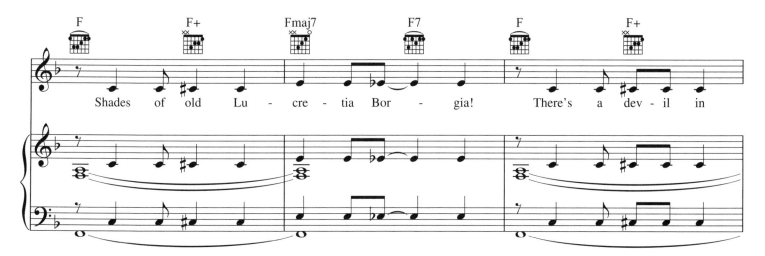

Shades of old Lu-cre-tia Bor-gia! There's a dev-il in

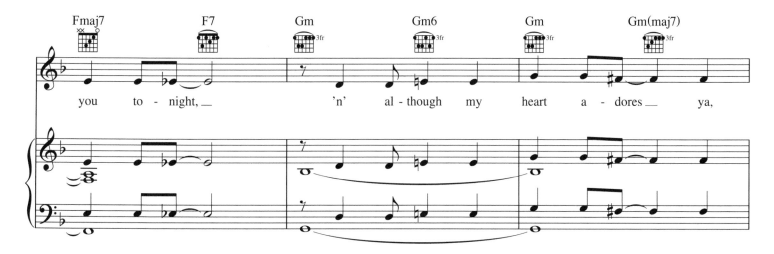

you to-night, — 'n' al-though my heart a-dores — ya,

my head says — it ain't right, — right to let you

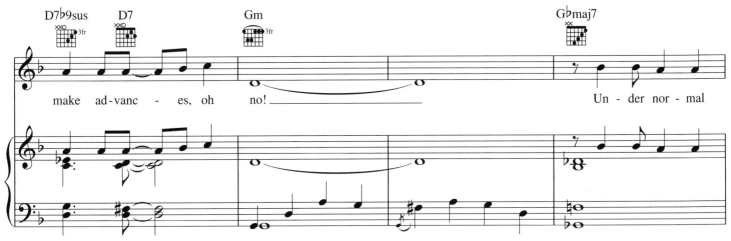

make ad-vanc - es, oh no! _____ Un - der nor - mal

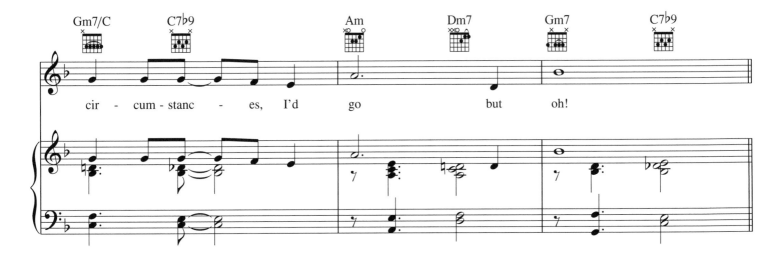

cir - cum - stanc - es, I'd go but oh!

Those fin - gers in my hair, ___ that sly, come -

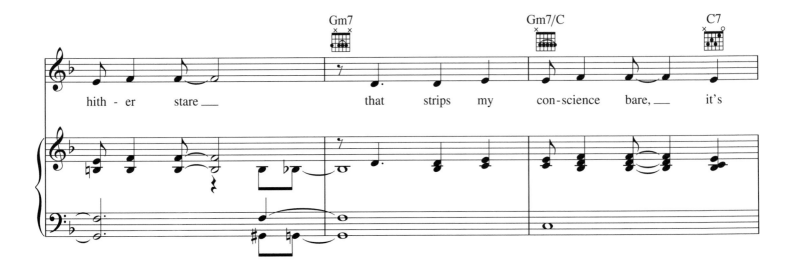

hith - er stare ___ that strips my con-science bare, ___ it's

witch - craft. _____ And I've got

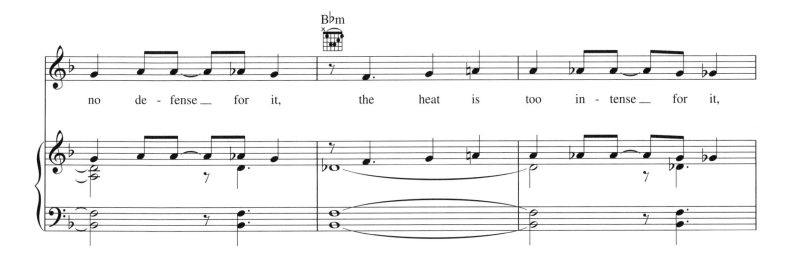

no de-fense ___ for it, the heat is too in-tense ___ for it,

what good would com-mon sense ___ for it do? _____

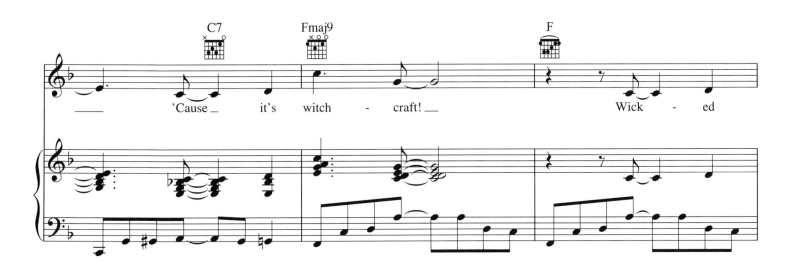

____ 'Cause ___ it's witch - craft! ___ Wick - ed

witch - craft. ___ And __ al - though I ____ know ___

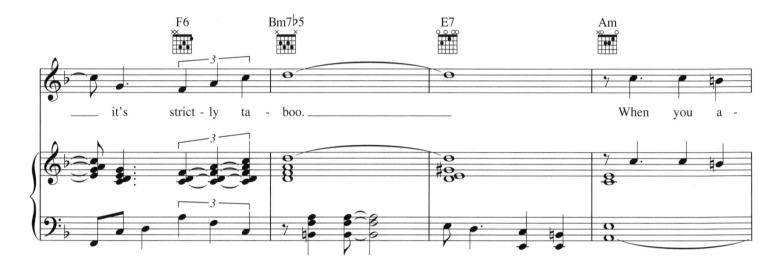

___ it's strict - ly ta - boo. _____ When you a -

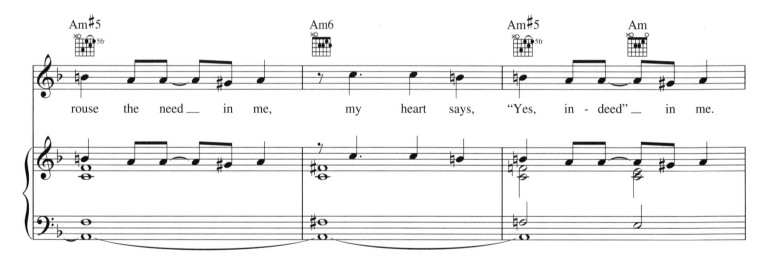

rouse the need __ in me, my heart says, "Yes, in - deed" __ in me.

"Pro - ceed with what you're lead - in' me to!" _____

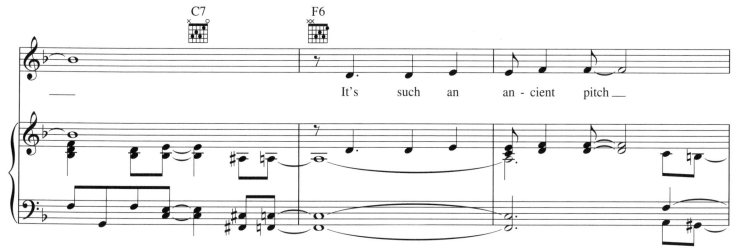

It's such an an-cient pitch ___

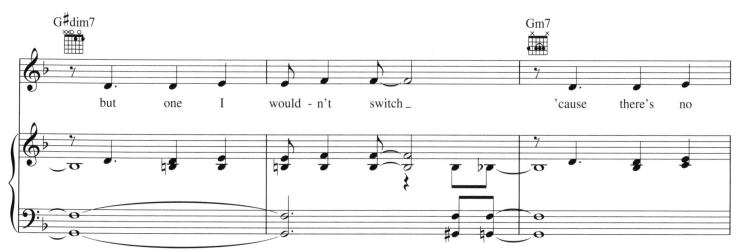

but one I would-n't switch ___ 'cause there's no

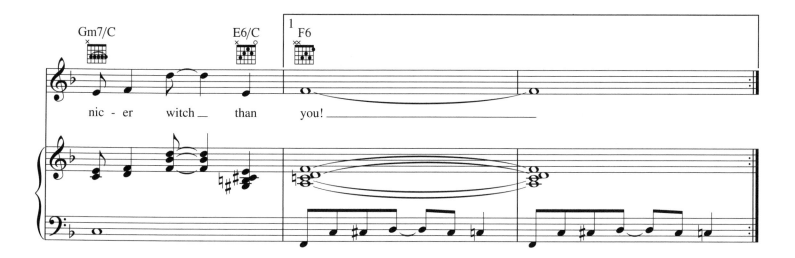

nic - er witch ___ than you! _____

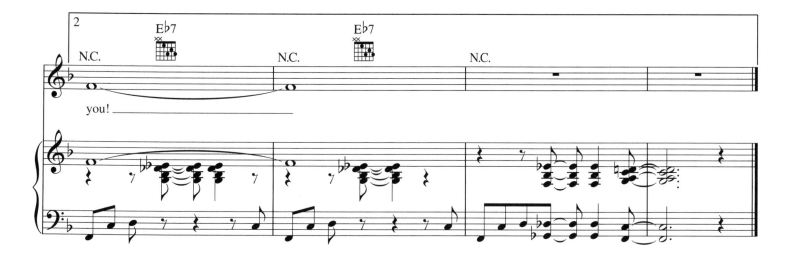

you! _____

YOU ARE THE SUNSHINE OF MY LIFE

Words and Music by
STEVIE WONDER

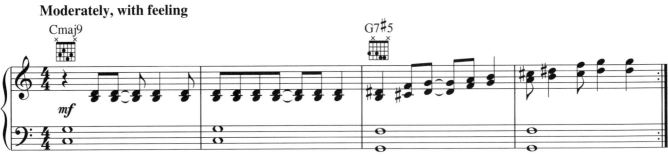

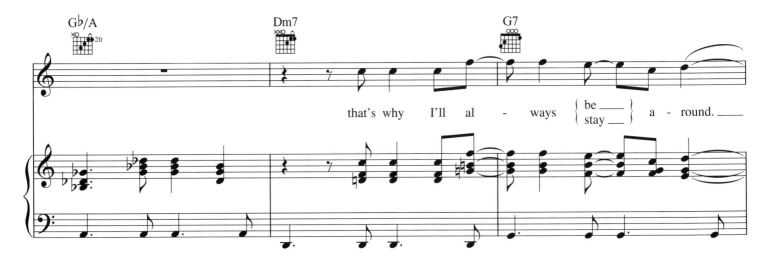

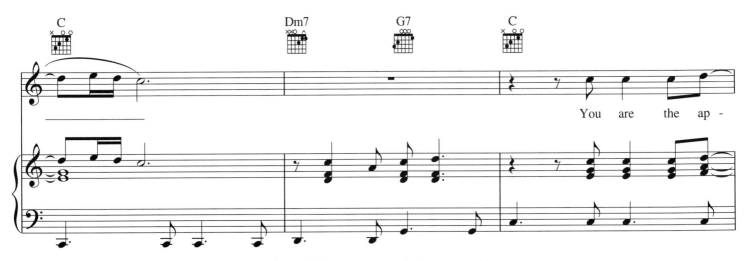

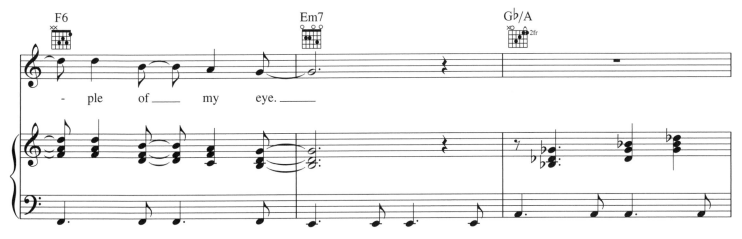

For-ev-er you'll stay in my heart,

I feel like this is the be-
You must have known that I was

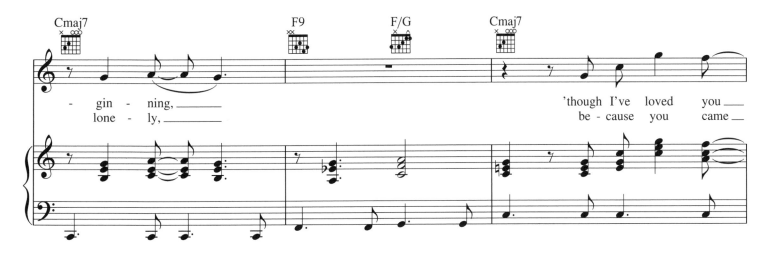

-gin-ning, 'though I've loved you
lone-ly, be-cause you came

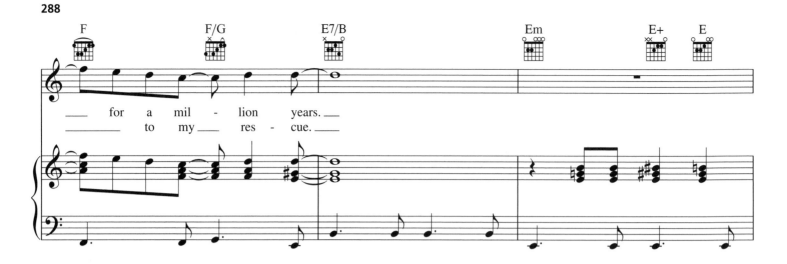

for a mil - lion years. ____
to my ___ res - cue. ____

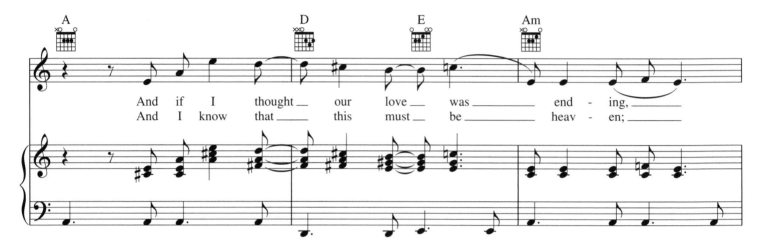

And if I thought ___ our love ___ was _____ end - ing, _____
And I know that ___ this must be _____ heav - en; _____

I'd ____ find ___ my - self ___ drown - ing in my ___ own
how could so ___ much love ___ be ___ in - side ___ of

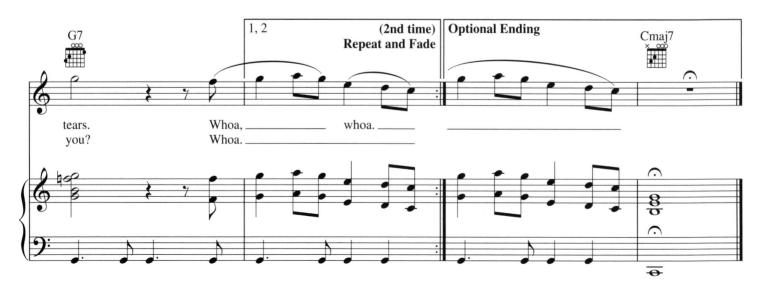

tears. _____ Whoa, _____ whoa. _____ _____
you? _____ Whoa. _____